WE ARE THE
WEATHER MAKERS

WE ARE THE
WEATHER MAKERS

The History of Climate Change

TIM FLANNERY

Adapted by **SALLY M. WALKER**

For the Generation Who Will Act on Global Warming

CANDLEWICK PRESS

First paperback edition 2010

Published by arrangement with Grove/Atlantic, Inc.,
and Text Publishing Company, Australia

Library of Congress Cataloging-in-Publication Data is available.

Library of Congress Catalog Card Number 2008939840

ISBN 978-0-7636-3656-2 (hardcover)
ISBN 978-0-7636-4656-1 (paperback)

09 10 11 12 13 14 MVP 10 9 8 7 6 5 4 3 2 1

Printed in York, PA, U.S.A.

This book was typeset in Stone Informal.

Candlewick Press
99 Dover Street
Somerville, Massachusetts 02144

visit us at www.candlewick.com

The interior of this book was printed using an eco-friendly printing
process involving low volatile organic compounds and energy-free curing.
The recycled paper was made from 30% post-consumer waste.

The cover was printed on Processed Chlorine-Free paper that
contains 100% recycled content (100% post-consumer).

To Malia and Sasha Obama,
in thanks for sharing your dad
so he can save the world
T. F.

To all people, everywhere, who take
that first step—no matter how small—
toward keeping Earth healthy.
You WILL make a difference.
S. M. W.

CONTENTS

Introduction

The Buzz about Global Warming

Global warming and climate change—it seems as if you can't turn around without reading or hearing these phrases. Newspapers, magazines, television and radio, even movie theaters are abuzz with news about Earth's climate and its future.

Simply defined, global warming is the increase in the average global surface temperature that has been caused by the presence of certain gases, called greenhouse gases, in Earth's atmosphere. A significant percentage of greenhouse gases have been added to the atmosphere as a result of human activity.

Is global warming something you should be concerned about? The majority of the scientific community says yes. Global warming skeptics, on the other hand, believe that the warming trend is just part of Earth's natural climatic cycles. While skepticism can be healthy, it can have drawbacks when society is called on to combat real dangers. For decades both the tobacco and asbestos industries found scientists who were prepared to cast doubt on discoveries linking their products with cancer. A nonspecialist cannot know whether any given view represents fringe or mainstream thinking, and so we may come to believe that there is a real division in the scientific community on these matters. In the case of asbestos and tobacco, the situation was made worse because cancers often appear years after exposure to carcinogenic products, and no one can say for certain just who among the many exposed will be affected.

In a similar manner, many people have reacted with rightful caution to news about climate change. They want proof. After all, they argue, it was only several decades ago that scientists said we'd soon run out of many of Earth's mineral resources. That hasn't happened. One reason that alarm ended up being a false one is that we can't see inside the ground and therefore can't precisely predict how much of a particular resource exists. The climate-change issue is different. Air pollution is causing a hefty share of global warming. And unlike the mineral resources belowground, we know with great precision the size of our atmosphere and the volume of pollutants that we are pouring into it.

Is climate change a terrible threat or just a lot of hoopla? Perhaps it's something in between—an issue that humanity must face eventually but not now. The world's media abound with evidence to support any of these views. Reading and listening to the stories makes one thing clear: climate change is difficult for people to evaluate dispassionately, because it strikes a chord that has deep environmental, political, economic, and personal implications. Some people fear changing their lifestyle. Some worry about losing money if business as usual is changed in any way. Others fear losing their livelihoods or their homes. This means that, as we seek to address this problem, winners and losers will be created. The stakes are high, and this has led to a proliferation of misleading stories as special-interest groups argue their cases.

What's more, climate change is a breaking story. Just over thirty years ago, the experts were at loggerheads about whether

Earth was warming or cooling—unable to decide whether an icehouse or a greenhouse future was on the way. By 1975, however, the first sophisticated computer models were suggesting that a doubling of carbon dioxide (CO_2) gas in the atmosphere would lead to an increase in global temperature of around 5° Fahrenheit (F) (2.8° Celsius (C)). Still, concern among both scientists and the community was not significant. There was even a period of optimism, when some researchers believed that extra CO_2 in the atmosphere would fertilize the world's croplands and produce a bonanza for farmers.

But by 1988, climate scientists had become sufficiently worried about CO_2 emissions to establish a panel named the Intergovernmental Panel on Climate Change (IPCC). The IPCC is a joint subsidiary body of the United Nations Environment Programme and the World Meteorological Organization that disseminates vital information about climate change and its effects. It reports its findings twice each decade on climate issues. The IPCC's third report, issued in 2001, sounded a note of sober alarm—yet many governments and industry leaders were slow to take an interest. The IPCC's most recent report, issued in 2007, has caused most governments, many businesses, and millions of people to sit up and take notice. Because concern about climate change is so new, many people are unfamiliar with the topic. Fortunately, scientists and other people who are concerned about climate change are spreading the word about global warming, what it will mean to the general public, and what we should do about it.

For the last 10,000 years, Earth's thermostat has been set to an average surface temperature of around 57°F (14°C). On the whole, this has suited our species splendidly, and we have been able to organize ourselves in a most impressive manner—

planting crops, domesticating animals, and building cities. Finally, over the past century, we have created a truly global civilization.

Earth's thermostat is a complex and delicate mechanism, at the heart of which lies CO_2, a colorless and odorless gas. The gas plays a critical role in maintaining the balance necessary to all life. It is also a waste product of the fossil fuels that almost every person on the planet uses for heat, transportation, and other energy requirements. On dead planets such as Venus and Mars, CO_2 makes up most of the atmosphere, and it would do so here if living things and Earth's processes did not keep it within bounds. Our planet's rocks and waters are packed with carbon itching to get airborne and oxidized. As it is, CO_2 makes up around 3 parts per 10,000 in Earth's atmosphere. It's a modest amount, yet it has a disproportionate influence on the planet's temperature. Because we create CO_2 every time we drive a car, cook a meal, or turn on a light, and because the gas lasts around a century in the atmosphere, the proportion of CO_2 in the air we breathe is rapidly increasing. Satellite images of Earth at nighttime show with startling clarity just how much energy we consume: our planet's surface shines in space as brightly as if it were strung with holiday lights.

Since the turn of the century, scientists have sounded alarms: our alpine forests are threatened; glaciers are melting ten times faster than previously thought; atmospheric greenhouse gases have reached levels not seen for millions of years; and plant and animal species are vanishing as a result of climate change. Reports of extreme-weather events, long-term droughts, and rising sea levels abound.

Finally, governments are responding to these issues. But we cannot wait for these problems to be solved for us. The most important thing to realize is that we can all make a difference and help combat climate change at almost no cost to our lifestyle.

The best evidence indicates that we need to reduce our CO_2 emissions by 70 percent by 2050. A family that replaces a four-wheel-drive car with a hybrid-fuel car can achieve a cut of that magnitude in a day rather than half a century. If your electricity provider offers a green option, for the cost of a daily cup of coffee you will be able to make equally major cuts in your household emissions. And when you reach voting age, if you vote for a politician who has a deep commitment to reducing CO_2 emissions, you might change the world. If you alone can achieve so much, so too can every individual and, in time, every industry and government on Earth.

The transition to a carbon-free economy is eminently achievable because we have all the technology we need to make it. It is only a lack of understanding and the pessimism and confusion generated by special-interest groups that is stopping us from going forward.

One statement frequently made by naysayers is that climate change may affect humanity in decades to come but is no immediate threat to us. It is far from certain that that is true, and it may not even be relevant. Chances are excellent that you will still be alive fifty years from now. You and your children will reap the results of the climate-change seeds that we all sow today.

The issue of certainty looms large in discussions of climate change. Some government leaders say they want "more certainty" before acting on climate change, yet science is about hypotheses, not truths, and no one can absolutely know the future. This should not stop us from making forecasts and modifying our behavior accordingly. When it comes to every-day matters, uncertainty hardly deters us: you and your family may be preparing to spend large sums on your college educa-tion, yet there's no guarantee of a good outcome. Except about death and taxes, certainty simply does not exist in our world, but that doesn't prevent us from managing our lives in the most efficient manner. Why should our response to climate change be any different?

To evaluate global warming and climate change in a truly skeptical spirit—to see how big it is and how fast it's moving—we need good information and careful thinking, so that we can prioritize our efforts and resources in ways that matter.

What follows is our best effort, based on the work of thou-sands of scientists, to outline the history of climate change, how it will unfold over the next century, and what people like us can do about it. With great scientific advances being made every month, this book is necessarily incomplete. That should not, however, be used as an excuse for inaction. It's time for all of us to act wisely.

PART 1

Earth and the Carbon Connection

Chapter 1

Earth's Carbon Cycle and You

The moment you were born, when you gulped in your first breath of air, you began a lifelong relationship with Earth via its atmosphere. Every minute of your life, the air you breathe into your lungs dissolves into your bloodstream. It spreads throughout your body, nourishing your cells, and becomes a part of you. This intimate relationship you have with Earth's atmosphere won't stop until you exhale your last breath at the moment when you die. And not even death will stop your last breath from continuing on a journey that will carry it all over our world.

Although Earth's atmosphere is crucial to our survival, we seldom think about it. After all, unlike Earth's vast blue oceans and towering mountain peaks, the atmosphere is invisible most of the time. Yet it's all that stands between us and the vastness of outer space. Alfred Russel Wallace, cofounder with Charles Darwin of the theory of evolution by natural selection, coined the phrase "the great aerial ocean" when he described the atmosphere. It's a far lovelier name, because in our minds, it conjures the image of swirling, churning currents capable of rivaling ocean currents in their ferocity and extent. Without this great aerial ocean, we could not exist. Gulped straight from the aerial ocean, the air we breathe is more than an old-fashioned tonic prescribed for good health. It is life itself. Thirty pounds of it are required by every adult every day of his or her life.

Earth's atmosphere contains the cumulative content of everything that has ever breathed, grown, and decayed on our planet. It has regulated our planet's temperature for nearly 4 billion years, providing us with the only known cradle of life in our universe. For nearly half that time, Earth's atmosphere would have been deadly for large organisms such as people, other mammals, and even dinosaurs. In Earth's "early days," life was microscopic, consisting of organisms such as algae and bacteria. And their hold on life was tenuous. By about 600 million years ago, oxygen levels had increased enough to permit the survival of larger creatures—ones whose fossils can be seen without using a magnifying lens. Clearly, Earth's atmosphere had undergone changes that had major effects on the development of life on Earth.

Carbon is an element that influences our planet's atmosphere in major ways. Carbon is found naturally in four main "storage" areas called reservoirs. Earth's soil and rock contain one carbon reservoir. Carbon is released into the soil by plant and animal remains as they break down during the decay process. The fossilized remains of ancient plants and animals that are found in sedimentary rocks, such as shale and coal, produce fuels that include oil, natural gas, and coal. Carbonate rocks, such as limestone, are made when carbon combines with other elements to form solid rock. A second carbon reservoir floats in our atmosphere as carbon dioxide (CO_2) gas. The third carbon reservoir is dissolved in ocean water. Marine organisms remove dissolved carbon from seawater when they build skeletons and shells. The last carbon reservoir is contained in the biosphere, where it is absorbed within living organisms. Your bones contain traces of carbon, absorbed from plants you have eaten that contain carbon—corn and wheat, for example. Carbon shifts naturally from rocks to the soil or the sea, in and out of our bodies, and from there to the atmosphere and back again via a process called the carbon cycle. This self-sustaining cycle is the basis for life on Earth, and the volume of carbon circulating around our planet is enormous. Around a trillion tons of carbon are tied up in living organisms. The amount of carbon buried underground is far greater.

When one atom of carbon combines with two oxygen atoms, the colorless, odorless gas CO_2 forms. Carbon dioxide is one of the keys that controls Earth's atmosphere. It helps regulate Earth's air and water temperatures, which play a critical role in maintaining the balance of life on Earth. Earth's average air temperature warms when a lot of CO_2 is in the atmosphere and cools when CO_2 levels drop. A substantial drop in CO_2 levels can drastically alter the face of our planet, and geological evidence proves it.

At around 710 million years ago and again at 600 million years ago, something altered the carbon cycle. Geologists know this because they have found a large amount of carbonate deposited in rocks that date from those periods. The formation of carbonate rocks removes carbon that otherwise would have been in the atmosphere. While geologists don't know exactly what caused the shift in the carbon cycle, they do know that it led to a runaway refrigeration of the planet. Earth crossed a temperature threshold that froze the planet right to the equator, killing off nearly all forms of life.

Whatever caused these two ice ages, Earth's periods of deep freeze were certainly aided by a powerful mechanism known as Earth's albedo. Albedo is the measure of how much of Earth's surface reflects the sun's rays. The word *albedo* is Latin for "whiteness," and all forms of ice and snow reflect sunlight. About one-third of all the sun's energy that reaches Earth is reflected back into space by white surfaces. Fresh snow reflects the highest amount, about 80 to 90 percent of the sunlight that strikes it. In contrast, water reflects only about 5 to 10 percent of sunlight. Once a certain proportion of the planet's surface is bright ice and snow, enough sunlight is lost that a runaway cooling effect is created, which freezes the entire planet. That threshold is crossed when ice sheets, which are thick blankets of ice that cover large areas of a continent, reach around 30 degrees of latitude—the latitude where cities such as San Antonio, Texas, and New Orleans, Louisiana, are now located.

Fortunately for the development of future life (particularly us), the carbon cycle was readjusted and Earth warmed up from these two major deep freezes. Oddly, it appears that tiny marine organisms may have helped turn Earth's carbon cycle around. In these two ice ages, as glaciers started to grow, the oceans would draw CO_2 out of the atmosphere, making Earth colder and promoting an even deeper ice age. About 540 million years ago, marine organisms began to build skeletons of carbonate, and to do this they absorbed CO_2 from seawater. Since they began doing so, there have been only two milder ice ages: one between 355 and 280 million years ago, and a second one that began when small glaciers formed in Antarctica, 33 to 38 million years ago. It is believed that the marine organisms' presence regulates ocean chemistry and prevents the ocean from absorbing large amounts of CO_2 from the atmosphere.

Plants play a crucial role in the carbon cycle and have influenced the balance in the carbon reservoirs. Forests first covered the land about 360 to 290 million years ago, during a geologic time period called the Carboniferous. During this period, Earth's widespread swampy regions were thickly forested with gigantic ferns and treelike plants. Forests have a lower albedo than snow and ice, so they absorb more sunlight. They also absorb CO_2. If it weren't for plants and algae, Earth's atmosphere would be awash in CO_2 and we would suffocate from lack of oxygen. Through photosynthesis, the process that plants use to create sugars using sunlight and water, plants take our waste CO_2 and use it to make their own energy.

Later, during respiration, a plant breaks down the sugars produced by photosynthesis and uses the energy for its growth. Oxygen and water are two of the by-products of respiration. In addition to pumping up the atmosphere's oxygen content, forests produce water vapor, which in turn affects cloud formation. As plants in the widespread Carboniferous forests died and decayed, they became layers of peat. Peat is the first stage of converting plant matter into coal. Most of Earth's coal deposits were formed during the Carboniferous period.

There is no doubt that ice and forests influence the carbon cycle. It's likely that the evolution of grasses and reef-building organisms called corals did too. The spread of modern coral reefs began around 55 million years ago. As the corals manufactured their skeletons, they drew unimaginable volumes of CO_2 from the atmosphere, which probably changed the balance of at least two segments of the carbon cycle.

The spread of grasses, about 6 to 8 million years ago, may also have changed the carbon balance, but in a very different way: grasses catch fire easily, and the rapidly spreading flames can destroy forests. Grasses contain less carbon than forests, and they also absorb less sunlight. When trees burn, they can no longer absorb large quantities of carbon, so there is likely to be more carbon in the air.

In the past 150 to 200 years, the Industrial Revolution added an unexpected twist in the carbon cycle. By heating homes, driving vehicles, and producing energy that uses fossil fuels— oil, natural gas, and coal—humans have been influencing the carbon cycle and increasing the level of atmospheric CO_2 by leaps and bounds.

Give-and-take has been the story of Earth's carbon cycle for millions of years. But many scientists are concerned about the balance of the carbon cycle and the increasing amount of CO_2 in one carbon reservoir: the atmosphere. As you have read, the amount of CO_2 in the atmosphere can substantially affect Earth's climates. If current trends continue, scientists believe that major climate changes will environmentally alter Earth and directly affect our future.

CALL TO ACTION

Lead the Green Charge

What programs does your school have to promote an eco-friendly environment? If there is no recycling program, start one. Because less energy is needed to transport, process, and manufacture recycled products than goods made from virgin materials, fewer fossil fuels are burned and less CO_2 is emitted. At the minimum, your school should have a recycling program that includes paper, glass, aluminum, and plastic. Every classroom and the administrative office should have a bin for recycling paper. There should be one next to every copying machine. Find out where the closest aluminum recycling drop-off facility is. Ask if they pay for empty cans. Use any money received to buy plants to place around the interior of the school or to plant outside it.

Check out the cafeteria—is the food served or packaged in recyclable or washable containers? If not, find out what you can do to get the school to make a change. Petitions signed by students and parents presented at a school board meeting can be effective. If not, a student boycott of environmentally unfriendly packaging could be another option.

Is there an environmental club? If not, start one. Educate the rest of your student body via posters and speakers at school assemblies. Ask your school's parent-teacher organization for funds if they are needed.

Chapter 2

The Ocean in the Sky

To understand climate change, we need to come to grips with three important yet widely misused and misunderstood terms: *climate change*, *greenhouse gases*, and *global warming*. But first, it's important to understand the difference between *climate* and *weather*. Climate is the average pattern of weather conditions that occur in a place or area *over a period of years*. "Snowbirds," the group of people who migrate to Florida and other states that are warm during January, February, and March, head south for one reason: to escape cold northern winters. Florida's warm climate is the draw. As a rule, you can expect the year-round temperatures in Florida to be well above freezing.

In contrast, weather is what we experience on any particular day. In Florida, there are rainy and sunny days, hot and muggy days, and occasionally a freezing-cold day. Although frost is rare, it does occur, and when it does, it can have devastating effects on crops that don't tolerate frost. In northern states like Maine and Alaska, temperatures rarely reach 100°F, but unusual as they are, hot days do occur. Weather varies from day to day.

Greenhouse gases are a class of gases that can trap heat near Earth's surface. Water vapor, CO_2, and methane are greenhouse gases. When greenhouse gases increase in the atmosphere, they trap extra heat in the lower atmosphere. That can lead to global warming, which is an average increase in temperature for Earth's atmosphere as a whole. And in some areas, an average temperature rise of two or three degrees is enough to cause a change in climate. The climate, greenhouse gases, and global warming are all generated in the atmosphere, a chiefly invisible zone where a whole lot is happening.

Earth's Atmosphere

Earth's atmosphere has four distinct layers: the *troposphere,* the *stratosphere,* the *mesosphere,* and the *thermosphere.* Each layer is defined by its temperature and by the gradient, or rate, at which the temperature in that layer increases or decreases.

The troposphere is the lowest part of Earth's atmosphere. The root of the word, *tropos,* is a Greek word that means "turning" or "changing," because the troposphere is in a constant state of flux, its air swirling and churning as it mixes vertically. The troposphere extends on average to 7 miles (11.3 kilometers) above Earth's surface, depending on where you are: it's about 6 miles up from the North and South poles and about 10 miles up from the equator. (The cruising altitude of a commercial airline jet on a cross-country flight from New York to San Francisco is about 7 miles high.). Eighty percent of all the atmosphere's gases are in the troposphere. The bottom third of the troposphere contains half of all the gases in the atmosphere and is the only part of Earth's entire atmosphere that is breathable.

If you were on a jet soaring vertically upward into the troposphere, you might expect the temperature outside the plane to be rising, since the plane would be getting closer to the sun.

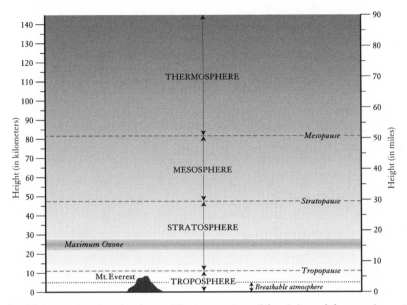

Earth's atmosphere has four layers. The temperature of the air in each layer varies, as does the amount of oxygen.

Oddly, however, the temperature gradient in the troposphere is reversed—it's warmest at the bottom, about 57°F (14°C), near Earth's surface, and plunges to a freezing –85°F (–65°C) near the top of the troposphere, referred to as the *tropopause.* As the cold, dense air in the higher parts of the troposphere sinks, it mixes with the warmer air that's rising from below. The troposphere's mixing air is what produces our weather systems: warm, rising air creates clouds and rain; colder, sinking air brings clear weather.

Another odd feature of the troposphere is that it is the only portion of our atmosphere whose northern and southern halves (divided by the equator) hardly mix. That's why smoggy air generated by factories and cars in large cities in the Northern Hemisphere doesn't affect visibility in the Southern Hemisphere.

The next layer of the atmosphere is known as the strato-sphere, through which fierce winds circulate. In contrast to the troposphere, the stratosphere gets hotter as one rises through it. This is because the upper stratosphere is rich in a form of oxygen called *ozone*. Ozone is like a supercharged molecule of oxygen. Usually a molecule of oxygen has two oxygen atoms. Ozone is produced when electricity—from thunderstorms, for example—causes a third oxygen atom to attach itself to the molecule. Ozone is very effective at capturing the energy from ultraviolet light (UV) rays that come from the sun. It prevents 95 to 99 percent of the sun's UV rays from reaching Earth's sur-face. That's to our benefit, because UV rays can cause certain types of skin cancer. Ozone does not cause global warming. What ozone does is reradiate the energy from UV rays as heat that warms the stratosphere.

The atmosphere's third layer, the mesosphere, begins about 30 miles above Earth's surface. At –130°F (–90°C), it's the coldest portion of Earth's atmosphere. Above it lies Earth's fourth atmospheric layer, the thermosphere, a thin dribble of gas that extends far into space. Temperatures in the thermosphere can reach almost 2,000°F (1,000°C), yet because the gas is so thinly spread, it would not feel hot to the touch.

The Air We Breathe

Earth's atmosphere, that great ocean in the sky, is com-posed of several gases. Nitrogen, the primary component, makes up 78 percent, followed by oxygen at 20.9 percent and argon at 0.9 percent. These three gases comprise more than 99 percent of the dry atmosphere that we breathe, but interestingly, water vapor can make up 1 to 4 percent of what we inhale, depending on the air's temperature: at 77°F (25°C), water vapor makes up 3 percent of what we breathe. However, it's the minor elements—the remaining one-twentieth of 1 percent—that spice the mix of Earth's atmosphere, and some of them are vital to life on our planet. These gases occur in such small amounts that scientists call them trace gases. Take, for example, ozone. Ozone makes up just ten molecules of every million tossed about in the currents of Earth's ocean in the sky. But without our ozone shield, we would soon go blind, contract cancer, and be plagued by a legion of other health issues.

Greenhouse gases are just as important to our continued existence. Carbon dioxide is the most abundant of the greenhouse gases, although with fewer than 4 of every 10,000 atmospheric molecules being CO_2, it can hardly be called common. Yet it's CO_2 that is partially responsible for Earth's current average surface temperature of about 57°F (14°C)—a temperature that keeps us all from freezing. And because CO_2 is still rare in our atmosphere, the lack of it keeps us from becoming overheated. Surprisingly, more gas lies dissolved in the oceans than floats in the atmosphere. For every molecule of CO_2 in the atmosphere, there are fifty in the oceans. And more heat energy is stored near the ocean's surface than in the atmosphere.

It seems hard to believe that people could affect such a large body of gases as Earth's atmosphere. But if you think of Earth's layers as an onion, with Earth's hot core at its center, our atmosphere, vast as it seems, would be no thicker than the parchment skin that covers the outer surface of the onion. The breathable portion of our atmosphere doesn't even completely cover Earth's surface. Mount Everest, Earth's tallest mountain peak, scarcely contains enough air for humans to breathe properly. That's why almost all the climbers who attempt the mountain's summit must bring canisters of air with them. If all the gas in our atmosphere could be turned into a liquid, it would make a puddle only one five-hundredth the size of the oceans. Because it's made of gases, however, the atmosphere spreads far and wide. It's likely that the CO_2 you exhaled a few seconds ago has already left the room you are in. And even if you've never left North America, breaths you exhaled last week may now be feeding a plant in Europe or Asia. There's no question that our atmosphere, the air we breathe, is dynamic and far-reaching. Because of this, the atmosphere is on intimate terms with every aspect of our planet. No volcano belches, no ocean wave churns, no car idles in a traffic jam, and no person breathes without it registering in the great aerial ocean.

Moreover, changes in Earth's atmosphere can manifest themselves simultaneously in distant regions. In response to heating or cooling, for example, the atmosphere can transform itself from one climatic state to another, allowing storms, droughts, floods, and wind patterns to alter on a global level at about the same time. Thus a driving rainstorm can cause flooding in California while drought withers corn crops in Illinois.

Earth's atmosphere is impenetrable to most of the sun's radiant energy. Obviously, daylight—visible light—reaches through the atmosphere. Our eyes depend on its bright rays to see. But the waves that constitute visible light are only a small portion of the sun's broad spectrum of radiant energy waves. There are many energy waves that the human eye can't see. And some of those wavelengths find Earth's atmosphere as impenetrable as a brick wall. The greenhouse gases in our atmosphere make up part of that brick wall. These gases trap the long wavelengths of solar energy known as *heat energy*, but in doing so, they become unstable, eventually releasing the heat, some of which radiates back to Earth. Compared to nitrogen and oxygen, the quantity of greenhouse gases in the atmosphere is minuscule, but their impact is massive. By trapping heat near Earth's surface, they both warm our world and account for the "upside-down" temperature gradient in the troposphere.

The enormous influence that greenhouse gases have on the temperature of a planet can easily be seen by examining the atmospheres of some of our neighboring planets. The atmosphere of Venus, our next-door neighbor, is 98 percent CO_2, and its surface temperature is 891°F (477°C). That's too hot for liquid water and more than hot enough to melt lead. If the CO_2 level in Earth's atmosphere were to reach the point at which it became even 1 percent of the atmosphere, the air temperature would hover right around the boiling point of water.

During the summer, people who say that the Arizona desert air feels cooler than the South Carolina seashore aren't crazy. The air truly does feel cooler, and this is due to the effect of a single greenhouse gas—the most powerful one of all—water vapor. Water vapor retains two-thirds of the heat trapped by all the greenhouse gases. The Arizona desert's hot air is mostly dry. Without the humidity and the added heat from water vapor, the temperature is bearable, especially at night after the sun sets. In contrast, the atmosphere along the South Carolina seashore is loaded with water vapor. Ocean breezes help make the heat bearable, but without them, the air is close enough to make you sweat without taking a step. The only saving grace of the high water-vapor content may be the clouds it generates. Like an atmospheric umbrella, clouds create a spot of shady relief from the sun's rays.

As recently as thirty years ago, less than half of the greenhouse gases had been identified, and scientists were still divided about whether Earth was warming or cooling. Without these molecules, our planet would be freezing cold—a frigid sphere with an average surface temperature of –4°F (–20°C), which is slightly lower than the temperature inside your refrigerator's freezer. But now we know that greenhouse gases have been accumulating.

Carbon dioxide, the most abundant of the trace greenhouse gases, is produced whenever we burn something and as living organisms decompose. In the 1950s, a climatologist named Charles Keeling climbed Mauna Loa, the largest volcano on our planet, to record the CO_2 concentrations in the atmosphere. He created a graph, known as the Keeling curve, with data he collected over a time span of nearly fifty years. Keeling's graph gives us a fascinating record of Earth's "breathing" pattern by season. Every spring in the Northern Hemisphere, sprouting greenery extracts CO_2 from the atmosphere, as though the Earth is breathing in. On the graph, the inhalation is recorded as a fall in CO_2 concentration. Then, in the following autumn, as leaves fall, decompose, and generate CO_2, there is an exhalation, which enriches the air with the gas. The exhalation is recorded as a rise on the graph. But Keeling's work revealed another CO_2 trend. He discovered that each exhalation ended with a little more CO_2 in the atmosphere than the one before. This ever-increasing climb in the Keeling curve was the first

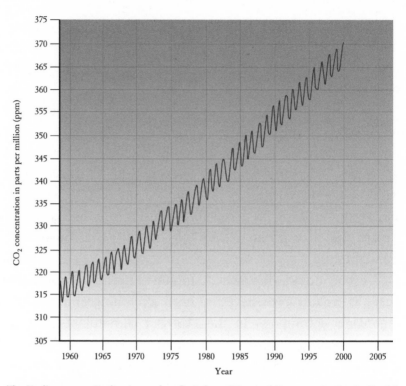

The Keeling curve: Keeling's graph reflects how CO$_2$, and its concentration in Earth's atmosphere, increases and decreases according to the season. It also shows the overall increase in CO$_2$ concentration in our planet's atmosphere during the last 40 years of the twentieth century.

definitive sign that Earth's great ocean in the sky might prove to be the Achilles' heel of our fossil-fuel-addicted civilization. Each rise and fall is like a photograph of climate change. And if you fast-forward the frames into the future, it appears that during the twenty-first century we may see a doubling of the CO$_2$ in the atmosphere—from the 3 parts per 10,000 that existed in the early twentieth century to 6 parts per 10,000. And that increase in CO$_2$ has the potential to heat our planet by around 5°F (2.8°C) and even perhaps as much as 10°F (5.6°C). An occasional increase of this amount on a summer day just makes us sweat more—that's *weather*. But if the average temperature remains that much higher throughout the year, it signals a climate change. And a climate change of that magnitude could be a recipe for disaster.

CALL TO ACTION

Energy Star

The U.S. Environmental Protection Agency (EPA) and the U.S. Department of Energy are serious about helping people take action. They created a joint program called Energy Star to educate people on how to save money and protect the environment by choosing energy-efficient products and incorporating some commonsense conservation practices into their daily lives. The EPA estimates that Energy Star programs from 1992 to 2003 have prevented the addition of more than 150 million tons of carbon emissions. In 2007, the program's advice and suggestions enabled Americans to curtail greenhouse-gas emissions equivalent to 27 million cars.

The Energy Star website, **http://www.energystar.gov,** has many informative features, including how to assess your home energy use, how to reduce it, and how to judge whether an appliance is energy-friendly or not. Before buying a new home appliance, television, cordless phone, DVD player, computer, printer, or any other electronic device, visit the Energy Star website and find out which products will best reduce greenhouse-gas emissions.

Chapter 3

The Greenhouse Story

The presence of greenhouse gases in Earth's atmosphere is well documented. So what are they actually doing as they float and circulate in the air around us? Scientists knew initially that CO_2 excelled at trapping longer wavelengths of sunlight. However, laboratory experiments showed that increasing the amount of CO_2 seemed to make no real difference in the amount of heat it trapped. Taking that and the small percentage of CO_2 present in Earth's atmosphere into account, scientists were stymied: How could such a small amount of gas change the climate of our entire planet? Further experiments revealed that the presence of CO_2, even in small amounts, acts as a trigger for retention of water vapor—an extremely potent greenhouse gas. When heated up by CO_2 even a little bit, the atmosphere can absorb and hold more moisture. That warms the atmosphere further. Scientists call this a positive-feedback loop: the increase of one gas helps another gas increase its effect.

Moreover, once CO_2 makes its way into the atmosphere, it has a lengthy life there: about 56 percent of all the CO_2 that humans have introduced into the atmosphere by burning fossil fuels is still floating around. And that, directly and indirectly, is the cause of about 80 percent of all global warming.

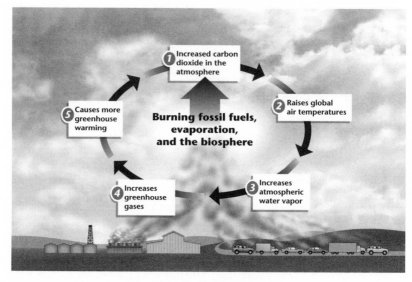

Positive-Feedback Loop

Increased carbon dioxide in the atmosphere

Raises global air temperatures

Increases atmospheric water vapor

Increases greenhouse gases

Causes more greenhouse warming

Burning fossil fuels, evaporation, and the biosphere

Yet concentrations of CO_2 have been in Earth's atmosphere for millions of years, and the concentrations have fluctuated in the past. Climatologists have collected proof of these fluctuations in ice cores sampled from glaciers and ice sheets in Antarctica and other areas.

By drilling more than a mile (3 kilometers) into the Antarctic ice sheet, scientists have drawn out an ice core that spans almost a million years of Earth history. The air bubbles contained in the ice core are like tiny pockets of ancient climates, with the deepest section of the core containing the oldest air. The ice-core record shows that during cold times, CO_2 levels dropped to around 160 parts per million, and that until recently they never exceeded 280 parts per million. That amount of carbon by weight, counting only the carbon found in a molecule of CO_2, equals approximately 588 gigatons (billion tons) of CO_2. (The conversion factor from ppm to gigatons is 2.1.) However, during the past 200 years, since the advent of the Industrial Revolution, the Earth's CO_2 level has started to climb. In 1958, when Keeling began his record on Mauna Loa, the CO_2 level was at 315 parts per million. And it's still going up. In 2008, the Mauna Loa Observatory reported that the figure stood at about 387 parts per million, or around 813 gigatons.

Where's all the CO_2 coming from? You don't have to look any farther than your driveway to find one source: the family car. The billions of engines we have built—including those in most of our cars—run on fossil fuels such as coal, gasoline, and oil-based fuels. They are the leading manufacturers of CO_2. The electricity that you use to light, and maybe heat, your home may have been generated by a coal-burning power plant, which is a major CO_2 producer. Coal's composition is 70 to 92 percent carbon, depending on the type of coal.

The carbon present in Earth's atmosphere is only one reservoir in the carbon cycle. After carbon leaves the atmosphere, it enters into the other carbon reservoirs, which are known as *carbon sinks*. Carbon sinks absorb and store more carbon than they release. All living organisms, including people, are carbon sinks, as are the ocean and some of the rocks beneath our feet. Some carbon sinks are very large, but the size of any given carbon sink can change through time. Fossil-fuel reservoirs are long-term carbon sinks buried beneath Earth's surface. Scientists calculate that if we could take all the carbon stored inside the Earth in the form of fossil fuels—like the coal made during the Carboniferous period—and return it to the atmosphere by burning it, we would use up all the oxygen in our atmosphere.

Soil is a carbon sink that contains carbon for a much shorter period of time. Gardeners prize black, moldy, carbon-rich soil because the nutrients it contains spur plant growth.

For the past couple of decades, scientists have been monitoring the CO_2 that humans produce by burning fossil fuels to see where it goes. This is possible because the gas derived from fossil fuels has a unique chemical signature that can be tracked as it circulates around the planet. In very round figures, scientists have discovered that each year 2 gigatons of CO_2 from burning fossil fuels are absorbed by the oceans and that a further 1.7 gigatons are absorbed by life on land.

The land, however, may not always be as reliable a carbon sink as it has been in the past. Mature forests don't absorb much CO_2, because they are already in a state of carbon balance, releasing CO_2 as old vegetation rots, then absorbing it as the new grows. For these reasons the world's largest forests—the coniferous forests of Siberia and Canada—and the tropical rain forests are not good carbon sinks, but new, vigorously growing forests are. The colonial people who arrived in America in the 1700s caused the vegetation's carbon "appetite" to increase by cutting and burning the great eastern forests, and later pioneers, spreading westward, burned and allowed their cattle to graze the western plains and deserts. As a result, most of America's forests are less than sixty years old. Each year, the vigorously growing vegetation absorbs around half a billion tons of CO_2 from the atmosphere, and newly planted forests in China and Europe may be absorbing an equal amount. The excess CO_2 being absorbed by these forests has helped cool our planet. However, as the Northern Hemisphere forests and shrubs mature into old-growth forests, they will extract less and less CO_2. Unfortunately, this will happen at the very same time that humans are pumping more CO_2 into the atmosphere.

But calculations indicate that there really is only one major carbon sink on Earth: the oceans. They have absorbed 48 percent of all carbon emitted by humans between 1800 and 1994, while life on land has actually added carbon to the atmosphere.

One of the fascinating aspects of oceans in their role as a carbon sink is that they vary in their ability to absorb carbon. The North Atlantic alone—a mere 15 percent of the ocean surface—contains almost a quarter of all the carbon emitted by humans since 1800. Even more curiously, it turns out that the CO_2 in the North Atlantic wasn't originally absorbed there at all. Instead, the North Sea, a shallow marine basin between Great Britain and northern Europe, has oddly stratified, or layered, waters that allow CO_2 to accumulate in areas below the surface, from which subsurface currents then carry the CO_2 to the North Atlantic. Just as a human kidney filters waste products from our blood, the North Sea acts as Earth's "carbon kidney." The sea's layering filters carbon from the atmosphere so efficiently that it has removed 20 percent of all CO_2 ever emitted by humans.

The discovery of this "carbon kidney" has, however, raised new concerns. Cold seawater holds more carbon than warm seawater. Global warming will warm Earth's oceans such that they will not absorb as much CO_2 as they do now.

Another critical aspect of seawater in regard to its capacity to absorb CO_2 is the amount of carbonate it contains. Carbon dioxide has an acidifying effect on seawater, and this effect is neutralized by the presence of carbonate, which is strongly alkaline, or basic. Carbonate enters the ocean from rivers that have flowed over limestone, a rock made of calcium carbonate, and reacts with the CO_2 in the seawater that has been absorbed from the atmosphere. At present, there is a balance in the ocean water between carbonate and CO_2 concentrations. However, as the oceans absorb more and more CO_2 from the atmosphere, the carbonate is being used up, causing the oceans to become more acidic. The more acidic an ocean becomes, the less CO_2 it can absorb.

An acidifying ocean could also pose a threat to marine organisms. Those creatures that build shells by extracting carbonate from the ocean water will have a reduced chance of survival if insufficient quantities of carbonate are available. In fact, scientists have discovered that the quantity of human-made CO_2 absorbed by the ocean is decreasing. During the 1980s the ocean was taking up about 2 gigatons of carbon per year, but by the 1990s that had dropped to below 1.8 gigatons. If the current reduction of CO_2 absorption by Earth's oceans persists, by the end of this century, oceans will be taking in 10 percent less CO_2 than today.

Since increased CO_2 is clearly affecting the atmosphere and oceans in ways that could disrupt life, the need to control our CO_2 emissions seems obvious. Responsibly run households adhere to a financial budget; it follows that responsible citizens of the planet should adhere to a carbon budget for humanity. Scientists calculate that to stabilize CO_2 emissions at a level twice that which existed before the Industrial Revolution (a level widely considered the threshold of dangerous change), we would have to limit all future human emissions to around 660 gigatons. Slightly more than half of these emissions would remain in the atmosphere, raising the CO_2 level from its current 813 gigatons to around 1,155 gigatons, which amounts to 550 parts per million, by the year 2100. This budget translates to an annual production of 6.6 gigatons of CO_2 if we use fossil fuels for only another century. Considering that during the 1990s an average of 14.6 gigatons of CO_2 accumulated each year, half of which were from burning fossil fuels, and that the human population is projected to increase to 9 billion by 2050, meeting such a budget will undoubtedly be a formidable task.

Carbon dioxide is a greenhouse gas with wide-ranging effects. It is, however, only one of about thirty greenhouse gases that can be found in Earth's atmosphere. Most of the other gases are rare, but because they absorb heat from energy wavelengths that are different from those absorbed by CO_2, any amount that they contribute is significant.

Although it makes up just 1.5 parts per million of the atmosphere, methane is the third most important greenhouse gas, after water vapor and CO_2. Over the last few years, its concentration has doubled, and when measured over a century-long timescale, methane is sixty times more potent at capturing heat energy than CO_2. Fortunately, it has a much shorter atmospheric life. Methane is often referred to as "swamp gas." It's created by microbes that thrive in environments that are anaerobic, or lacking in oxygen. Methane is produced in swamps, stagnant pools, and inside your bowels after a hearty bean supper. Garbage dumps and pig and cattle farms also produce methane gas. Scientists estimate that methane will cause 15 to 17 percent of all global warming experienced this century, which makes it an important factor in creating the positive-feedback loops that have on occasion heated Earth.

Nitrous oxide, also called laughing gas, is 270 times more

efficient at trapping heat than CO_2, and although it's far rarer than methane, it lasts 150 years in the atmosphere. Nitrous oxide is produced naturally by the activity of microbes, especially in tropical waters and soils, but a far greater volume is now being produced by humans as we add nitrogen fertilizers to soil, burn fossil fuels and forests, and operate sewage- and manure-treatment facilities. Our contributions have put 20 percent more nitrous oxide in the atmosphere than there was at the beginning of the Industrial Revolution.

The rarest of the greenhouse gases are members of the hydrofluorocarbon (HFC) and chlorofluorocarbon (CFC) families of chemicals. These gases did not exist before industrial chemists began to manufacture them. Some of them are 10,000 times more potent at capturing heat energy than CO_2. They can last in the atmosphere for hundreds of years. This class of greenhouse gases plays an important role in the health of Earth's ozone layer (see chapters 13 and 21).

Having gotten a glimpse of how the carbon cycle and Earth's greenhouse gases interact in our planet's atmosphere, we can now consider the problem of global warming—and there's no better way to do that than to look back at the work of the pioneers who first realized that something was amiss.

CALL TO ACTION

Start a Low-Carbon Car Diet Today

The average American's slice of the CO_2 "pie" comes to a whopping 122 pounds per person per day. Half of the poundage comes from emissions generated by industry and businesses, like those that heat, cool, and light our buildings, make our cars, sell us clothing, show the latest movies, cook our fast foods, and serve up our double lattes. The individual carbon emissions for the rest of the world, for example, a person in Jamaica or Romania, average 24 pounds per person per day.

While you can't immediately control the carbon emissions of businesses and industry, you can make immediate changes to lower the carbon diet of your family's car.

1. Go carless. Every gallon of gasoline burned by a car or truck produces 24 pounds of CO_2. Don't hop into the car for trips less than a mile and a half. A walk that distance takes only about

twenty minutes and counts toward the medical community's (and the government's) recommended daily exercise of thirty to sixty minutes. You'll walk off pounds, both fat- and carbon-related. If you or your parents drive you to school and a school bus is available, think about using the bus a couple of times a week. When global warming and carbon emissions are at stake, it's cool to ride a school bus.

2. Start riding your bike more often. It's a carbon-free vehicle. But always wear a helmet.

3. If you must take a car, combine all your errands into one circular trip. Multiple trips waste time, gas, and money, *and* generate more CO_2.

Chapter 4
A Grand Discovery

The land surfaces where glaciers exist today exhibit certain physical characteristics such as oddly placed boulders, scratched bedrock, and U-shaped valleys. The features are clearly the plucking and sculpting effects of moving ice. By the early seventeenth century, European scientists noticed that those same features existed in places far from any existing glaciers. From that, they drew the conclusion that sheets of ice had once covered a far more extensive area. In 1837, a Swiss scientist named Louis Agassiz proposed the first hypothesis of glacial ages. By the end of the century, scientists accepted Agassiz's concept and began theorizing about what produced these different ages.

Born in what is now Serbia in 1879, Milutin Milankovitch spent most of his life working as a civil engineer. Like many other people of his time, he pondered the puzzle of the great ice ages. An internment during World War I in Budapest, Hungary, where he was permitted to work in the library of the Hungarian Academy of Sciences, gave Milankovitch the opportunity to delve into the issue of ice-age formation with vehemence. He was determined to explain how *insolation,* the effect of solar radiation, might have contributed to changes in Earth's climate. By 1941, Milankovitch published his great work, *Canon of Insolation and the Ice-Age Problem.*

Milankovitch identified three principal cycles that drive Earth's climatic variability. The first and longest cycle concerns the shape of Earth's orbit around the sun. This shape changes from a circle to an ellipse in a cycle that takes about 100,000 years to complete and is known as Earth's *eccentricity.* The more elliptical the orbit is, the higher the eccentricity. When Earth's orbit is strongly elliptical, the planet travels both closer to and farther away from the sun, which means that the intensity of the sun's seasonal rays varies considerably throughout the year. At present, the orbit is not very elliptical, with only a 6 percent difference between January and July in the radiation reaching Earth, but when Earth's orbit is at its most eccentric, the difference is 20 to 30 percent. This is the only cycle that changes the total amount of the sun's energy reaching Earth, so its influence is considerable.

The second of Milankovitch's cycles takes about 42,000 years to run its course, and it concerns the tilt of Earth on its axis. This varies anywhere from 21.8 to 24.4 degrees, and it determines which areas of Earth will receive the most radiation. At the moment, Earth's axial tilt is in the middle of its range.

The third and shortest cycle lasts about 22,000 years and concerns the wobble of Earth on its axis. If you could trace the wobbling path of Earth's axis, the shape created would look like a cone with the tip against Earth's surface. At present, Earth's axis of rotation in the Northern Hemisphere points in the direction of a star named Polaris, also known as the North Star. During this cycle, Earth's axis of rotation will gradually shift until it points at another star, named Vega, which at that point will become the new North Star. The direction in which the axis of rotation points affects the intensity of Earth's seasons. Winters can be bitter cold and summers scorching hot when Vega marks true north.

However, Milankovitch's cycles can cause ice ages only when continental drift brings large parts of Earth's land surface near the poles. Then, when the cycles are just right, mild summers and harsh winters allow snow to accumulate on the polar lands, eventually forming great ice domes.

Even at their most extreme, Milankovitch's cycles result in an annual variation in the total amount of sunlight reaching Earth of less than one-tenth of 1 percent. But that small difference has a whopping effect on Earth's temperature, causing it to rise or fall by about 9°F (5°C). Scientists are still mystified by how such small inputs of solar rays result in big changes in Earth's climate, but they are certain that greenhouse gases play a role, based on evidence from computer models.

Computer models of Earth's surface and the processes at work there are the basic tools used in climate-change prediction. By varying the data inputs, scientists can, for example, see how our climate might respond to a doubling of CO_2 in the atmosphere or how the ozone hole affects climate. As evidence of greenhouse gases' impact, computer models can't create a virtual ice age south of the equator by using Milankovitch's cycles alone: they must also lower the atmospheric levels of CO_2.

By 1969, the year Milankovitch's work was translated into English, oceanographers were already finding evidence in cores of deep-sea sediments of the kinds of impacts Milankovitch's cycles had predicted. Today, Milankovitch's discovery is considered one of the greatest breakthroughs in climate studies. But in addition to his cycles, there are still other factors to consider.

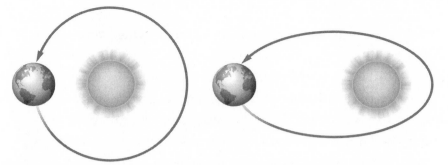

ORBIT

During a cycle that lasts about 100,000 years, Earth orbits the sun in a path that changes from a circle to an ellipse and then back to a circle.

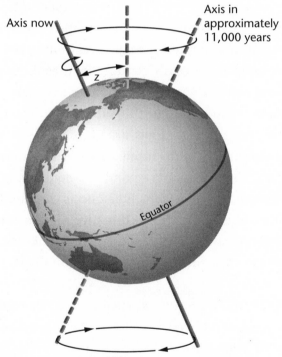

Wobble of Axis

WOBBLE

During a cycle that takes about 22,000 years to complete, Earth's axis "wobbles" in a pattern shaped like a cone. The intensity of Earth's seasons is affected by the direction in which the axis points during the cycle. Angle z is the number of degrees that Earth's axis wobbles during the cycle.

Milutin Milankovitch's theory proposes that the shape of Earth's orbit around the sun in combination with the tilt of Earth's axis and the amount of wobble in the axis at any given time are related to the amount of glaciation found at the North Pole. The farther the orbit takes the Earth away from the sun, the greater the contrast between summer and winter temperatures. When the tilt of the Earth is at its minimum, solar radiation is reduced at the pole, resulting in colder temperatures. In addition to the cooling effects of the orbit and tilt, the degree of Earth's wobble can prevent the pole from receiving direct solar radiation, resulting in the onset of widespread glaciation and/or ice ages.

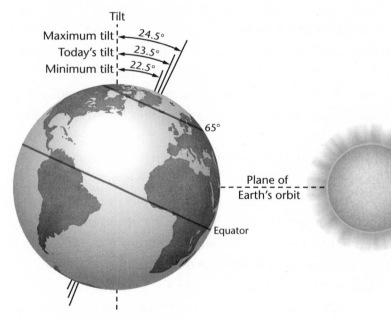

Period: 42,000 years

TILT

As Earth orbits the sun, it also rotates on its axis, which is tilted. The angle of the tilt changes over a period of about 42,000 years.

One of these factors is the intensity of radiation emitted from the sun. One-third of the sun's rays that strike Earth are reflected back into space; substances with a high albedo—ice, for example—play an important role in this process. The other two-thirds of the sun's rays that reach our planet are absorbed and used for energy needs here on Earth, powering our weather, climate, and most of life on Earth. But the sun's intensity varies. More than 2,000 years ago, ancient Greek and Chinese astronomers wrote about dark spots they observed on the sun's surface that shifted positions and changed shape. In April 1612, the Italian astronomer Galileo, armed with an early telescope, made detailed observations of these sunspots, demonstrating that they were not, as previously thought, celestial bodies orbiting the sun's surface but phenomena that originated from the star itself. At that time, sunspot activity was exceptionally low, so the observation received something of a ho-hum reception for several centuries.

Interest in sunspots spiked in the nineteenth century, when scientists discovered that their activity seemed to follow two patterns: an eleven-year cycle as well as a longer cycle of centuries. Sunspots are slightly cooler than the rest of the sun's surface, so one might think that the sun is emitting fewer rays when a lot of sunspots are present. However, satellite measurements have shown that the opposite is true: the emission of solar rays increases when sunspots form, causing global temperatures to rise. During the years 1645 to 1715, when relatively few sunspots formed, the paradox appears to have held true: temperatures in Europe plummeted, and rivers such as the Thames, in England, regularly froze over. Whether sunspots played a part in lower temperatures is challenged by some scientists, because despite the coincidence in timing, no testable physical mechanism has yet been identified that confirms exactly how, or if, sunspots affect Earth's temperature.

However, scientists have recently acknowledged that variations in solar radiation and greenhouse-gas concentrations affect Earth's climate in fundamentally different ways. Solar radiation warms the upper levels of the stratosphere through the UV rays absorbed by ozone there. In contrast, greenhouse gases warm the troposphere, and mostly at the bottom, where their concentration is greatest. At the moment, Earth is experiencing both stratospheric cooling (due to a hole in the ozone) and tropospheric warming (due to increased greenhouse gases).

Orbital variations, sunspots, and greenhouse gases can all be thought of as "forcing" changes in the temperature of our planet. As scientists sought to understand these changes, they looked to the geologic record—Earth's history as reflected by rock materials—for evidence that would support and confirm this belief. They discovered that the fossil record in particular is characterized by sudden shifts from one steady, long-lasting climatic state to another. It appears that Earth responded in jolts to the factors believed to influence climate. The fossil record told a tale of a series of wild shifts in which entire habitats changed from one end of a continent to another, causing many extinctions, yet keeping conditions just tolerable enough for life to survive on Earth.

CALL TO ACTION

Happy (Green) Holidays!

Electricity consumption soars during the December-to-January holiday season, when holiday trees and the exteriors of homes are festooned with strings of sparkling holiday lights. Each year approximately 159.4 million sets of holiday lights are sold in the United States; one-third to one-half of the bulbs will need replacement within three years. When one bulb burns out, the entire strand can go dark. At that point, many people toss the strand and buy a new one.

According to the U.S. Department of Energy, you can make a difference if you scrap those old holiday lights and go green with strings of *light-emitting diode (LED)* bulbs. A light-emitting diode is a semiconductor that emits a ray of visible light when an electric current passes through it. (When replacing your strings, look for "LED" on the package.) LEDs take the cake when it comes to saving energy: the average bulb lasts more than 100,000 hours indoors, half that outdoors. It uses one-tenth the energy that an incandescent miniature holiday bulb uses, and it doesn't get hot, which reduces the risk of fire. The whole strand remains lit if one bulb burns out. It's also made of plastic, so you don't have to worry about broken glass shards.

A string of LED bulbs costs more to buy than a string of incandescent bulbs; they range up to $30 for a string of 100, compared to $10 to $15 for a similar string of incandescents. But LEDs are more economical in the long run. In 2006, when the Idaho State House replaced the incandescent lights on its holiday tree with 10,000 LED bulbs, the cost of electricity to light the tree dropped to 1 percent of what it cost to light the tree in previous years. Decorate with LED bulbs and feel good about turning on your holiday lights. Or perhaps you will choose to go even greener and forgo holiday lights completely.

Chapter 5
Time's Gateways

Earth's history spans more than 4,500 million years. Scientists divide that history, the geologic record, into time segments that reflect major changes that have occurred on Earth. *Eras* are the longest segments. They are divided into shorter segments called *periods,* which in turn are subdivided into *epochs.* The divisions of the geologic timescale are easily told apart because of what geologists call *faunal turnover,* times when species first appear or disappear. For example, the Mesozoic era is called the Age of Dinosaurs; the Devonian period is often called the Age of Fishes. We can think of these divisions or episodes as time's gateways—occasions when one age, and often one climate, gives way to the next.

The shifting of continents, cosmic collisions, and climate-driving forces such as greenhouse gases are the only agents of change sufficiently powerful to open a gateway in time. They all act in different ways, but the result is the same: death for some species and opportunity for others.

Time's gateways come in three "sizes"—small, medium, and large. The smallest are those opening on brief and local slices of time, occurring within a geological epoch or less. The Bering land bridge is an example of a small gateway. About

21,000 years ago, during an ice age in the Pleistocene epoch, enough water became locked in ice to cause the sea level in the Bering Sea, between North America and Asia, to drop about 400 feet (120 meters). That left a bridge of land called the Bering land bridge exposed. This bridge, which in some places was almost 1,000 miles (1,609 kilometers) across, became a migration highway for animals and probably some humans. Horses and camels, which had previously lived only in North America, crossed into Asia and spawned new populations. As the ice age ended, the sea level rose and flooded the land bridge. By 10,000 years ago, rising seawater had completely separated the two continents. Today, most of the land bridge lies 82 to 180 feet (25 to 55 meters) below sea level. Ironically, after their migration to Asia and after the land bridge disappeared, horses and camels became extinct in North America. It wasn't until the Spanish arrived in the 1500s that horses were reintroduced. A land bridge is only one example of a small time gateway. Shifting continents that bump into one another or the Earth heating up or cooling are other factors that open time gateways. These gateways are marked by the sudden arrival of new species to a single continent, often with the extinction of local competitors.

The medium-size divisions of time separate geological time *periods,* such as the Cretaceous from the Tertiary. These time divisions are global in scale and usually result from factors such as greenhouse gases, which alter the climate and habitats found over widespread areas. In the fossil record, this type of time gateway is evidenced by the extinction of a number of species followed by the slow evolution of new life-forms that adapt to the changed conditions.

Time's greatest divisions are those separating *eras,* when massive upheavals have caused as much as 95 percent of all species to vanish. Earth has experienced mass extinctions of this type five times, driven by various causes. The most recent of these occurred 65 million years ago, when an asteroid smacked into Earth in the area of the Caribbean Sea and Mexico's Yucatan peninsula. Although the impact occurred primarily in North America, the devastation that followed was worldwide: every living thing that weighed more than about 77 pounds, including the dinosaurs, plus a vast number of smaller species, died. Why? The extinctions were caused by the huge quantity of material—dust, ash, gases—that was injected into the atmosphere, causing climate change, and CO_2, it turns out, played a major role in the event.

We know this from the work of paleobotanists studying *stomata*—the tiny "breathing" holes found on the epidermis of a leaf—in 65-million-year-old fossil leaves. The scientists noticed that the plants that survived the extinction had fewer stomata than those that existed before the extinction. Plants need fewer stomata when CO_2 is readily available. A study of the precise number of stomata indicates that atmospheric CO_2 rose by thousands of parts per million. When the asteroid crashed, it smashed into limestone-rich rock, and the chemical reactions that occurred generated huge volumes of CO_2. The greenhouse gas would have caused a rapid spike in temperature, and species that couldn't cope with the sudden heat perished, including many reptiles.

The geologic record stretches back thousands of millions of years. Unfortunately, the further back in time we go, the more likely it is that details of past climates are erased as rock and sediments are altered by geological processes inside the Earth. For that reason, paleontologists who hope to correlate past climate changes with possible future trends tend to work on rocks

ERA	PERIOD	EPOCH	SIGNIFICANT EVENT	YEARS AGO
				present day
Cainozoic	Quaternary	Holocene	The Long Summer	
				8000
		Pleistocene	Ice Ages *First modern humans*	
				1.8 million
	Tertiary	Pliocene	*First upright human ancestors*	
				5.3 million
		Miocene	*Decline of widespread rain forests*	
				23.8 million
		Oligocene	*Diverse vertebrate communities*	
				33.7 million
		Eocene	*Final separation of Australia from Antarctica*	
			Clathrate release 55 million years ago	55.5 million
		Paleocene		
			Cretaceous–Tertiary extinction about 65 million years ago	65 million
Mesozoic	Cretaceous		*First flowering plants*	
				145 million
	Jurassic		*First birds*	
				213 million
	Triassic		*First dinosaurs*	
			Permian–Triassic extinction about 251 million years ago	248 million
Paleozoic	Permian		*First conifers; early reptiles*	
			Ice Ages about 350 to 250 million years ago	286 million
	Carboniferous		*Early amphibians*	
			Late Devonian extinction about 364 million years ago	360 million
	Devonian		*First insects*	
				410 million
	Silurian		*First fish*	
			Ordovician–Silurian extinction about 439 million years ago	440 million
	Ordovician		*Marine invertebrates*	
				505 million
	Cambrian		Cambrian explosion	
				544 million
Proterozoic			Ice Ages about 800 to 600 million years ago	
				2500 million
Archean			*First life*	
				3800 million
Hadean			*Earth takes form*	
				4500 million

Geologic Timescale

65 million years old or younger, and nowhere is there a bigger jackpot of information than in the deep oceans. Scientists drilling more than a mile deep into the fossil-bearing rock in the seafloor have retrieved cores that offer clues to ancient temperature, salinity, and other environmental conditions. Most of the cores corroborate climate trends indicated by Milankovitch's cycles. But the cycles couldn't explain three baffling climatic aberrations discovered in the cores.

The oldest of the three climate aberrations occurred about 55 million years ago. Because the Earth's surface heated abruptly—by 9°F to 18°F (5°C to 10°C)—during the event, it seems relevant to our situation today. Until November 2003, we had little detailed knowledge of this event. But three sediment cores drilled from the Shatsky Rise (32°N, 158°E), a submarine mountain range more than a mile deep in the North Pacific, opened an astonishing window on a planet-altering climatic event.

At a point 656 feet below the seafloor, the drill encountered a 10-inch-thick layer of ooze resting atop a section of the seafloor that had been eaten away by acid, powerful proof that the oceans had turned acidic. Scientists have observed this trend today and know that it occurs when seawater is absorbing large amounts of CO_2.

The core revealed that this influx of CO_2 profoundly affected marine organisms in the deep ocean. Foraminifera, often called forams, are tiny marine creatures living on the ocean floor that play an important role in the oceanic food chain, where they are eaten by small marine invertebrates and fish. The shells of forams fossilize well and are easily identified, which makes them ideal as evidence to explain how climatic change has affected ecosystems. Comparisons of forams from above and below the acid-eaten layer reveal that there were massive extinctions in the ocean depths, and it seems that no creature in the oceanic food chain, from the tiniest ocean dweller to the bizarre deep-sea fishes, sharks, and squid, escaped the shock. Even the surface levels of the ocean were affected by the acidic water, as evidenced by the appearance of new species of forams in shallow water and in the open oceans.

Evidence of the high CO_2 level 55 million years ago and the abrupt warm climate it would have fostered is evident in the fossilized remains of terrestrial flora and fauna from that period. At that time, land bridges across the Arctic Circle connected North America, Asia, and Europe. The warmer temperatures favored the migration of warmth-loving species, and they took advantage of the brief window of opportunity to spread.

So what caused the climate to warm up? Scientific analysis has revealed that a mind-boggling 1,650 to 3,300 gigatons of carbon were injected into the atmosphere. The warming trend seems to have occurred over the course of decades or centuries, a very short period of time on the geologic timescale. But during that time, the atmospheric concentrations of CO_2 rose from about 500 parts per million to around 2,000 parts per million.

Norwegian scientists have recently located a structure that points to where the gas came from. They noticed that 55-million-year-old sediments in the north and central Atlantic Ocean lacked any carbonate at all, indicating that these areas were far more acidic than elsewhere and suggesting that the gas source was nearby. When the scientists looked at seismic data from the sea off Norway, they discovered several craterlike structures, up to 62 miles (100 kilometers) across, which reach from deep inside Earth up to the level that would have been the sediment surface 55 million years ago. At the base of these structures lay narrow bands of volcanic rock.

These scientists believe that the bands of volcanic material acted like a wick leading to dynamite. The craterlike structures had formed in sediments that contained huge accumulations of hydrocarbons (organic compounds made of hydrogen and carbon)—fossil fuels, in other words—and also may have contained an icy, methane-rich substance known as clathrates. When the molten volcanic rock reached the hydrocarbons and clathrates, the gases they contained heated and expanded. The result was a huge submarine explosion that ripped craterlike holes in the ocean floor.

The scientists theorize that most of the methane chemically combined with oxygen contained in the seawater, creating CO_2 as a by-product. What life remained in the ocean depths scrambled to survive in the oxygen-depleted water. As the CO_2 rose to the surface, it turned the water acidic, a result leading directly to the extinction of countless marine organisms. In fact, ever-mounting fossil evidence indicates that many of the deep-sea creatures that exist today evolved after the explosion.

Scientists are still analyzing this information, trying to determine if the explosions alone were responsible for the change in climate. Whatever happened, it took at least 20,000 years for the Earth to reabsorb all of the additional carbon, which was apparently soaked up by a bloom of surface plankton, small organisms that float in freshwater and salt water.

It's likely that the rapid rise in greenhouse gases that occurred 55 million years ago offers a reasonable parallel with our current situation. There are, however, significant differences. First, Earth today is still in an "icehouse" phase from the recent

Pleistocene ice ages, whereas 55 million years ago the climate was already warm, with CO_2 levels around twice what they are today. There were no ice caps then, and presumably fewer cold-adapted species such as narwhals and polar bears. It's unlikely that the ancient warm world had the incredible diversity found today on Earth's colder mountains and in the depths of the sea. Our modern Earth stands to lose far more from rapid warming than the world of 55 million years ago. Back then, the warming closed the Paleocene epoch. We, with our greenhouse-gas-producing activities, may bring an entire era to an end.

CALL TO ACTION

Plug the Leaks

Plugging air leaks around windows and doors is a fast way to make your home more comfortable, and it's an immediate energy saver.

To test windows and doors for air leaks, light an incense stick or a candle and hold it near your windows, doors, and even electrical outlets. If the trail of smoke blows horizontally or the candle flame flickers, you've got air leaks—and they're year-round energy wasters. Plug the leaks:

- Caulk or weather-strip around the windows and doors. Ask at the store which product is best for your situation.
- Install rubber or foam gaskets around electrical outlets located on the walls along the perimeter of your home.
- Caulk around ductwork in exterior walls, such as dryer vents.

Do you have a fireplace? If so, make sure the damper is closed after the fire is completely out. Eight percent of your home's heat can drift right up the chimney. And in the summer: keep the damper closed so that your air-conditioned air doesn't seep out.

- Install glass doors across the fireplace.
- If you use starter logs, check out the new kind made with recycled coffee grounds. They produce 14 percent less CO_2.

Chapter 6

Markers of Change

On the geologic timescale, the history of human life on Earth is about equivalent to the amount of time it would take to light and blow out a match. We are, most definitely, one of the new kids on the block. Our species, *Homo sapiens,* evolved in Africa during the Pleistocene epoch, and the ice age we evolved in has its roots in small glaciers that formed about 2.4 million years ago.

The earliest humans and their ancestors lived in an environment very different from the one we live in today. For a long time, an icehouse climate dominated their world. Had Milankovitch's cycles not altered, ushering in a widespread hospitable climate, it's possible the human species would have become extinct. But by 60,000 years ago, the climate had changed in a manner that favored our migration from Africa. Humans spread across the Sinai peninsula and out into Europe and Asia; by 46,000 years ago, they had reached Australia via sea voyages. People had definitely reached the Americas by 13,000 years ago and may have arrived earlier than that. Humans thrived as they spread into new lands. Yet for thousands of years, these intelligent people, who were like us in every way physically and mentally, remained hunters and gatherers. Was it because the climate favored this lifestyle? If so, might climate changes during the past 10,000 years have influenced the change toward a more urbanized lifestyle? To explore this possibility, we have to know more about the climate that gave birth to our species.

One of the best sources of information about climate is timber. A tree's growth rings, as seen in a cross section of the trunk, supply a reliable record of what the growing conditions were like during the tree's life. Widely spaced rings, a sign of growth, tell of warm and bountiful growing seasons, when sunlight and rainfall were plentiful. Compressed rings, recording little growth in the tree, tell of adversity, when long, hard winters or drought-blighted summers tested life to the limits.

Groves of bristlecone pines dotting the rocky slopes of California's White Mountains are the home of Earth's oldest living organism, a tree more than 4,600 years old. Located in the aptly named Methuselah Grove, this tree holds a detailed, year-by-year record of California's climate during the tree's life. By matching the growth pattern at the heart of this tree with that of a dead stump nearby, researchers found that the trees' climatic timeline extends back as far as 10,000 years. Tree-ring records of this length have now been obtained in the Southern Hemisphere as well, and scientists hope that New Zealand's kauri pines will help them establish a tree-ring record that spans 60,000 years of climatic change.

Tree-ring records can shed light on climatic events that affected human life. In 1609 to 1610, Jamestown, the first permanent English settlement in America, was almost eradicated when more than two-thirds of the colonists died, mostly of starvation. A tree-ring record established using a series of bald cypress trees proffers evidence that a severe drought existed during the years prior to the colonists' arrival. The resulting shortages of food, both meat and plants, had devastating effects on the colonists.

The climate record provided by trees is useful but relatively limited in what it can tell us. For a really detailed record, we must turn to ice—but only in special places does it yield all its secrets. One such place is the Quelccaya ice cap in the high mountains of Peru, where 10 feet (3 meters) of snow can fall in a summer. There the ice is laid down in a banded annual pattern, each year's snowfall separated by a band of dark dust blown up from the deserts below during the winter dry season. The snowfalls of subsequent seasons compress the layers below, changing the snowflakes first to *firn* (compacted snow) and then to ice. In the process, bubbles of air are trapped and act as minute archives documenting the condition of the atmosphere. By drilling and removing long cores of ice, scientists can analyze the levels of methane, nitrous oxide, and CO_2 found in the different bubbles to reveal a climatic story about the past conditions of the biosphere. Even the banded layers of dust are informative, since they tell of the strength and direction of the winds and of conditions below the ice cap.

The ice sheets of Greenland and Antarctica yield Earth's longest ice-core climatic records. In the 1990s, European researchers drilled into the Greenland ice plateau and obtained a core containing a detailed climatic record extending back 123,000 years. Using this unique record, the team was able to show that spectacular shifts in the North Atlantic climate occurred over just five annual ice layers, and that 115,000 years ago Greenland experienced a hitherto-unknown warm phase that was not mirrored in the Antarctic.

In June 2004, an ice core almost 2 miles (3.2 kilometers) long was drawn from a region of the Antarctic known as

Dome C, located about 300 miles (483 kilometers) from the Russian Vostok research station. The results of this core were even more spectacular. The core from Dome C takes us 740,000 years back in time. Obtaining this core was an enormous triumph, because it allows us to glimpse how things stood around 430,000 years ago—the last time that the Milankovitch cycles brought Earth into a position similar to that which it occupies today. Back then, the ice revealed, the warm (interglacial) period was exceptionally long, suggesting that our planet may have continued to experience mild conditions for a further 13,000 years.

Warm phases—even far briefer ones than the present—were, however, anomalies during the ice age. Cold periods are more typical, including a span of time called the glacial maximum, when the extent of the ice is at its greatest. The last time this happened was between 35,000 and 20,000 years ago. Back then, the sea level was more than 300 feet (91 meters) lower than it is today, affecting the very shape of the continents. Miles of ice covered what are now the most densely inhabited landscapes of North America and Europe.

By the end of the ice age, widespread and rapid climate changes were well under way. So it's no surprise that climatologists are especially interested in the period from around 20,000 to 10,000 years ago—as the glacial maximum began to wane—because during those ten millennia the overall surface temperature of Earth warmed by 9°F (5°C)—the fastest rise recorded in recent Earth history.

It is worth comparing the rate and scale of change during this period with what is predicted to happen this century if we do not reduce our emissions of greenhouse gases. If we pursue business as usual, an increase of 5°F (2.8°C) over the twenty-first century seems inevitable. While the scale of the change is less than that seen at the end of the last glacial maximum, the fastest warming recorded back then was a mere 2°F (1°C) per thousand years. Today we face a rate of change thirty times faster—and because living things need time to adjust, speed is every bit as important as scale when it comes to climate change.

Despite the keen focus of scientists on this period, details of how the world shifted from glacial maxima to warm interglacial periods, where we are now, have been slow in coming. In 2004, a study of sediments in the Irish Sea basin revealed that 19,000 years ago, over a period of just 100 to 500 years, sea levels rose abruptly by 10 to 15 yards (9 to 14 meters), indicating a massive thaw that began far earlier than anyone had imagined. What puzzled scientists was the fact that the world did not continue warming, but when the cause of the sea rise was determined, the answer to that puzzle became clear. The water generated by the thaw, it turned out, had come from the collapse of a Northern Hemisphere ice sheet, which poured somewhere between one-quarter and two Sverdrups' worth of freshwater into the North Atlantic. (The volume of water transported by ocean currents is measured in a unit called a Sverdrup, named after the Norwegian oceanographer Harald Ulrik Sverdrup. A Sverdrup is an enormous flow of water—1.3 million cubic yards (993,921 cubic meters) of water per second per 0.4 of a square mile.) The huge influx of freshwater into the North Atlantic disrupted an ocean current called the Gulf Stream. The Gulf Stream starts in the western Caribbean Sea, then flows through the Gulf of Mexico and the Straits of Florida, where it veers northward to North Carolina. At Cape Hatteras, it veers northeast until it passes the Canadian provinces of Nova Scotia and New-foundland. The disruption of the Gulf Stream had profound consequences.

The Gulf Stream transports vast amounts of heat northward from near the equator—almost a third as much warmth as the sun brings to western Europe. The heat is borne in a stream of warm, salty water that is 11°F to 18°F (6°C to 10°C) warmer than the surrounding cold northern water. As the warm water cools, it sinks, because cold water is denser than warm water, and this sinking draws more warm, salty water northward. Importantly, if the Gulf Stream's saltiness is diluted with fresh-water (as from melting glaciers), it does not sink as it cools, because freshwater is less dense than salt water, and no more warm water is drawn northward in its wake.

Without the heat the Gulf Stream brings, melting glaciers begin to grow again. The land cools as the increasing ice reflects more of the sun's heat back to space. Animals and plants migrate or die, and temperate regions such as the state of New York are plunged into a Siberian chill. The heat, however, does not vanish. Most of it pools around the equator and in the Southern Hemisphere, where it can cause the melting of gla-ciers in the south. When that happens, the sun's rays fall on a dark sea surface instead of on ice and are absorbed. This heats the world from the bottom up, so to speak, which eventually reestablishes the Gulf Stream, and the northern Atlantic enters another cycle of warming.

It takes about two Sverdrups of freshwater to significantly slow the Gulf Stream, and the geological record confirms that that happened repeatedly between 20,000 and 8,000 years ago. Thus the transition from the ice age to the warmth of today was no gentle segue but instead the wildest of roller-coaster rides, whose high and low points had the sharpness of a saw's teeth.

The seesawing climate changes in the Northern and Southern Hemispheres drew Earth jerkily yet inexorably toward its present state. And then the climatic madness gave way to a long mild period, whose summery warmth and stability were very people-friendly. The long summer that has been the last 8,000 years is without doubt *the* crucial event in human history. Climate conditions, including a rise in CO_2 levels, permitted the expansion of agriculture, the domestication of animals, and the establishment of cities.

Until recently, it was thought that this long summer was just a cosmic fluke resulting from Milankovitch's cycles and other natural phenomena. But environmental scientist William Ruddiman proposed a controversial new theory to explain the stability of Earth's long summer. He looked for a unique factor—something that was operating in this last warm cycle but in none of the earlier ones. That unique factor, he decided, was humans.

Earlier, several scientists had already suggested that we had entered a new geologic epoch. They christened it the Anthropocene—meaning the age of humanity—and marked its dawn at AD 1800, when methane and CO_2 brewed up by the gargantuan machines of the Industrial Revolution began to influence Earth's climate. Ruddiman added an ingenious twist to this argument, because he detected what he believes to be human influences on Earth's climate that occurred long before 1800.

Ruddiman discovered from air bubbles trapped in the Greenland and Antarctic ice sheets that until around 8,000 years ago, the volume of methane in the atmosphere was mostly controlled by Milankovitch's 22,000-year-long orbital-insolation cycle, which controls the intensity of the seasons. This makes sense, since methane is produced in large volume by swamps, which abound in warm, wet times.

But at the start of the last insolation cycle, 8,000 years ago, methane should have dropped as the climate cooled and swamps disappeared. Instead, after a shallow dip, its concentration inside the air bubbles that had been trapped in the ice 5,000 years ago showed a slow but emphatic rise. Ruddiman is convinced that the beginnings of agriculture—particularly wet agriculture, such as that practiced in flooded rice paddies in eastern Asia—tipped the methane balance, because such agricultural systems can be prodigious producers of the gas. This, Ruddiman argues, is evidence that humans had wrested control of methane emissions from nature, and so he believes we should mark the Anthropocene's dawn as occurring 8,000 years ago rather than 200 years ago.

Also based on evidence from the air bubbles, Ruddiman suggests that the concentration of CO_2 in the atmosphere was being influenced by humans far earlier than first imagined. The pattern of CO_2 concentrations in the atmosphere through the glacial cycles is well established. Basically, CO_2 levels rise rapidly as the glacial stage ends, then begin a slow decline toward the next cold period. Over the last 8,000 years, atmospheric CO_2 rose from around 160 parts per million to its preindustrial high of 280 parts per million. If natural cycles were still in control of Earth's carbon budget, Ruddiman states, CO_2 should have stood at around 240 parts per million by 1800, 40 ppm less than actual. At first glance his argument seems incredible. After all, early humans would have needed to emit more than half as much carbon as our industrial age did between 1850 and 1990 (when carbon rose from 280 ppm to about 353 ppm, an increase of 73 ppm)—an output made possible only by an unprecedented population using coal-burning machines. The key, notes Ruddiman, is time. Eight thousand years, in human terms at least, is a long span, and as humans cut and burned forests and fields around the globe, their activities acted like a hand slowly placing feathers in the pan on one side of a balance scale: eventually, enough feathers piled up to tip the balance. And thus, posits Ruddiman, the Anthropocene was created.

During the past 8,000 years, there were times when the CO_2 level lowered by 5 to 10 parts per million. Ruddiman sees a clear correlation with times of low atmospheric CO_2 and several plagues such as that caused by the bacterium *Yersinia pestis*—the "black plague" of medieval times. The plagues themselves had nothing to do with the CO_2 level, but the fact that they killed off a large percentage of the human population did. Because so many people died, agricultural lands were left untended. Forests had sufficient time to grow back on these lands, absorbing CO_2 and lowering atmospheric concentrations of the gas in the process. Global temperatures then fell, and periods of relative cold ensued in places such as Europe. But each time this happened, human activity rebounded, adding sufficient greenhouse gases to keep the Earth "just right," warm enough to stave off the onslaught of another ice age.

The new ice core from Dome C challenges Ruddiman's theory because it reveals that, although our current interglacial period is different from the past four (which Ruddiman examined), it's similar in some ways to the fifth before our own, which occurred around 430,000 years ago. During that time, the combination of Milankovitch's cycles and levels of CO_2 was similar to today's, and the warm spell was exceptionally long—26,000 years, as opposed to 12,000 for the others. Further scientific analysis is necessary to determine whether Ruddiman's provocative theory is correct in placing the beginning of the Anthropocene at 8,000 rather than 200 years ago.

Regardless of its origin, today there are unmistakable signs that the Anthropocene is turning ugly. So great are the changes that scientists are detecting in our atmosphere that time's gates appear once again to be opening. Will the Anthropocene become the shortest geological epoch on record?

CALL TO ACTION

The Sweater Test

Overheating or overcooling a building is a colossal waste of energy, and it produces unnecessary greenhouse-gas emissions. If it's a warm-weather month in your area and you're wearing a long-sleeved shirt or a sweater in school or at home, the air-conditioner thermostat is set too low. A summertime room temperature of 76°F to 78°F is plenty cool enough. Wear a short-sleeved shirt if you feel hot.

Conversely, if it's winter and you're wearing short-sleeved shirts, the room is probably too warm. Many schools seriously overheat their classrooms. When it's 80°F in the room, you're likely to doze off. You'll feel a lot more alert if the room temperature is between 68°F and 72°F.

If you think your school or home falls into either of these categories, *take action.* Get hold of a thermometer and start taking room temperatures. Then talk to the principal or your parents about doing something that will make a difference not only to the school and your ability to learn but also to Earth's environment. Don't accept the answer, "The building heats/cools unevenly." Ask if a heating/cooling specialist could solve the problem. As the cost of fossil fuels rises, fixing the problem will, in the long run, save money. Mention that according to the U.S. Department of Energy, for each degree the thermostat is lowered in winter, the heating bill shows a savings of 3 percent. Do the math in your own home: how much money could your family save by turning down the heat?

Chapter 7

An Energy Blast from the Past

The pace at which humans consume natural resources to produce energy is skyrocketing, and it's changing the composition of Earth's atmosphere in ways that point toward future disaster.

Fossil fuels—coal, oil, and natural gas—are all that remain of organisms that drew carbon from the atmosphere many millions of years ago. The carbon remained locked in place after they died and sediments buried them. When we burn wood, we release carbon that has been out of atmospheric circulation for a few decades—in other words, for the life of the tree. But burning fossil fuels releases carbon that has been out of atmospheric circulation for eons. Digging up long-dead organisms in this way does not serve the living well.

In 2005, the burning of fossil fuels released more than 30 million tons of CO_2 into the atmosphere. Of this amount, coal contributed 41 percent; oil, 39 percent; and gas, 20 percent. These percentages, however, don't reflect the tonnages burned, because some fuels contain more carbon than others. The energy we liberate when we burn these fuels comes from carbon and hydrogen. Because carbon causes climate change, the more carbon-rich a fuel is, the more danger it presents to humanity's future. The best black coal is almost pure carbon. Burn a ton of it, and you create four tons of CO_2. The fuels derived from oil are less carbon-rich, because they contain two hydrogen atoms for every carbon in their structure. So burning oil releases less CO_2 per unit used than coal. Methane gas, with only one carbon atom for every four hydrogen atoms, contains the least carbon.

How efficiently a fossil fuel burns plays an important factor in determining how much CO_2 is produced. Anthracite is the hardest and oldest type of coal. Using the most advanced methods, burning anthracite to generate electricity results in 67 percent more CO_2 emissions than burning methane does (and unfortunately, most coal-fired power plants come nowhere near this level of efficiency). Brown coal is a younger, less pure type of coal. When brown coal burns, it produces 130 percent more CO_2 emissions than methane. From a climate-change perspective, then, there's a world of difference between using coal or gas to power an economy.

Found on every continent, coal is our planet's most abundant and widely distributed fossil fuel. Coal is often referred to as "buried sunshine," and in a sense that is an accurate description, because coal is the fossilized remains of plants that grew in swamps millions of years ago. In the United States, you can see the initial stages of the coal-forming process in the 7,000-year-old Okefenokee Swamp in Georgia and Florida. There, trees topple over and sink into the muck, where a lack of oxygen impedes rotting. Dead vegetation builds up, forming a thick layer of sodden plant matter. Sand and silt, carried into the swamp by rivers, compress the vegetation, squeezing out moisture and other impurities. As the matted layer is buried deeper and deeper, heat and time alter the chemistry of the wood, leaves, and other organic matter. The altered matter is called peat and is the first stage toward becoming coal.

Over millions of years, pressure and heat convert peat to brown coal, which, in turn, becomes bituminous coal, the type of coal most often used for generating electricity and heat. If further pressure and heat are applied to bituminous coal, even more impurities are removed and the organic matter finally becomes anthracite, which is 90 percent carbon.

Despite the inroads made by oil and gas on coal's empire, more coal is burned today than at any time in the past. In 1990, coal-fired power plants produced 39 percent of the world's CO_2. That slice of the global carbon emissions "pie" had grown to 41 percent in 2005. Projections are that by 2030 coal-fired plants will produce 44 percent of global carbon emissions. As the cost of oil increases, so does talk of building more coal-fired plants in many countries, including the United States, India, and China—all countries with large populations that would place heavy demands on the plants, thus pumping more CO_2 into the atmosphere. The average life of a coal-fired power station is fifty years, and the CO_2 that new plants produce will continue to warm the planet for centuries after they shut down.

Manufacturing processes turned the nineteenth century into the century of coal. While we still rely heavily on coal—it generates more than half the electricity used in the United States— the twentieth century could accurately be called the century of oil. Indeed, the dawn of the hydrocarbon age has been put down as January 10, 1901, when on a small hill called Spindle-top near Beaumont, Texas, Al Hamill was drilling for oil. After his drill penetrated more than 1,000 feet into the sandstone below, a sudden roar filled the air and thick clouds of methane gas blasted from the hole. A gushing column of liquid shot hundreds of feet into the air and then fell back to earth as an oily, dark rain. Although the first purpose-drilled oil well had been put down forty years earlier in Pennsylvania, Hamill's discovery of oil in such deep strata was novel. As drilling became more widespread and ever deeper, such flows became commonplace, ensuring that oil would quickly drive coal from the fields of transport and home heating. The trouble with oil, however, is that there is far less of it than coal, its distribution is patchier, and it's harder to find.

Oil is the product of life in ancient oceans and estuaries. It is composed primarily of the remains of plankton—in particular, single-celled plants known as phytoplankton. Scientists believe most of the world's oil reserves originated in quiet, deep, oxygen-poor ocean basins in areas where upwelling currents carry cold, nutrient-rich bottom waters to the sunlit surface. The nutrients supercharge the phytoplankton into mass reproduction. When they die, their remains settle to the oxygen-free depths, where their organic matter can accumulate without being consumed by bacteria. Earth's oceans are vast—more than double the area of its land—so why is the world not literally swimming in oil? Part of the reason is that the ocean crust is always being recycled. Another reason is that oil is slippery stuff, and unless something obstructs it, it's likely to ooze out of the rocks and dissipate.

The geological process for making oil is as precise as a recipe for making a soufflé. First the sediments containing the phytoplankton must be buried and compressed by other rocks. Then the absolute right conditions are needed to squeeze the organic matter out of the source rocks and transfer it, through cracks and crevices, into a suitable storage stratum. This stratum must be porous, but above it must lie a layer of fine-grained, impervious rock, strong enough to withstand the pressures that shot the oil and gas high into the air above Spindletop and thick enough to forbid escape. In addition, the waxes and fats that are the source of oil need to be "cooked" at 212°F to 275°F (100°C to 135°C) for millions of years. If the temperature ever exceeds these limits, all that will result is gas, or else the hydrocarbons will be lost entirely. The creation of oil reserves is the result of pure chance—the right rocks being cooked in the right way for the correct time, usually in a dome-shaped structure where a "crust" that prevents the oil's escape overlies the porous oil-rich level.

In order to use petroleum to make products such as gasoline, home heating oil, and petrochemicals, it must be refined at an oil refinery. The crude, or unprocessed, oil is heated to separate it into chemical groups called hydrocarbons. It is also separated by chemical treatment, which dissolves some of the compounds while causing others to form solids.

After separation, a catalyst such as a clay mineral is added to some of the less useful compounds to force them to chemically change into compounds that can be more readily used to improve the quality and quantity of a product, for example, gasoline. Finally, the separated compounds are treated chemically to remove impurities. Still, vapors from smokestacks and leaks in refinery equipment allow pollutants to seep into the atmosphere. Refineries also use water as part of the production and cooling processes. The wastewater is released into rivers, bays, and oceans and can potentially pose a hazard to fish and other wildlife. Toxic chemicals such as benzene can be released during refining, and oil spills are always a concern.

The oil-rich countries of the Middle East lie atop a bonanza of oil. Before it was tapped, just one Saudi Arabian oil field, the Ghawar, held a seventh of the entire planet's oil reserves. Until 1961, the world's oil companies were finding more and more oil every year, much of it in the Middle East. Since then, the rate of discovery has dwindled, yet rates of use have gone up. By 1995, humans were using an average of 24 billion barrels of oil per year, but an average of only 9.6 billion barrels was discovered. Possible oil shortages and the rising costs of oil suggest that something else will need to power the economies of the twenty-first century.

That something else, many in the industry believe, is natural gas, which is 90 percent methane. Only thirty years ago, gas supplied just 20 percent of the world's fossil fuel, while coal supplied 31 percent and oil provided nearly half the total. By the beginning of the twenty-first century, however, gas had supplanted coal in importance. If current trends continue, by 2025, it will have overtaken oil as the world's most important fuel source. There are proven reserves of gas sufficient to last fifty years. Only our filthiest fuel, coal, holds greater promise by way of reserves.

The twentieth century opened on a world that was home to little more than a billion people and closed on a world of 6 billion. Every one of those 6 billion is using on average four times as much energy as his or her forefathers did 100 years before. This helps account for the fact that the burning of fossil fuels has increased sixteenfold over that period.

Taking into account how plants gather carbon and hydrogen from sunlight, how efficiently plant matter is preserved and changed into fossil fuels, and how efficiently we retrieve those fuels from the earth, biologist Jeffrey Dukes has calculated that approximately 100 tons of ancient plant life is required to create one gallon of gasoline. Given the vast amount of sunlight needed to grow 100 tons of plant matter and the rate at which we are using fossil fuels, it should come as no surprise that during each year of our industrial age, humans have required several centuries' worth of ancient sunlight to keep the economy going. In 1997 alone, for example, we burned through 422 years' worth of blazing light from a Carboniferous sun.

But weaning ourselves off of fossil fuels isn't going to be easy. In 1961, there were just 3 billion people on Earth, using only half of the total resources that our global ecosystem could sustainably provide for us. Twenty-five years later, in 1986, our population topped 5 billion, and so great was our collective thirst for resources that we were using *all* of Earth's sustainable production.

Since then, we have been running the environmental equivalent of a deficit budget, plundering our savings account to pay for our overspending habits. The plundering takes the form of overexploiting fisheries, overgrazing pasture until it becomes desert, destroying forests, and polluting our oceans and atmosphere, which in turn leads to the large number of environmental issues we face. In the end, though, the environmental budget is the only one that really counts.

By 2050, when the population is expected to level out at around 9 billion, the burden of human existence will be such that we will be using nearly two planets' worth of resources—assuming they can be found. But for all the difficulty we'll experience in finding those resources, it's our waste—particularly the greenhouse gases we produce by burning fossil fuel—that may prove to be our downfall. This increasing waste is straining Earth's climates to the limit. A global warming of 1.13°F

(0.6°C) has occurred since the dawn of the Industrial Revolution, the principal cause of which has been an increase in atmospheric CO_2. While a little over a degree may not seem like much, many signs show that even this small increase is having an impact on life on Earth.

CALL TO ACTION

Reduce the Hidden Oil in Your Life

It's obvious that we use petroleum and other fossil fuels for heat, air-conditioning, electricity, and as fuel for vehicles. In 2007, the United States used 20.7 million barrels of petroleum products every day, according to the U.S. Energy Information Administration. The lion's share of that amount was used for heating fuel, diesel fuel, and gasoline. But petroleum products are used in the manufacture of many other less obvious products. About 10 percent of the products you use in your home contain petroleum and/or fossil fuels.

Take a look at the ingredients listed on your shampoo bottles, the deodorants you use, the eye and face makeup that you wear, and the household cleaners you use. Most of them contain petrochemicals derived from oil. Some common ingredients that signal the presence of petrochemicals include: propylene glycol, petrolatum, parabens (four different kinds), quaternium-15, benzene, toluene, acetone, vinyl chloride, and methylene chloride. If a product contains any of these, it was made from a petroleum derivative and adds carbon to the environment, some in the form of gases that contribute to global warming.

Take action: reduce your carbon consumption and buy products that don't contain petrochemicals. (Or at least commit to buying fewer of them.) The companies Seventh Generation, Sun & Earth, and Ecover produce a wide variety of environmentally-friendly products. The Aveda Corporation, which makes makeup and personal-care products, is committed to eliminating the use of petrochemicals in its products. Many stores stock environmentally-friendly products. Just ask where they are shelved.

PART 2

Endangered Habitats

Chapter 8
The Unraveling World

Global warming changes the climate in sudden jerks, during which climate patterns jump from one stable state to another. The best analogy is perhaps that of a finger on a light switch. Nothing happens for a while, but if you slowly increase the pressure, a certain point is reached, a sudden change occurs, and conditions swiftly alter from dark to light.

Climatologist Julia Cole refers to the leaps made by climate as "magic gates," and she argues that since temperatures began rising rapidly in the 1970s, our planet has seen two such events—in 1976 and 1998. Like the time "gateways" that divide the classical geologic record, these dates are important because, again, they mark the onset of remarkable phenomena.

The first evidence of the 1976 magic gate was found on the faraway coral atoll of Maiana in the central Pacific nation of Kiribati. Climate information found in the Maiana area is important because it's the region where El Niños, a major climate force around the globe, are first detected. An El Niño is a phenomenon during which the sea-surface temperature in the central Pacific goes up. In Maiana, the magic gate manifested as a sudden and sustained increase in sea-surface temperature of about 1°F (0.6°C) and a decline in the ocean's salinity of 0.8 percent.

Maiana is also where one of the oldest corals ever found lived and grew. Corals can record climate change in much the same way that annual tree rings do. So when scientists drilled into the 155-year-old coral, they were thrilled to find that it contained a detailed record of climate change extending back to 1840.

Between 1945 and 1955, the temperature of the surface of the tropical Pacific commonly dipped below 66.5°F (19.2°C), but after the magic gate opened in 1976, it has rarely been below 77°F (25°C). This degree of temperature change directly affects other regions, especially the United States. Among other things, the tropical Pacific controls most tropical precipitation and the position of the jet stream, a high-speed wind current that brings snow and rain to North America. In 1976, the rise in sea-surface temperature and decline in salinity caused a shift in the path of the jet stream. This ultimately led to wacky weather conditions in the United States, including unprecedented mild conditions in Alaska and blizzards in the lower forty-eight states.

The magic gate's rising sea-surface temperature spawned extreme weather conditions in other places, including a drought in the Galápagos Islands. The Galápagos became well known when Charles Darwin used the islands' finches to illustrate his theory of evolution by natural selection. In modern times, biologists who were studying the native finch *Geospiza fortis* watched helplessly as the 1977 drought all but exterminated the species on one of the islands. Of the population of 1,300 that existed before the drought, only 180 survived, all of them individuals with the largest beaks, which enabled them to feed by cracking tough seeds. Of those 180 survivors, 150 were males, so at mating season, the males faced tough competition for mates. Again, it was those with the biggest beaks that won out. This natural-selection "double whammy" weeded out all individuals except those with the very largest beaks, resulting in a measurable shift in beak size in the island population. Thanks to Darwin, scientists have nearly two centuries' worth of beak measurements to look back on, which confirmed what biologists believe to be the evolution of a new species.

What Julia Cole calls the second magic gate since the 1970s occurred in 1998. It was also connected with El Niño. El Niño alternates with La Niña, which is a cooling of sea surface in the Pacific, in a two- to eight-year-long cycle that brings extreme climatic events to much of the world. During the La Niña phase, which until recently seemed to be the dominant part of the cycle, winds blow westward across the Pacific, bringing warm surface water away from the Pacific coast of South America and toward the coast of Australia and the islands lying to its north. As the warm surface waters are blown westward, the Humboldt Current, a cold current that is normally deeply submerged, rises off the South American Pacific coast. The upwelling current carries nutrients from the seafloor that feed the most prolific fishery in the world (18 to 20 percent of the world's fish catch, which includes sardines, anchovies, and mackerel, is caught off the west coast of South America). The El Niño part of the cycle begins when the tropical winds weaken, allowing the warm surface water to flow back eastward, thus overwhelming the Humboldt Current and releasing humidity into the atmosphere. The resulting rains cause floods in the normally arid Peruvian deserts. Meanwhile, back in the far western Pacific, cool water upwells as the warm water flows eastward. Because cool water does not evaporate as readily as warm water, a dry period strikes Australia and Southeast Asia. When an El Niño

Global Wind Currents

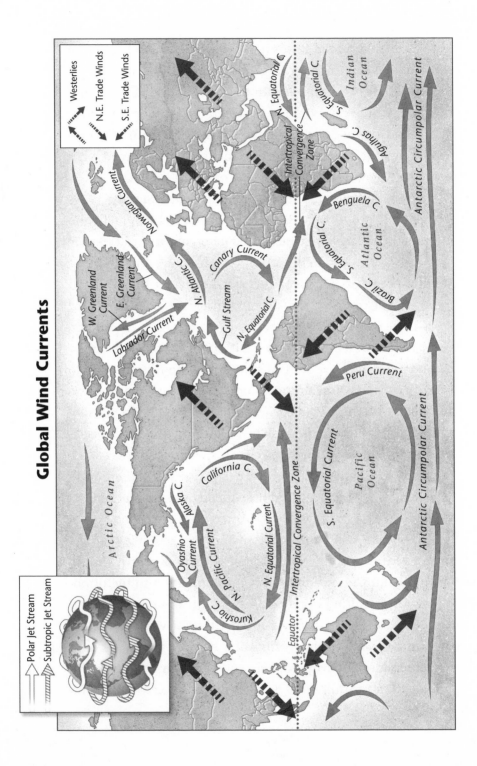

Oceans' Surface Currents

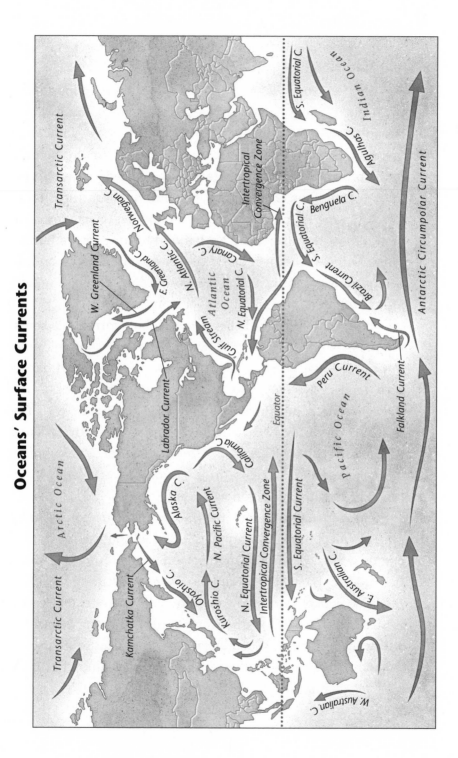

is extreme enough, it can afflict two-thirds of the globe with droughts, floods, and other extreme weather.

The 1997 to 1998 El Niño year has been immortalized by World Wildlife Fund as "the year the world caught fire." Drought had a stranglehold on a large part of the planet, and fires raged on every continent. However, the normally wet rain forests of Southeast Asia were the most devastated. There, approximately 25 million acres burned, of which half was ancient rain forest. On the island of Borneo, 2 million acres were lost—an area almost the size of the Netherlands. Many of the burned forests will never recover on a timescale meaningful to human beings, and the impact that this has had on Borneo's unique fauna will, in all probability, never be fully known.

Some climatologists believe that global warming is stressing the El Niño–La Niña cycle. Ever since the 1976 magic gate, the cycles have been exceptionally long—one would expect such long cycles only once in several thousand years—and there has been an imbalance between the phases, with five El Niños and only two La Niñas. Computer-based modeling supports the climatologists' belief, indicating that as greenhouse-gas concentrations increase in the atmosphere, a semipermanent El Niño–like condition will result.

It appears that severe El Niño events can permanently alter global climate. During the 1998 magic gate, enough heat energy was released to spike the global temperature by around 0.5°F (0.3°C). The temperature rise seems to occur as a result of the large pool of warm seawater that builds up over the central western Pacific. The warm water is drawn from across the entire Pacific Ocean. When greenhouse gases cause small rises in global temperatures, the warm-water pool amplifies them, and this rise in temperature in turn feeds back to the seawater and amplifies the intensity of the El Niño cycle.

Some of the changes spawned in 1998 were permanent, because ever since then, the waters of the central western Pacific have frequently reached 86°F (30°C), while the jet stream has shifted toward the North Pole. The new climatic regime also seems prone to generating more extreme El Niños, a topic we will return to later.

What are the consequences of these new climate patterns? For one thing, they are affecting various plant and animal populations. Notes taken by bird-watchers, fishermen, and other nature watchers are some of the most powerful tools to help us trace how the behaviors and habits of animals and plants have changed over time. In 2003, researchers Camille Parmesan and Gary Yohe analyzed a database drawing on more than 200 years' worth of historical observations, including detailed records of the migration, breeding habits, and distribution of birds by amateur bird-watchers, the jottings of botanists about the flowering and shooting of plants, and captains' logs from whaling ships. The researchers sought to find out if there was an underlying trend toward change in all regions.

They found that while before 1950 there is little evidence of any trend, since that date a strong pattern has emerged worldwide: the distribution of species has shifted toward the poles an average of 4 miles (6 kilometers) per decade. At the same time, species have retreated up mountainsides about 20 feet (6.1 meters) per decade, and spring activity—migrating and mating behaviors, for example—has begun about 2.3 days earlier per decade. These trends correlate with the scale and direction of temperature increases brought about by greenhouse-gas emissions. So strong is the correlation, in fact, that the pattern has been called a "fingerprint of climate change." And CO_2 is the driving force that is pushing these trends.

One of the most remarkable changes in distribution concerns the tiny marine organisms called copepods, which have been detected up to 620 miles from their usual habitat. Copepods are near the base of the world's *food chain*—the sequence of who eats whom in order to get the nutrition needed for survival. Changes in copepod distribution can have major effects on larger forms of life that prey on them. Changes are occurring for some insects too. Thirty-five nonmigratory species of Northern Hemisphere butterflies have extended their ranges northward, some by as much as 150 miles, while at the same time becoming extinct farther south because the habitat is no longer suitable. Even tropical bird species are on the move: Costa Rica's lowland birds have extended their range 11.7 miles (18.8 kilometers) northward over a twenty-year period.

The early onset of spring activity is a distinctive manifestation of climate change. In the bird world, the common murre, a seabird, has begun to lay its eggs an average of twenty-four days earlier each decade over the period its nesting has been studied. European butterflies are appearing 2.8 to 3.2 days earlier per decade, while migrating birds are arriving in Europe 1.3 to 4.4 days earlier per decade. In Europe, numerous plant species have been budding and flowering 1.4 to 3.1 days earlier per decade, while their relatives in North America have been doing so 1.2 to 2 days earlier.

Such shifts can disrupt an ecosystem's network of connections, for example, the system's food chain. If a prey species migrates in response to a change in climate and its predator doesn't, the food chain is compromised. And if the predator species that remains behind can't adapt to a change in diet, it will die.

An example of this type of situation involves the caterpillars of Europe's winter moth, whose sole food source is young oak leaves. A problem arises because oaks and moths have different cues to tell them when spring has arrived. Warm weather causes the moth's eggs to hatch. Oaks count the short cold days of winter as their guide for when to leaf out. In the winter moth's European range, spring is warmer than it was twenty-five years ago; however, the number of cold days in winter has remained the same. As a result, the winter moths now hatch up to three weeks before the oaks bear their first leaves. Because the caterpillars can survive only two to three days without food, there are now far fewer of them, and those that do survive generally grow faster because there is less competition for the food that exists.

It seems likely that natural selection will act upon the moth to alter the timing of its hatching, but this will occur only through mass mortality of early-hatching caterpillars, and for several decades at least we can expect the species to be rare. Whether the birds, spiders, and insects that prey on the moths can survive the collapse of their food source is another matter.

Marcel Visser of the Netherlands Institute for Ecology, the researcher who discovered the moth's plight, believes that if people look for these kinds of effects, they will find them everywhere. If this is true, then we should be very concerned about the species at the top of the food pyramid, such as those that prey on winter moths, because they are likely to be losing many potential sources of food. Indeed, this statement justifies concern for the ecosystem as a whole, because it implies that all around the world, the delicate web of life is being torn apart.

Some reptiles face even more direct threats from global warming, since their sex ratios are determined by the temperature at which the eggs are incubated. The American alligator is one well-studied species that definitely stands to lose if global temperatures rise a few degrees. Only males are produced when the eggs hatch at higher than 89.6°F (32°C), and only females when eggs are hatched at less than 87.8°F (31°C). The North American painted turtle faces a similar situation, but in reverse: high incubation temperatures produce all-female populations.

Africa's Lake Tanganyika, one of the world's oldest and deepest freshwater bodies, is located just south of the equator and is home to a host of unique species. Like most lakes, its waters are stratified, with the warmest water on top. If the oxygen-rich upper layers don't mix with the nutrient-rich layers below, plants in the sunlit layers will starve from a lack of nutrients, while those in the deeper layers starve from a lack of oxygen. In the past, the lake's stratification was seasonally broken down by the southeast monsoons, which stirred its waters and drove the spectacular biodiversity.

Since the mid-1970s, however, global warming has so heated the surface layers that the monsoons are no longer strong enough to mix the water. As a result, nutrients no longer surface and oxygen no longer penetrates to any depth. Inevitably, the lake's plankton population, which is a crucial component in the food chain, has now declined to less than one-third of its abundance of twenty-five years ago, with noticeable effects on other creatures. The spectacular spined snail *Tiphoboia horei*, which is found only in the lake, has lost two-thirds of its habitat. Today it's found only at depths of 100 yards (91.4 meters) or less, whereas twenty-five years ago it ventured three times as deep. This kind of ongoing change threatens to collapse the lake's entire ecosystem. While from a biodiversity standpoint Lake Tanganyika is one of the world's most important lakes, it's not unique in its vulnerability to climate change. All over the world, the surfaces of lakes are warming, thereby preventing the mixing of their waters and threatening the basis of their productivity.

Even remote and seemingly pristine rain forest is being affected by global warming. In areas of the Amazon far distant from any direct human influence, the proportions of trees that make up the canopy are changing. Spurred on by increased CO_2 levels, fast-growing species are powering ahead, crowding out slower-growing species. The birds and other animals that in turn depend on those slower-growing species as food are diminishing as well.

In tropical and temperate regions, where the pace of climate change isn't exceptionally rapid, species have time to try to adapt to the changes. Near the poles, however, climate change is occurring now at *twice* the rate seen anywhere else. Animals in those areas may not have the luxury of time to adapt. The impact of rapid climate change in the cryosphere, Earth's polar realms of eternal ice and snow, will affect the entire planet.

CALL TO ACTION

Time to See the Light

How many CFLs are in your house? If you just said "Huh?" chances are, not many. CFLs are compact fluorescent lightbulbs—those lightbulbs that sometimes look like twisty ice cream cones. The traditional round lightbulbs are called incandescent bulbs, and when it comes to cutting-edge technology, they are dinosaurs. They haven't changed much since Thomas Alva Edison invented the first commercially practical incandescent light back in 1879. Replacing just one incandescent bulb with a CFL makes a difference in more than one way. An Energy Star–qualified CFL lasts up to ten times longer than an incandescent bulb and uses two-thirds less energy. In fact, if every household in the United States replaced just *one* incandescent bulb with a CFL, it would reduce CO_2 emissions equivalent to removing almost one million cars from the roads. Replacing five of your most frequently used incandescent bulbs could also save up to $60 a year on your family's energy bill. There are many types of Energy Star CFLs available, so with a bit of comparison shopping, you should be able to find ones to fit your home's lighting needs.

So great are the energy savings from CFL use that Australia's government plans to phase out incandescent bulbs across the country and replace them with compact fluorescents. They estimate that this move will cut green-house-gas emissions by 4 million tons by 2012 and will cut electric bills to homes by as much as 66 percent. In its 2007 Federal Energy Bill, the United States passed legis-lation that, while not banning incandescent bulbs, requires that their efficiency standards be increased. Given the technology that these bulbs use, many will become obso-lete because they cannot meet the new standards.

For more information about CFLs (and other energy savers) see the Department of Energy's website: http://www.energystar.gov.

Chapter 9

Peril at the Poles

In the final days of 2004, the cities of the world received some astonishing news: beginning at its northern tip, Antarctica was turning green. Antarctic hair grass is one of just two kinds of higher plants that occur south of the fifty-sixth degree of latitude. It usually appears as sparse tussocks crouched behind the north face of a boulder or some other sheltered spot. In the southern summer of 2004, however, great swaths of the grass appeared and formed extensive green meadows, an uncommon sight in Antarctica. But this kind of anomaly pales in significance when compared to the disappearing sea ice.

The subantarctic seas are some of the richest on Earth, and the semifrozen edge between salt water and the floating ice promotes remarkable growth of the microscopic plankton that are the base of the food chain. Despite the months of winter darkness, plankton thrive under the ice, allowing the krill (tiny shrimplike creatures) that feed on them to complete their seven-year life cycle. When winter sea ice is extensive, plentiful food exists for the krill. Penguins, seals, and great whales rely on krill populations as part of their food supply. When krill thrive, so do they.

However, the extent of the sea ice has reduced as the water temperature has warmed, and since 1976, the krill population—

whose young feed better when there is a cover of sea ice—has experienced a sharp decline, reducing at the rate of nearly 40 percent per decade. As the krill numbers have decreased, numbers of another major grazing species, the jelly-like salps, have increased. Previously confined to more northerly waters, salps, unlike krill, don't require a great density of plankton to thrive. They easily survive on the meager pickings offered by the ice-free parts of the Southern Ocean. Unfortunately, salps are so devoid of nutrients that an ocean stocked to the choking point with them is useless. Indeed, none of the Antarctic's marine mammals or birds finds it worthwhile to feed on them. That profoundly influences the Antarctic food chain. Again, climate change threatens an entire ecosystem.

Already, there are signs that some Antarctic fauna are feeling the pinch. The emperor penguin population is half what it was thirty years ago. The number of Adelie penguins has declined by 70 percent. These decreases suggest that in the near future a point will be reached when, one after another, krill-dependent species will be unable to feed. Southern right whales, humpback whales, and innumerable seals and penguins will have to shift their habitats, or they will starve. And instead of a rich, biologically diverse Southern Ocean, we'll have an ocean full of jelly-like salps, the ultimate inheritors of a defrosting cryosphere, the portion of the ocean surrounding the Antarctic that is frozen solid.

The Arctic is a region that is almost a mirror image of the south, because while the Antarctic is a frozen continent surrounded by an immensely rich ocean, the Arctic is a frozen ocean almost entirely surrounded by land. It's also home to 4 million people, which means it is better studied.

Most of the Arctic's inhabitants live on its fringe, and it's there, in places such as southern Alaska, that winters are 4°F to 5°F (2.2°C to 2.8°C) warmer than they were just thirty years ago. Among the most visible impacts of climate change anywhere on Earth are those wrought by the spruce bark beetle. Over the past fifteen years, it has killed some 40 million trees in southern Alaska, more than any other insect in North America's recorded history. Two hard winters are usually enough to control beetle numbers, but a run of mild winters in recent years has left them raging out of control.

Anything that lives in the treeless Arctic has got to be tough and versatile. Collared lemmings are true offspring of the extreme north; they survive even on the hostile northern coast of Greenland. They're the only rodents whose coat turns white in winter and whose claws in that season grow into capacious, two-pronged shovels used for tunneling through snow, superb adaptations to life in the cryosphere. Their population fluctuates on a cycle of around four years, at the end of which their abundance is such that they exhaust the food supply of seeds, plants, lichen, and berries in the area. Because of this, they may be forced to migrate en masse in search of food, thereby giving rise to the idea, erroneously propagated, that they commit suicide by running off cliffs. For the collared lemming, the tundra and life itself are inseparable, and indications show a likelihood that the species will be extinct before the end of this century. Perhaps all that will be left then will be a folk memory of the small "suicidal" rodent. But the real tragedy will be that the lemmings didn't jump. They were pushed.

Despite the hardiness of its inhabitants, the Arctic ecosystem is especially fragile, and subtle changes such as a season with less snow but more rain can have enormous impacts. The caribou is vital to the Inuit, the Arctic's indigenous people. The Peary caribou is a small, pale subspecies found only in west Greenland and Canada's Arctic islands. Autumn rains now ice over the lichens that are the creature's winter food supply, causing many to starve. The number of Peary caribou dropped from 26,000 in 1961 to 1,000 in 1997. In 1991, it was classified as endangered, which meant that it couldn't be hunted, thus becoming irrelevant to the Inuit economy.

The Sami people of Finland have also noticed an icing over of lichens, similar to the icing seen in Canada. Again, rains due to mild weather seem to be the cause. Other factors are also acting to deplete the caribou herds, including changed patterns of snowfall, which blankets food resources, and flooding of rivers, which kills thousands of calves as they migrate. In short, as climate change advances, it seems that the Arctic will no longer be a suitable habitat for caribou.

Ironically, spreading forests will wreak havoc in the Arctic. Scientists predict that if global warming trends persist, forests will expand northward to the edge of the Arctic Sea, destroying the tundra. Several hundred million birds migrate to these treeless regions to breed, and as the forest encroaches northward, the great flocks will lose out. Indeed, the birds look set to lose more than 50 percent of their nesting habitat this century alone.

If anything symbolizes the Arctic, it is surely the polar bear, or *nanuk*, as it is called by the Inuit. For thousands of years, every inch of the Arctic has lain within its grasp: polar bears have been sighted more than a mile up on the Greenland ice cap; their dens have been found at the southern edge of Canada's Hudson Bay. They've even been spotted striding the ice within 100 miles of the North Pole. They can go anywhere in

✱ TESTAMENT TO ENVIRONMENTAL CHANGES ON BAFFIN ISLAND

Dick Gordon is a journalist and radio and TV correspondent. In February 2007, he interviewed Pitseolak Alainga, an Inuit man who lives in Iqaluit, the southernmost community on Baffin Island in Canada. For more than seventeen years, Alainga has worked as a Canadian ranger. He is also a respected hunter in the Inuit community. Both jobs require that he spend a lot of time outdoors, especially on the ice.

Pitseolak Alainga has spent his entire life in the Arctic, and he has seen many changes, such as the sky being clear more often. One of his duties as a ranger is to keep the main roads free of ice and snow for governmental and local transit. Alainga stated in the interview that in the 1970s, when the pavement was first put down, there was a lot of snow and wind. However, he said, "Today on our roads we have barely any snow, and today we feel like we're in the fall, even throughout the winter." The roads around Iqaluit were built on *permafrost,* a permanently frozen layer below the soil surface in cold regions. "But," Alainga continued, "the new roads sometimes become spongy because of the permafrost melting. There are getting to be more potholes from the asphalt sinking. In the past, we never used to repair pavement."

Alainga also reported changes in animal behavior. "The seals in the springtime, when they're out suntanning . . . like to lie on their backs more and have their tummies showing to the sun. We have caught a few seals [recently that] have absolutely no hair on their tummies from suntanning. We never would have seen that in the past." The Inuit also now see a difference in the seals when they prepare them for food. The seals appear thinner; they have less fat on their bodies. Alainga thinks this may occur because the seals are spending more time basking in the sun. Because they go underwater less, they are catching and eating less food.

The insects are changing too. When Alainga was a boy, there were no wasps in the area. "There are wasps that are starting to come up [and] bumblebees that are different from our bees up here. There are different ladybugs. . . . The elders here in town are saying, 'What type of insect is that? What type of bird is that?'"

Hundreds of years of experience living and hunting in a frozen climate have taught the Inuit people how to "read" the ice to navigate on top of it and hunt safely. This knowledge is passed from one generation to the next through the oral tradition. But some information can no longer be relied upon: due to climate change, the ice isn't as predictable as it used to be. "In the 1970s and '80s, we'd go 130 to 140 miles down the bay and we'd be snowmobiling on the ice. Today we can only snowmobile 45 miles down the bay. Past that, it's open water. Where there used to be some glaciers, there's bare rock. Those are the changes I have seen in the past twenty to twenty-five years," Alainga reported. These days, Alainga and other hunters drag a dinghy behind their snowmobiles as a safety precaution. They can no longer rely on the ice being thick enough to support their weight. ✳

the Arctic, as long as they can find food. But the presence of sea ice—lots of it—is crucial to the polar bear's food source: the Arctic's seals.

Polar bears, it's true, will deign to catch lemmings or scavenge dead birds if the opportunity presents itself, but the seals that live and breed on sea ice are a polar bear's main diet. In 1978, an Inuit hunter and his attendant biologist saw a polar bear make a seal kill in open water, but such an event is as rare as a spring blueberry—the exception that proves the rule.

The ringed seal is the most abundant mammal of the far north; at least 2.5 million of them swim in its iceberg-cooled seas. Yet at times climatic conditions are such that they simply cannot breed. In 1974, too little snow fell over the Amundsen Gulf for the seals to construct their snow-covered dens on the sea ice, so they left, some traveling as far as Siberia. Polar bears followed, but many had not fed well enough the previous season to produce sufficient storages of body fat to complete the journey. Sadly, they starved to death on the way.

The plight of the harp seals living in the Gulf of St. Lawrence gives us a clear idea of the shape of things to come. Like the ringed seals, they can't raise pups when there is little or no sea ice—something that happened in 1967, 1981, 2000, 2001, and 2002. The run of pupless years that opened this century is worrying. When a run of ice-free years exceeds the reproductive life of a female seal—perhaps a dozen years at most—the Gulf of St. Lawrence population, which is genetically separate from the rest of the species, will become extinct. Other species of seals give birth and nurse on the sea ice. Even the mighty walrus lives under the spell of a frozen sea, because the highly productive ice edge is its prime habitat.

Research shows that polar bears are slowly starving as

each winter becomes warmer than the one before. A long-term study of 1,200 individuals living around Hudson Bay reveals that the feeding season has become too short for the bears to find enough food, and they are 15 percent skinnier on average than they were a few decades ago. With each year, starving females give birth to fewer cubs. Decades ago, triplets were common; now they are unheard of. And back then, around half the cubs were weaned and feeding themselves at eighteen months. Today that number is less than one in twenty; scarcer prey means they must continue to rely on their mothers for nourishment. Those females that successfully give birth face dangers unknown in times past. Increasing winter rain in some areas may collapse birthing dens, killing both the mother and cubs sleeping within. The early breakup of the ice can separate denning and feeding areas. If young cubs cannot swim the distances required to find food, they will starve to death.

If the level of greenhouse-gas emissions keeps rising, even more sea ice will melt. As the polar-bear population declines in response, so will those of other Arctic wildlife such as arctic fox and ivory gulls, which scavenge on seal carcasses left by polar bears. Some of these animals also depend on sea ice for their survival. Indeed, the ivory gull has already declined by 90 percent in Canada over the past twenty years and, if it continues at that rate, will not see out the century. Scientists fear that the loss of *nanuk* may mark the beginning of the collapse of the entire Arctic ecosystem. And it's possible that few polar bears will live in the wild as soon as the year 2030.

If nothing is done to limit greenhouse-gas emissions, it seems certain that sometime this century a day will dawn when no summer ice will be seen in the Arctic—just a vast, dark, turbulent sea. The changes we're witnessing at the poles are of the runaway type, and unless we do something to curb greenhouse gases, there can be no winners among the fauna and flora unique to the region. Instead, we should expect that the realm of the polar bear, the narwhal, and the walrus will simply be replaced by encroaching forests and cold, ice-free oceans. In areas where forest does not take over, increasing temperatures (and thus increasing evaporation) will give rise to polar deserts, because surprisingly large areas of the Arctic receive very little precipitation.

You might think that the encroaching forests, by taking in CO_2 as they grow, would help abate climate change. However, scientists estimate that any such gains will be more than offset by the loss of albedo, since a dark green forest absorbs far more sunlight, and thus captures far more heat, than snow-covered tundra. The overall impact of foresting the world's northern regions will be to heat our planet ever more swiftly, with repercussions that cannot be reversed. The north polar cryosphere will have vanished forever.

CALL TO ACTION

Choose Green Power

We all use electricity in our homes. Power companies generate the electricity in several ways. How does your electricity supplier generate your electricity? Call and ask what percentage of the electricity they supply comes from renewable energy sources, like wind and solar power. ("Renewable" energy resources are those that can be produced, unlike petroleum, which cannot and in time will be gone.) If the percentage is low, see if you can switch your provider to a company that uses a higher percentage of renewable energy. For information on buying green power in your state, see the U.S. Department of Energy's Energy Efficiency and Renewable Energy website at **http://www.eere.energy.gov/greenpower/buying/buying_power.shtml.**

Chapter 10

Australia's Great Stumpy Reef?

Of all the ocean's ecosystems, none is more diverse or filled with beauty of color and form than a coral reef. Tens of thousands of species of marine organisms depend on coral reefs for their survival. Yet no other ecosystem, climate experts and marine biologists tell us, is more endangered by climate change.

Can it be that the world's coral reefs are really on the brink of collapse? It's a question of considerable self-interest to humanity, because coral reefs yield around $30 billion in income each year, mostly to people who have few other resources, such as Pacific island fishers. Financial loss, however, may prove to be a small thing compared with the loss of the "free services" that coral reefs provide. The citizens of five nations live entirely on coral atolls, while for tens of millions more people, fringing reefs are all that stand as protective barriers against the relentless waves of the invading sea. Destroy these fringing reefs, and the Pacific nations they shield will be inundated—the equivalent of bulldozing Holland's dikes.

Most commonly, coral reefs grow in clear, tropical seas where the water temperature remains above 64°F (18°C). There are a few species of coral that live in colder water, but they are only a small percentage of the world's coral. Coral polyps are small, filter-feeding anemone-like marine organisms with tentacles. They secrete calcium carbonate, which forms coral, the skeletal structure of a coral reef. Coral polyps have a symbiotic relationship with certain types of green, red, and purple algae known as zooxanthellae, which live inside the polyps. Under normal circumstances, the relationship is a happy one: the coral polyp provides a home and some nourishment to the algae, while the algae provide the polyp with food from photosynthesis and with its bright color. Because algae rely on sunlight for their survival, coral polyps can live only in water shallower than 330 feet (100 meters), the depth sunlight can penetrate in ocean water.

One of every four inhabitants of the oceans spends at least part of its life cycle in coral reefs. Such biodiversity is made possible by both the complex architecture of the corals, which provides many hiding places, and the lack of nutrients present in the clear, tropical water.

Climate-change-induced damage to reefs sometimes comes from unexpected quarters. The 1997 to 1998 El Niño saw the rain forests of Indonesia burn like never before, and for months the air was thick with a smog cloud rich in iron. Before those fires occurred, the coral reefs of southwestern Sumatra were among the richest in the world, boasting more than 100 species of hard coral, including massive formations more than a century old. Then, late in 1997, a "red tide" appeared off Sumatra's coast. The color was the result of a bloom of minute organisms that fed on the iron in the smog that had settled over the water. Known as dinoflagellates, the organisms produced toxins causing so much damage that it will take the reefs decades to recover, if indeed they ever do.

The smog cloud generated over Southeast Asia during the

2002 El Niño was even larger than that of 1997 to 1998—it was the size of the United States. On such a scale, smog can cut sunlight by 10 percent and heat the lower atmosphere and ocean, all of which causes problems for corals. Dinoflagellate blooms are now devastating coastlines from Indonesia to South Korea and causing hundreds of millions of dollars' worth of damage to aquaculture. The prospect of recovery for any East Asian coral reefs looks dimmer than ever.

It's the direct impact of higher temperatures, however, that is proving to be the most threatening aspect of climate change to coral reefs. High temperatures lead to coral bleaching, or the whitening and ultimately killing of formerly vibrant corals. Coral bleaching occurs whenever sea temperatures exceed a certain threshold. As the temperature of the seawater rises, the algae that live inside the coral polyps lose their ability to carry out photosynthesis; at that point, it costs the polyp more energy to maintain its partner than it gets in return. As in many a failing relationship, this unequal situation leads to a split, though precisely how the polyp ejects the algae (if they do not leave of their own volition) remains a mystery. If temperatures remain high for a month or two, the polyps starve to death without their algae, leaving a skeletal reef that will eventually become overgrown with soft corals (which are not reef-building) and green algae (which are a different type of algae from the symbiotic algae that live inside coral polyps).

To confirm that warm water can cause coral bleaching on its own, scientists examined a coral reef far from human interference, where no pollution, fishermen, or tourists have affected it. Myrmidon Reef, lying far off the coast of Queensland, Australia, sees almost nothing of humans. Every three years scientists from the Australian Institute of Marine Science survey the reef, and in 2004 they took along environmental writer James Woodford. He described Myrmidon as looking "as though it's been bombed." This was the result of the reef crest being severely bleached, leaving a forest of dead, white coral. Only on the deeper slopes did coral survive.

Coral bleaching was little heard of before 1930, and it remained a small-scale phenomenon until the 1970s. It was the 1998 El Niño that triggered the global dying. Some coral reefs were studied intensively before and after this event, which taught scientists a great deal. In the Indian Ocean, the Scott and Seringapatam reefs were severely affected, with bleaching to a depth of 100 feet. Before 1998, the percentage of hard-coral cover on these reefs was a healthy 41 percent; then it dropped to 15 percent. On Scott Reef there has been a complete failure of coral recovery since; Seringapatam is recovering slowly.

Australia's Great Barrier Reef, off the coast of Queensland, is 1,200 miles long (2,000 kilometers). The Great Barrier Reef is the most vulnerable reef in the world to climate change, and due to higher temperatures near the coast and the debilitating impact of pollution, the corals growing nearer the shoreline have been harder hit than those on the outer portion of the reef. In all, 42 percent of the Great Barrier Reef bleached in 1998, with 18 percent suffering permanent damage. In 2002, with the renewal of El Niño conditions, a pool of warm water around 200,000 square miles developed over the reef. This triggered another massive bleaching event that on some inshore reefs killed 90 percent of all reef-forming corals and left 60 percent of the Great Barrier Reef complex affected. In the few patches of cool water that remained, however, the coral was undamaged.

A survey conducted in 2003 revealed that the live coral

cover had dropped to less than 10 percent on half of the reef's area, with large declines evident even in the healthiest sections. Public outrage made political action inevitable, and the Australian government announced that 30 percent of the reef would be protected. This meant that commercial fishing would be banned and other human activities severely curtailed in the newly protected zone. But it is not fishing or tourists that are killing the reef; that is being done by spiraling CO_2 emissions.

In 2002, a panel of seventeen of the world's leading coral-reef researchers warned in an article in the journal *Science* that "projected increases in CO_2 and temperature over the next fifty years exceed the conditions under which coral reefs have flourished over the past half-million years." By 2030, they say, catastrophic damage will have been done to the world's reefs, and by 2050, even the most protected of reefs will be showing massive signs of damage. The message was reinforced in October 2002, when fifteen of the world's greatest authorities on coral reefs met in Townsville, Queensland, to discuss the plight of the Great Barrier Reef. According to reef scientist Dr. Terry Done, a further rise of 1.8°F (1°C) in global temperature would see 82 percent of the reef bleached, a 3.6°F (2°C) increase would bleach 97 percent, and a 5.4°F (3°C) rise in temperature would yield "total devastation." Because it takes the oceans around three decades to catch up with the heat accumulated in the atmosphere, it may well be that four-fifths of the Great Barrier Reef is doomed to become one vast zone of the living dead—just waiting for time and warm water to catch up with it.

Extinctions caused by climate change are almost certainly under way on the world's reefs, and a tiny species of coral-reef-dwelling fish known as *Gobiodon* species C may be emblematic of them. Most of the habitat used by this diminutive creature was destroyed by coral bleaching and associated impacts during the 1997 to 1998 El Niño, and it can now be seen only on one patch of coral in one lagoon in Papua New Guinea. "Species C" indicates that it has not yet been formally named, and its situation is so tenuous that it may become extinct before it gets named. We know about *Gobiodon* species C only because a scientist interested in these small fish has spent months documenting changes in their abundance. So great is the diversity of coral reefs, and so few are the marine biologists that study them, that it isn't an exaggeration to say that we need to multiply the loss of this one little fish a thousandfold to gain a sense of the cascade of extinctions that is probably occurring right now.

Despite the enormous damage already evident on the world's coral reefs, some scientists are hopeful that the reefs may yet survive climate change. They pin their hopes on the fact that 15,000 years ago, the sea level was 300 feet lower than at present. All the locations where coral reefs exist today were high and dry, yet species of hard coral managed to survive. Just how corals survived is unclear, though it was almost certainly only in special refuges. Some scientists think they altered the chemistry of their skeletons; others argue that, for a time, they did away with skeletons altogether. Corals may be forced to such extremities again in the future, because as CO_2 accumulates in the atmosphere and then diffuses into the ocean, it turns the seas acidic and prevents the coral organism from secreting its hard skeleton.

There are two ways that the species that constitute coral reefs might survive the looming threat of climate change: adaptation or migration. Recent research has found that a rare type of symbiotic algae named *Symbiodinium* strain D can tolerate higher temperatures than others, and on reefs destroyed by bleaching, its abundance has increased. If corals can adapt in this way, there is hope that some of them will survive in the locations where they grow right now. Yet the extent of this adaptation would need to expand many times over and occur swiftly to save the majority of coral reefs from devastation.

Another escape route may lie in corals migrating south to cooler waters. In the case of the Great Barrier Reef, the coast south of the corals' present distribution lacks the extensive shallow continental shelf required to support large reefs. A few species might find refuge in places like Sydney Harbor, but only a fraction of the diversity of even mobile reef species could exist in such limited spaces.

So what is the prognosis for the world's coral reefs? The complexity of their ecology, and our limited knowledge of key aspects of them, makes the response of the reefs toward warming among the most difficult of climate-change outcomes to determine. Nevertheless, the damage already sustained is a strong indication that reefs are sensitive to climate change, which doesn't bode well for their future.

Let's imagine what the Great Barrier Reef might look like fifty years from now. Only 50 of the 400 species of hard coral currently inhabiting the reef complex are likely to have adapted to using *Symbiodinium* strain D as partners, and almost all of these heat-hardy species are lumpy, rocklike forms or thick, sturdy types. Not only are such corals relatively unattractive, but they also do not form the mazelike structures so necessary to the reef's biodiversity. It is hard to believe that anything more than a small proportion of the reef's creatures could survive this transformation.

Could visitors to Queensland by 2050 see the Great Stumpy Reef? A lot more than a tourist attraction is at stake. Continuing on our present course is likely to destroy not only one of Earth's most beautiful and diverse ecosystems but also the lives of those people who depend on reefs to sustain their livelihoods.

CALL TO ACTION

Urge Local Businesses to See the Light

Some Saturday morning, before the stores in your town are open, check out the stores' lights. Many stores are as brightly lit as if they were open. Some stores even leave their computer terminals on. Both situations are a colossal waste of energy. It's time to take action:

1. Write a short note to the manager or owner. Explain that you are concerned about CO_2 emissions and that you couldn't help but notice how brightly lit the store was at a time when it was closed. Ask if the owner or manager would consider turning half the lights off, or if they could use a timer to periodically switch the lights on and off to conserve electricity. Mention that it would save the store money. Thank the store representative for his or her time. Send a copy of your note to the mayor of your town.

2. Wait and watch for a response to your note. Follow up a positive response by thanking the store owner in writing, letting him or her know that you intend to shop at that store. If you receive a negative response, again thank the owner in writing, but state that you won't be shopping there any longer. Take your hard-earned money to a business that is both environmentally responsible and interested in keeping costs down.

3. Take the same action for multi-storied office buildings that are overly lit at nighttime. Perhaps the lights on certain floors or a system of randomly spaced lights could be turned off. Turning off the lights in even a few of the offices will make a difference!

Chapter 11

A Warning from the Golden Toad

There is no doubt that climate change is affecting Earth's richly diverse flora and fauna. But is there proof that climate change has driven any species to extinction? If this has happened in remote places, such as New Guinea's forests and coral reefs, there's been no biologist on hand to document the event. In contrast, researchers flock to the Monteverde Cloud Forest Reserve in Costa Rica. Soon after our fragile planet passed through the climatic magic gate of 1976, abrupt and strange events were observed by the ecologists who spend their lives conducting detailed field studies in the Costa Rican forests.

One strange occurrence the ecologists noted was the keel-billed toucan, a lowland bird, nesting alongside the resplendent quetzal, known as the spiritual protector of the Maya, in the Monteverde Cloud Forest Reserve. The intrusion of the toucan into the quetzal's misty forest nesting area could ultimately be disastrous for quetzals. The quetzal is still seen in Monteverde, but it is not as common as it once was, in part because the keel-billed toucan eats its eggs and young. Some more sensitive bird species have already vanished from the site altogether.

Then, during the winter dry season of 1987, in the mossy rain forests that blanket the mountain's slopes about a mile above the sea, thirty of the fifty species of frogs known to inhabit the 12-square-mile study site vanished. Among them was a spectacular toad the color of spun gold. The creature lived only on the upper slopes of the mountain, but there it was abundant, and at certain times of year the brilliant males could be seen by the dozen, gathering around puddles on the forest floor to mate. It was aptly named the golden toad, and its disappearance particularly worried researchers, because it was one of the most spectacular of the region's amphibians and was found nowhere else.

The golden toad was discovered and named in 1966. Only the males are golden; the females are mottled black, yellow, and scarlet. For much of the year, it's a secretive creature, spending its time underground in burrows amid the mossy root-masses of the woodland. Then, as the dry season gives way to the wet in April to May, it appears aboveground en masse for just a few days or weeks. With such a short time to reproduce, the males fight with one another for top spot and take every opportunity to mate.

In her book *In Search of the Golden Frog,* amphibian expert Marty Crump described what it was like to see the creature in its mating frenzy:

> I trudge uphill . . . through cloud forest, then through gnarled elfin forest. . . . At the next bend I see one of the most incredible sights I've ever seen. There, congregated around several small pools at the bases of dwarfed, windswept trees, are over one hundred Day-Glo golden orange toads poised like statues, dazzling jewels against the dark brown mud.

On April 15, 1987, Crump made a note in her field diary that was to have historic significance:

We see a large orange blob with legs flailing in all directions: a writhing mass of toad flesh. Closer examination reveals three males, each struggling to gain access to the female in the middle. Forty-two brilliant orange splotches poised around the pool are unmated males, alert to any movement and ready to pounce. Another fifty-seven unmated males are scattered nearby. In total we find 133 toads in the neighborhood of this kitchen sink–sized pool.

Again, on April 20:

Breeding seems to be over. I found the last female four days ago, and gradually the males have returned to their underground retreats. Every day the ground is drier and the pools contain less water. Today's observations are discouraging. Most of the pools have dried completely, leaving behind desiccated eggs already covered in mold. Unfortunately, the dry weather conditions of El Niño are still affecting this part of Costa Rica.

As if they knew the fate of their eggs, the toads attempted to breed again in May. This was, as far as the world knows, the last great golden toad orgy ever to occur, and Crump had the privilege to record it. Despite the fact that 43,500 eggs were deposited in the ten pools she studied, only twenty-nine tadpoles survived for longer than a week, because the pools once again quickly dried.

The following year Crump was back at Monteverde for the breeding season, but this time things were different. After a long search, on May 21, she located a single male. By June, the still-searching Crump was worried: "The forest seems sterile and depressing without the bright orange splashes of color I've come to associate with this [wet] weather. I don't understand what's happening. Why haven't we found a few hopeful males, checking out the pools in anticipation . . . ?" Yet even after the season closed without another sighting, there was no undue pessimism. A year was to pass before, on May 15, 1989, a solitary male was again sighted. Since it was sitting just 10 feet from where Crump made her sighting twelve months earlier, it was almost certainly the same male, who, for the second year running, held a lonely vigil, waiting for the arrival of his fellows. He was, as far as we know, the last of his species, for the golden toad has not been seen since.

Lizards also suffered population crashes in the years following 1987, especially the anoles, small relatives of the iguanas; by 1996, two species had vanished entirely. Today, the mountain's rain forests continue to be stripped of their jewels, with many reptiles, frogs, and other fauna becoming rarer by the year. While still verdant enough to justify its name, the Monteverde Cloud Forest Reserve is beginning to resemble a crown that has lost its brightest and most beautiful gems.

Suspecting that some odd weather event might be the cause of the changes, researchers studied the reserve's temperature and rainfall records. In 1999, they announced that they had identified what killed the golden toad and its neighbors. Their findings revealed that ever since Earth had passed through its first climatic magic gate in 1976, the number of mistless days experienced each dry season had grown, eventually combining into runs of mistless days. By the dry season of 1987, the number of consecutive mistless days had passed some critical threshold. Crossing that threshold, which was so subtle that the researchers hadn't detected it, plunged the entire ecosystem of the mountaintop into crisis. Mist, you see, brings vital moisture. Without it, some of the animals die.

What caused the mist to dry? The cloud line in Monteverde is the level at which clouds sit against mountainsides. That creates misty conditions. Beginning in 1976, the bottom of the cloud mass had risen until it was above the level of the forest. The change was driven by the abrupt rise in sea-surface temperatures in the central western Pacific that signaled the magic gate of 1976. A hot ocean had heated the air, elevating the condensation point for moisture. By 1987, the rising cloud line still shaded the forest but no longer provided mist.

The golden toad's habit of wandering about in daylight hours left its porous skin exposed to a new, drier climate. By the time the researchers announced their conclusion, in 1999, the golden toad had been extinct for a decade.

The golden toad's extinction, however, was not in vain, because when the explanation of its demise was published in the journal *Nature,* the scientists could make their point without equivocation: the golden toad was the first documented victim of global warming. We had killed it with our wasteful use of coal-fired electricity and our oversize cars just as surely as if we had flattened its forest with bulldozers.

Since 1976, other researchers have observed frogs, toads, and other amphibian species vanish. It now appears that climate change is responsible for their disappearance as well.

In the late 1970s, a remarkable creature known as the gastric brooding frog disappeared from southeastern Queensland, Australia. This brown, medium-size frog astonished the world in 1973, when it was discovered. The surprise came when a

This frog is not eating a smaller frog. The litle frog is actually the offspring of the larger one. The baby "hatches" in its mother's stomach.

researcher looked into a female's open mouth and saw a tiny frog sitting on her tongue! It turns out that the strange brown frog was not cannibalistic; it just had bizarre breeding habits. The female swallows her fertilized eggs, and the tadpoles develop in her stomach until they metamorphose into frogs, which she then regurgitates into the world.

When this novel method of reproduction was announced, some medical doctors understandably got very excited. How, they wondered, did the frog transform its stomach from an acid-filled digesting chamber into a nursery? They thought the answer might assist in treating a variety of stomach complaints. Alas, they were unable to carry out many experiments, because in 1979—six years after its existence was announced to the world—the gastric brooding frog vanished. It hasn't been seen since.

When the first global survey of amphibians was completed in 2004, it revealed that almost a third of the world's 6,000-odd species were threatened with extinction. Many of these endangered species began their decline after 1976, and according to Simon Stuart of the International Union for the Conservation of Nature, "There's almost no evidence of recovery." Research suggests that climate change is the likely cause for the disappearances.

The results of a North American research study led scientists to hypothesize about the amphibian decline that was occurring in the northwestern United States. Amphibians of the genus *Bufo* are commonly known as toads. One fundamental discovery of the American study was that ultraviolet (UV) light hinders the development of the toad's embryos. This in turn makes them more vulnerable to a fungal disease known as *Saprolegnia ferax*, a killer of amphibians worldwide. The reason the toad embryos received more UV light was that their nursery ponds were shallower. Why? Because persistent El Niño–like conditions since 1976 have brought less winter rain to the Pacific Northwest. And for toad embryos, even a small change in pond depth can be critical. In ponds 19.5 inches (50 centimeters) deep, 12 percent of tadpoles die from the fungus. When the water is only 7.8 inches (20 centimeters) deep, 80 percent die. At worst, some ponds dried up completely, killing all the tadpoles in them.

To compensate, some frogs tried to breed in larger bodies of water, but these contained fish that ate the hatching tadpoles. Between the fungus, the drying ponds, and the fish, the region's amphibians had nowhere to go, and so they joined the long list of species in free fall toward extinction.

The study led scientists to link a variety of impacts under a single dominant factor. In various parts of the world, researchers have documented one or more of these changes at work. In the case of the golden toad, it was the loss of mist. Australia's frogs have been reported to be infected with a fungus similar to the one found in North America, while elsewhere failing rains or tadpole deaths mean that reproduction is in decline. It now seems obvious that the change in weather patterns brought about by the magic-gate years of 1976 and 1998 is the hidden cause of amphibian extinctions.

CALL TO ACTION

Save the Animals

Any changes you make in your life that conserve energy or reduce greenhouse-gas emissions, no matter how small, will make a difference. The tipping points that lead to the extinction of a species are the cumulative result of many small changes, such as temperature rates or annual rainfall, which can result in an environment that is no longer suitable for some of its inhabitants. Anything you can do to slow down those changes is a plus.

Several organizations actively work to protect animals by seeking conservation legislation, sponsoring sanctuaries, and helping distressed animals. Donations to these organizations ensure that animals are treated fairly. Consider becoming a member of one of these groups, including the following three reputable organizations:

- The World Wildlife Fund. This group seeks to preserve nature and its biological diversity. Globally, its membership numbers almost 5 million people. Visit their website at http://www.worldwildlife.org.

- The Sierra Club. For more than 100 years, the Sierra Club has advocated the preservation of wilderness areas and the plants and animals that inhabit them. Many conservation laws and parklands are the result of grassroots movements initiated by the club. Visit their website at **http://www.sierraclub.org**.
- The Nature Conservancy. The Conservancy takes action by protecting the land and water that animals and plants need to survive. Visit their website at **http://www.nature.org**.

Each website offers a wealth of information plus suggestions on how you can become active.

Chapter 12

Liquid Gold: Changes in Rainfall

From the poles to the equator, our earth spans a range of temperatures from around −104°F to 104°F (−75.6°C to 40°C), and air at 104°F can hold 470 times as much water vapor as air at −104°F. The low temperature and lack of water vapor explains why Earth's poles are frozen deserts. The capacity of warm air to hold more water vapor also dictates that, for every degree of warming we create, our world will experience an average 1 percent increase in rainfall. But it's critical to note that this rainfall increase will not be evenly distributed in time and space. Already, rain is appearing at unusual times in some places and not at all in others.

Over large parts of the world, rainfall is increasing; however, more rain is not always a good thing. One of the most certain predictions of climate science is that as our planet warms, increasing amounts of rain will fall at high latitudes in winter, since the air won't be cold enough to freeze the water vapor into snow. Flooding, of course, is expected to increase wherever rainfall does, but as extreme-weather events become more common, the incidence of flooding will grow even higher. For example, in 2004 in England, heavy spring rains so soaked the land that in many regions haymaking was difficult or impossible.

In other regions, climate change will lower the amount of rainfall. A major decrease in rainfall could transform these areas into new Saharas or at least into regions untenable for human habitation. A lack of rainfall is often referred to as a drought, yet droughts are by their nature transient: they end within a few years. But in the areas affected by climate change, there is no prospect that the rain will return. Instead, what occurs is a rapid shift to a new, drier climate.

We already have evidence that this kind of climate shift occurred in Africa's Sahel region during the 1960s. The area affected was huge—an enormous swath of sub-Saharan Africa extending from the Atlantic Ocean to Sudan. Four decades have now passed since the sudden decline in rainfall, and there is no sign that the life-giving monsoon rains will return. Even before the decline, the Sahel was a region of marginal rainfall where life was tough. In areas with better soils and more rain, farmers eked out a living growing crops, while in the drier areas, semi-nomadic camel herders followed the vegetation from one place to another in pursuit of feed for their herds. The decreased rainfall has made life difficult for both groups: herders struggle to find grass in what is now a true desert, while the farmers rarely get sufficient rain to stir their fields to life. The world's media periodically show images of the result—starving camels and desperate families struggling in a dust-filled wasteland.

For decades many people in more industrialized nations maintained that this disaster was brought on by the people in Africa themselves. The argument was that overgrazing by camels, goats, and cattle, as well as people gathering firewood, had destroyed the region's thin covering of vegetation, exposing the dark soil and changing the albedo of the area. With constant updrafts of hot, dry air and no plants to transpire moisture into the atmosphere, the rain-forming clouds had failed to gather. As this human-made "drought" lengthened, the soil began to blow away. It's an argument that has proved to be wrong in almost every respect.

The true origin of the Sahel disaster was revealed in November 2003, when climatologists at the National Center for Atmospheric Research in Boulder, Colorado, published a painstaking study that used computer models to simulate rainfall regimes in the region between 1930 and 2000. It was a massive exercise, since everything from sea and land temperatures to changes in the region's vegetation needed to be fed into the computer.

In the end, the model simulated past and current climate in the region, and it revealed that the amount of human-caused land degradation there was far too insignificant to have triggered the dramatic climate shift. Instead, climatologists found that one climatic variable was responsible for much of the rainfall decline: rising sea-surface temperatures in the Indian Ocean, which resulted from an accumulation of greenhouse gases. The Indian Ocean is the most rapidly warming ocean on Earth, and the computer study showed that as it warms, the conditions that generate the Sahelian monsoon, or rainy season, weaken. As a result, by the 1960s the Sahelian "drought" had begun.

As is commonly the case in such studies, not all of the observed rainfall decline could be explained, which means that some unidentified mechanism was at work. But now some scientists think that they have found the cause, which they've dubbed "global dimming."

Global dimming is a phenomenon that cuts down the amount of sunlight reaching Earth's surface. It has caused a cooling of the oceans around Europe, which has further weakened the monsoon. Global dimming is in large part due to particles spewed out into the air by coal-fired power plants, automobiles, and factories. This bolsters the argument that the Sahelian catastrophe was not the result of ecological mismanagement by irresponsible farmers or herders. In fact, one could argue that the greenhouse-gas-producing countries were equally, if not more, responsible. In 2005, scientists published more results of climate modeling for this region. The conclusion? It seems seriously possible that the drought will persist, and perhaps worsen, in the twenty-first century.

The Sahelian climate shift is so big that it could influence the climate of the entire planet. This was first noted by researchers Joseph Prospero and Peter Lamb, who studied the dust that blows from the Sahel.

Dust is important stuff, because its tiny particles can scatter and absorb light, thereby lowering temperature. Dust particles also carry nutrients into the ocean and to distant lands, promoting the growth of plankton and plants, thereby increasing the absorption of CO_2. Around half of the global dust in the air today originates in arid Africa, and the impact of the drying is so great that the planet's atmospheric dust loading has increased by a third. Climatologists are still calculating what will result, but Earth's systems are so interconnected that a phenomenon of this scale is certain to have an impact.

The citizens of the industrialized world tend to feel that their technology will protect them from Sahelian-scale disasters, but nature has been busy proving them wrong. Australia is a dry country, and Australians—even urban ones—are obsessed with rainfall. The southwestern corner of western Australia once enjoyed one of the most reliable of rainfall regimes. Traditionally, the rain fell during the winter, with more than 40 inches (1 meter) falling annually at some locations. The area gained fame as the western wheat belt and was one of the largest and most predictable centers of grain production on the continent. Later, vineyards spread throughout the wetter areas and began producing some of the finest and most expensive wines made in the Southern Hemisphere.

During the first 146 years of European habitation of the southwest of Australia (1829 to 1975), the reliable winter rainfall brought prosperity and opportunity. But then things changed, and ever since, the region has endured a decrease in rainfall averaging 15 percent. Climate models indicate that about half the decline results from global warming, which has pushed the temperate weather zone southward. The Australian climatologist David Karoly thinks that the other half results from destruction of the ozone layer, which has cooled the stratosphere over the Antarctic, thus hastening the circulation of cold air around the pole and drawing the southern rainfall zone even farther southward.

While a 15 percent loss may seem trivial, its impact has been considerable. Farms in the region's drier margins particularly felt the change, because a variation of only a few inches makes the difference between a good crop and failure. In these areas, wheat is the principal crop, and it's grown in an unusual manner. In the 1960s, the goal of the western Australian farmers was to clear a million acres of native vegetation a year. When the bulldozers had done their work, farmers found themselves staring at sterile stretches of sand—some of the most infertile soil to be found anywhere on Earth—because here, as in rain forests, the region's natural wealth was bound up in its native vegetation. This, however, was what the farmers wanted, since wheat growing in the southwest was a gigantic version of hydroponic gardening: farmers planted their wheat seed, dusted the sterile sand with nutrients, and then waited for the never-failing winter rains to add water.

By 2004, after decades of nature refusing to "just add water," the wheat-growing region began shifting westward, replacing dairy farming in country once considered too wet for wheat. But because of the Indian Ocean, wheat farming can shift westward only so far. As conditions worsen over the coming century, one high-rainfall activity after another must face being pushed into the sea.

The situation is further complicated by the summer rainfall, which has increased, but in very erratic downfalls. Because summer rains cannot be depended upon, farmers do not plant summer crops, so the rain falls on bare fields, allowing the water to soak down to the water table. There it meets salt, which steady westerly winds have been blowing in from the Indian Ocean for millions of years.

Under every square yard of this land lies an average of between 150 and 250 pounds of salt. Before land clearing, this didn't matter, because the diverse native vegetation used every drop of water that fell from the heavens, and the salt stayed in its crystalline form. As the summer rains began to fall on the vacant wheat fields, however, water far saltier than seawater began to creep upward, killing everything it touched. The first sign of trouble was a salty taste in the previously sweet brooks of the region. In many cases the brooks' water quickly became undrinkable and brookside vegetation died; within a decade or two, many brooks had turned into collapsed, salty drains. Today, impoverished and bankrupt farmers are facing the worst case of dry-land salinity in the world. Neither science nor government has been able to provide solutions, and the damage bill is in the billions. Roads, railways, houses, and airfields are now besieged by salt, and unless the original vegetation can be returned and induced to grow in the drier and saltier conditions that now prevail, there appears to be no hope of a turnaround.

Western Australia's capital is Perth, a city of 1.5 million people and the world's most isolated metropolis. For Perth, the most crucial impact from the decline in winter rainfall was less water in the city's reservoirs, because after 1975 the rain tended to fall in light showers that sank into the soil rather than replenishing the reservoirs. Between 1975 and 1996, the city's surface water supply dropped 50 percent lower than in the early part of the twentieth century. Between 1997 and 2004, it dropped even lower—to little more than a third of the flow received three decades earlier.

Severe water restrictions were put in place in 1976, but the situation was soon eased by drawing on a reserve of groundwater known as the Gnangara Mound. For a quarter of a century, the city mined this subterranean water, but the failing rains meant that it was not being recharged. By 2004, the situation of the Gnangara Mound was critical, with the state's Environmental Protection Authority warning that drawing more water from it would threaten some species with extinction. Today, the western swamp tortoise, which is a living fossil, survives only because water is pumped into its habitat.

By early 2005, nearly thirty years after the crisis emerged, the city's water experts rated the chances at one in five that a "catastrophic failure of supply"—meaning no water coming out of the tap—could occur. Were that to happen, the city would have no choice but to squeeze what water it could out of the Gnangara Mound and in doing so destroy much ancient and wondrous biodiversity. Even then, the fix would be only temporary.

In response to the growing water crisis, a desalination plant was constructed in Perth. The plant, which began operation in November 2006, converts seawater from the Indian Ocean into freshwater that is pumped into the city water supply system. Government officials expect that the desalination plant, which is Australia's first large-scale operation of its kind, will supply 17 percent of Perth's drinking water. An added bonus is that the plant buys its power from a power plant that generates electricity with wind turbines, reducing the desalination plant's carbon emissions.

Across the Pacific Ocean, much of the American West is experiencing drought. Research shows that such dry conditions have not been seen in the region for around 700 years, since a time when the American Southwest was even warmer than it is today. This suggests a relationship between drought and warmer conditions, and as with the Sahel, the link seems to lie in rising ocean temperatures.

Between 1998 and 2002 the Pacific Ocean was in an unusual state. Waters in the eastern tropical Pacific were a few degrees cooler than normal, while those in the central western Pacific were about 86°F (30°C), far warmer than average. These conditions shifted the jet stream northward, pushing storms that would usually track at around latitude 35°N, about the location of San Luis Obispo, California, to north of latitude 40°N, which is about 250 miles north of San Francisco. The rising sea-surface temperature caused a shift in winds that ultimately affected areas far away. And, of course, what was driving warmer ocean temperatures was CO_2 in the atmosphere.

Some people, including some climatologists, claim that the drought conditions in the American West are just part of a natural cycle. The only way to be absolutely sure if this is the case is to wait the decades or hundreds of years required for any natural cycle to play itself out. But the fact that the changes are consistent with those expected from global warming and that they have been observed during warm times in the past is worrying. Furthermore, the potential of climate change to spawn drought almost anywhere on the planet is so great that leading climatologists have recently warned that "it would be a mistake to assume any region is safe from megadrought." It is worth pointing out that the near-record rains the United States experienced over the winter of 2005 in parts of the Southwest were not sufficient to make up for the preceding dry years.

Much of the water in the American Southwest comes in the form of winter snow that accumulates in its high mountains. When this snow melts during the spring and summer, it provides stream flow when it is most needed by farmers. In effect, the snowpack has offered an inexpensive form of water storage that has minimized the need for dams, which are used to create reservoirs. The amount of snow that falls has always varied considerably from year to year, and this variability can hide any long-term trend from the casual observer. Over the last fifty years, however, there has been a decline in the average amount of snow received. If this trend continues for another five decades, western snowpacks will be reduced by up to 60 percent in some regions, which could cut summertime stream flow in half. This will devastate not just water supplies but hydropowered electricity and fish habitats as well.

Changes in the overall volume of snowfall, however, are not nearly as worrying as changes in the way the snowpack forms and melts. Over the past fifty years, the Southwest region has warmed by 1.4°F (0.8°C)—slightly more than the global average, and even in regions that are now receiving more snow, this warming, along with seasonal changes in rainfall and temperature are affecting water supply. These factors have conspired to reduce the snowpack. This is because the higher temperatures are melting the snow before it can consolidate as snowpack. On the whole, the snowpack is melting earlier, which means that the peak of runoff into streams is now occurring three weeks sooner than in 1948. This leaves less water for the height of summer, when it's most needed, and increases water flow in winter and spring, which may lead to more flooding. With temperatures in the region set to rise between 3.6°F and 12.6°F (2°C and 7°C) over this century (unless we significantly reduce CO_2 emissions), it can be anticipated that most streams will eventually flow in winter, when the water is least needed.

Some people suggest that the solution is to build more dams: they would hold the water in reserve for summer. It's possible this will happen. But there are a limited number of sites suitable for dams in the Southwest, and dams mean that farmers will pay for water storage that was once provided by nature. Unfortunately, the changes under way are so vast that even a new program of dam building may be insufficient to counter them. Researchers forecast that snowpack changes could lower farm values by 15 percent, costing billions. The biggest problem, however, will certainly be for cities like Los Angeles in the western United States that are tethered to ever-dwindling water supplies.

These vast metropolises are impossible to relocate, and some may, if the rate of change accelerates, have to be abandoned. If this sounds extreme, it's important to remember that we are only at the beginning of the West's water crisis. Five thousand years ago, when the American Southwest became a little warmer and drier even than it is today, the Native American cultures that had flourished across the region all but vanished. Only when conditions cooled again was the region habitable. For more than a millennium, the Southwest was little more than one big ghost town.

CALL TO ACTION

Eat Locally

Chances are the shelves in the produce section of your local supermarket are overflowing with fresh fruit and vegetables. If you live in Chicago and see strawberries in the market in February, you can bet they were shipped from out of state. Ask where your produce comes from. If it isn't grown locally, transporting it increases CO_2 emissions.

In the summer, whenever possible, buy locally grown produce. Try shopping at farmers' markets. If your town does not host a farmers' market during the summer months, suggest that the town governing body investigate the possibility of starting one. Ask your grocer or local food cooperative if it is possible to buy from suppliers who don't transport produce from hundreds, maybe even thousands, of miles away. Eat fruits and vegetables when they are in season. For example, in the fall and winter, choose butternut squash, apples, and broccoli. In the spring, look for strawberries, lettuce, and peas. You'll find that the fruits and vegetables have a lot more flavor when they are in season.

Chapter 13
Weather Gone Wild

Scientists continuously monitor Earth's atmosphere, because its variations can strongly influence climate change. The tropopause—the boundary between the troposphere and the stratosphere—is a particular area of the atmosphere that climatologists have been watching closely. Normally, the tropopause varies in altitude from approximately 5 miles (8 kilometers) at the poles to approximately 11 miles (18 kilometers) at the equator. In 2003, climate scientists announced that over just a few years the tropopause had risen by several hundred meters. Why should this small adjustment between layers of the atmosphere occurring several miles above our heads worry us? For the excellent reason that climatologists now realize that the tropopause is where much of our weather is generated. Change it, and you alter not only weather patterns but extreme-weather events as well.

Human-caused pollution—ozone-destroying chemicals and greenhouse gases—is responsible for the tropopause change. Chlorofluorocarbons (CFCs) are man-made chemicals that destroy ozone. In Earth's atmosphere, ozone is six times as abundant in the stratosphere as it is at sea level, yet if all the planet's stratospheric ozone were brought down to sea level, it would form a layer just one-tenth of an inch thick. Because

CFCs have destroyed ozone, the stratosphere has cooled and shrunk. Meanwhile, in the troposphere, ever-increasing levels of greenhouse gases are trapping more heat, causing it to expand. These two effects "push" the tropopause upward. At the same time, there are signs that the warming troposphere and its resulting ability to hold more water vapor are changing the weather patterns globally and increasing the likelihood of extreme-weather events.

You needn't look far to find examples of such events. As the troposphere has warmed over the past decade, the world has seen the most powerful El Niño ever recorded (1997 to 1998), the most fatal hurricane in 200 years (Mitch, 1998), the hottest European summer on record (2003), the first recorded South Atlantic hurricane (Catarina, 2004), the most economically devastating hurricane (Katrina, 2005), unprecedented flooding in Myanmar (2007 and 2008), and more Arctic sea ice melted during the summer than ever before recorded (2007). This series of events, many would argue, indicates that the potential for the new climate to generate extremes is already increasing.

How can global warming cause extreme-weather events? Hurricanes and cyclones are fueled by warm, moist air. Global warming raises the temperature of the oceans and the air, and in a positive-feedback loop, the warm ocean water warms the air. This is similar to the way warm sweat from your body evaporates and transfers your body's heat to the air; the ocean simply does this on a much larger scale. As you know, warm air can hold significantly more water vapor, or "hurricane fuel." The amount of water vapor that air can hold doubles for every 18°F (10°C) increase in air temperature; thus air at 86°F (30°C) can hold four times as much hurricane fuel as air at 50°F (10°C).

There are signs that hurricanes are becoming more frequent in North America. In 1996, 1997, and 1999, the United States endured more than twice the number of hurricanes experienced annually during the twentieth century. Moreover, what 1998's hurricanes lacked in numbers, they more than made up for in intensity. Hurricane Mitch tore through the Caribbean in October of that year, killing more than 10,000 people and making 3 million homeless. With wind speeds of up to 180 miles per hour, Mitch was the fourth-strongest Atlantic Basin hurricane ever recorded. It was also the most damaging storm to hit the Americas in 200 years; only the Great Hurricane of 1780, which occurred near Barbados and killed at least 22,000 people, was more severe in its impact.

After a few years of relative calm, hurricanes returned with a vengeance in 2004, when four major tropical storms crossed the Florida coast in quick succession. Many of the homes damaged by these storms are still uninhabitable.

In August 2005, Hurricane Katrina devastated the states of Louisiana and Mississippi, with property damage exceeding that of all other natural disasters to strike the United States. Katrina began as a thunderstorm off the Bahamas. As it moved across the ocean, it picked up more water vapor and increased in intensity, first to tropical-storm status, and then to a category-one hurricane, making landfall in Florida on August 25. Katrina killed eleven people as it crossed the Floridian peninsula. During the next four days, the hurricane swung southwest into the Gulf of Mexico, and then north in a scythe-shaped path toward the cities of New Orleans and Biloxi, Mississippi. Along the way, the Gulf's warm water fueled Katrina's power and increased the storm's strength to a category-five hurricane, the strongest of all.

By the time Katrina reached New Orleans, it had been downgraded to a category-three storm, the eye of which passed 30 miles (50 kilometers) east of the city. At first, people heaved a sigh of relief: Katrina wasn't at its fiercest when it reached land, nor had it scored a direct hit on the city. But within hours, unimaginable catastrophe struck.

The city of New Orleans, located between the Mississippi River and Lake Pontchartrain, is home to more than half a million people. Levees along the river and lake protect the city, which lies an average of 6 feet (2 meters) below sea level, from inundation. Tragically, the levees were not designed to withstand a storm of Katrina's strength. On Monday, August 29, water began to breach the levees and flooded almost 80 percent of the city.

In 2008, with many people still trying to rebuild from Katrina, another hurricane threatened the city. As they watched videos of Hurricane Gustav wreaking havoc on Cuba, moving into the Caribbean, and then heading straight for New Orleans, city officials feared another Katrina-like disaster. To avoid this, they ordered a mandatory evacuation of New Orleans. Fortunately, Gustav weakened in strength; its path veered slightly westward, and despite heavy rain, the rebuilt levees held. And while some people grumbled about the mandatory evacuation, they may have to accept the possibility of more frequent periodic evacuations in the future.

While many of a hurricane's most devastating aftereffects are not related to global warming, ample evidence shows that global warming is changing the atmosphere and oceans in ways likely to promote more powerful hurricanes and cyclones. Satellite measurements reveal that the oceans are rapidly warming from the top down as the result of additional heat in

✳ KATRINA SURVIVOR NOW TAKES HURRICANE WARNINGS SERIOUSLY

Katherine Hart has been a resident of New Orleans since 1994. During this time, she has heard many weather forecasts predicting the approach of a big storm, and at times, even a hurricane.

"It seems like almost every year there is a hurricane heading this way. Hurricane George was huge, and it was my first big scare. For us, though, George was nothing. Just a little bit of wind," Hart recalled. "We've gotten used to evacuating. We go away for a couple of days, and then we come back. We disrupt our lives for nothing." After repeated evacuations without a serious storm making landfall, forecaster warnings of an approaching hurricane began to resemble the story about the boy who cried "Wolf!"

Because Hart works for the media, she stayed in New Orleans during the storm. She did not, however, remain in her home, which is located at the base of a small rise in an old, established neighborhood. Instead, she grabbed a sleeping bag, a change of clothes, and some toiletries, and she and some of her colleagues settled in on the third floor of the building where they work, which is a secure, sturdily constructed building.

Initial predictions forecasted that the eye of Katrina was going to pass over New Orleans. But like other storms, including Hurricane George, at the last minute Katrina veered toward Mississippi. Early Monday morning, Hart ventured out into the building's parking lot, where she noticed that water covered some of the lot. At first, Hart experienced a sense of relief. The building was intact; they had an electric generator up and running. Everything seemed calm. Hart returned to work.

Later, after the rain and wind had stopped, Hart went out again. "The water in the parking lot was higher than it had been. I got this strong feeling of dread. It was clear the city was filling with water." Soon after, it became evident that the levees had been breached, and large areas of New Orleans did indeed fill with water. "Nobody was really prepared psychologically, physically—in any way—for what happened."

At that point, Hart and her colleagues were ordered to leave the city. She climbed onto a truck owned by her company and, without knowing where she was going, left New Orleans. Getting out of the city was a surreal experience. She saw highways empty of cars, helicopters flying overhead, and police cars blocking the exit and entrance ramps of the major highways. She was in the truck for nine hours before reaching a safe haven in Baton Rouge. "At that point," Hart remembers, "I switched into survival mode. All I cared about was getting air, water, and going to the bathroom." She had arrived .

Hart's home was damaged by what she refers to as "the man-made disaster"—floodwaters that resulted from the breach of the levees. "There was a brown line, visible throughout the city, that marked the level of the water at each stage—where it went up and where it went down. On my street, there was three feet of water. My house is on a slight rise, so inside it the water level went up to [only] one foot deep, then it settled back to six inches and stayed there a long time."

Making her home habitable again took months of work; it had to be completely gutted. She and her husband had to drag out rugs and other wet materials, including ruined upholstered furniture, and spray the walls with bleach to prevent the growth of mold. The refrigerator, filled with rotted food, had to be hauled out and cleaned. "For a long time," Hart recalled, "refrigerators were everywhere." While it was possible to eliminate the horrible smell that clung stubbornly to the interior of some refrigerators, most people found it impossible to completely rid them of the insects that had moved into the appliances' cracks and crevices.

Hart and her husband lived in a FEMA trailer for about sixteen months before they could move back into their home. But they consider themselves lucky: thousands of people whose homes were completely covered by water lost everything.

There is one thing Hart is certain about: "People definitely take [hurricanes] more seriously. Some people are taking them so seriously that it's the major reason they aren't coming back to New Orleans." ✴

the atmosphere. Because of this, the amount of water vapor—hurricane fuel—in the air over the oceans has increased by 1.3 percent per decade since 1988. Both the warmer ocean and increased water vapor are key agents in transforming tropical storms into hurricanes and in making category-one hurricanes grow into category fives. Since 1974, the global number of category-four and category-five hurricanes has almost doubled, from a 1970s annual average of ten storms to almost eighteen per year since the 1990s. Historically, hurricanes haven't occurred in the winter because sea temperatures are too cold, but that might change in a warming world.

Globally, the increase in hurricane-related flood damage over recent decades has been profound. In the 1960s, around 7 million people were affected by flooding annually. By 2005, that figure reached 150 million. And in the wake of floods come plagues. The bacterium that causes cholera breeds in stagnant and polluted water, as do mosquitoes that can spread malaria, yellow fever, dengue fever, and encephalitis. As Katrina proved, oil spills from flooded petrochemical plants foul the environment and kill plant and animal life. Katrina killed more than 1,200 people, and its financial costs associated with property damage may exceed $200 billion. In light of this figure, the failure to address climate change and the future extreme-weather events it spawns will carry a very high price tag.

The United Kingdom has experienced a significant increase in severe winter storms, a trend that is predicted to continue. In January 2007, hurricane-strength windstorm Kyrill ripped across England and then moved on across Europe, killing at least forty people.

On the continent, more alarming events have occurred. The European summer of 2003 was so hot that, statistically speaking, such an outlandish event should occur no more often than every 46,000 years. The heat wave was so extreme that more than 30,000 people died during June and July, when temperatures exceeded 104°F (40°C) across much of the continent and the United Kingdom. Heat waves, incidentally, kill a large number of people worldwide each year. In the United States, heat-related deaths exceed those from all other weather-related causes combined.

In terms of extreme-weather events, it's worth recording that the United States already has the most varied weather of any country on Earth, with more intense and damaging tornadoes, flash floods, thunderstorms, hurricanes, and blizzards than anywhere else. With the intensity of such events projected to increase as our planet warms, in purely human terms the United States would seem to have more to lose from climate change than any other large nation. And the climate in the United States seems to be warming. The National Oceanic and Atmospheric Administration acknowledged that 2006 was the warmest year on record for the contiguous United States. The 2006 annual average temperature was 55°F (12.7°C), which is 2.2°F (1.2°C) above the twentieth-century mean. Can Americans afford to risk an unchecked temperature rise due to greenhouse gases? If the ever-spiraling insurance bill resulting from severe weather events such as droughts and hurricanes is any indication, the United States is already paying dearly for its CO_2 emissions.

Some regions of the world, however, have so far recorded little change. In India, apart from Gujarat and western Orissa, there is less drought than twenty-five years ago. Extreme temperatures also seem to be less frequent, although northwestern India is experiencing a marked increase in extremely hot days, and the heat waves there are exacting a heavy toll in human lives. On the other hand, in 2005, record monsoon rains and storms in Mumbai and the surrounding regions resulted in widespread floods.

Extreme-weather events affect Earth's continents locally. But global warming is affecting all continents equally in one sense: all of them are shrinking. Why? Because as the atmosphere and sea temperatures rise and ice melts in Antarctica and the Arctic, the oceans are expanding. Is this a threat to humanity? That depends on how far the ocean waters will rise—and at what speed.

CALL TO ACTION

Energy-Smart Schools

Many school districts are expanding and building new school buildings at an increasingly rapid rate. If you live in one of those districts, become active in the energy choices being made for the new schools. Attend a school board meeting with a group of your friends. Request speaking time. Request that wind and/or solar energy sources be incorporated into the plans for any new buildings. Also ask that sustainable architecture and natural-daylight lighting be considered during the buildings' construction. An increasing number of schools have small photovoltaic panels, devices that convert sunlight directly into electricity. They generate a small percentage of the school's electricity and serve as teaching tools for the students. Many of these types of projects are eligible for grants to implement them. Request that the school board look into renewable energy grant programs for schools added to your district—and maybe even retrofit some of the older buildings.

Visit the U.S. Department of Energy's website at **http://www1.eere.energy.gov/buildings/energysmart schools/** for information on how you can encourage energy-smart planning in your school district. Also visit the Green Schools Initiative website at **http://www.greenschools.net** for information about environmentally healthy schools and how to generate support for them in your community.

Chapter 14
The Rising Ocean

Water is a necessary "ingredient" for human life. Without it we would be nowhere, because water makes up about 60 percent of our bodies. While lakes dot Earth's continents and rivers flow across the land, no body of water fascinates us as endlessly as the ocean. Earth's oceans are richly filled with seaweeds and myriad creatures, from the tiniest shrimp to the largest whales. We play in the blue water, surf the crashing waves, and build fanciful castles on the beaches that fringe the seas. Beginning with our earliest ancestors, oceanfront areas have always been prime real estate. Even knowing that these areas may be prone to flooding, we still crowd Earth's shorelines: today, two out of every three people on Earth live within 50 miles of the seacoast. So what effects will global warming have on the sea level in the future, and will any changes affect us?

Climate change and greenhouse gases are already causing sea levels to rise. Geologist Kenneth Miller and other researchers at Rutgers University, in New Jersey, drilled into the sediments along the eastern coast of the United States, sampling the many layers of different sediments. The character of the sediments each layer contains reflects whether they were deposited in an ocean-covered or a beach environment. Using chemical techniques to date the layers, Miller showed that before 1850, going back in time as long as 5,000 years, the global rate of sea-level rise was about 1 millimeter per year. During the twentieth century, the rate sped up to 2 millimeters per year. That rate, beginning in 1993, has increased to 3 millimeters per year globally. According to Miller, "The rate has tripled since anthropogenic emissions of the industrial age. It is virtually certain that humans are responsible."

Although 3 millimeters seems like a small amount, scientists are concerned about the momentum of the rise. The ocean is the most massive force on our planet, and when movements within it reach a certain pace, no amount of human effort can slow them down. When you think of the atmosphere changing the oceans, imagine a compact car pushing a tank down a steep hill. It may take a lot to get the monster moving, but once it gets going, there's little anyone can do to stop it. We can't stop the ocean from expanding; its momentum is out of our control.

One factor that slows the oceans' reaction to the current climate change is the fact that ocean waters are stratified, or layered. If all the oceans' water were homogenized to one temperature, it would be a chilly 38°F (3.3°C). But in fact, ocean water forms three layers separated by their temperatures. The top 300 feet or so vary enormously in temperature; near the poles this top layer can be below freezing, while at the equator it can exceed 86°F (30°C). Below this familiar, light-filled world, to a depth of around half a mile, is a zone of temperature transition—the deeper you go, the colder it gets. At around half a mile down, you reach the world's deep ocean water. This layer, from bottom to top, is remarkably stable in temperature— varying between 23°F and 39°F (–5°C and 4°C). (It can be below freezing and not turn to ice because of its salt content.) Most of the water in this lightless realm has flowed there from Antarctica, where it has been chilled to near freezing by submarine currents.

Cooling the surface layer of ocean water helps mix the layers, because cool water sinks. But as the oceans heat up in response to warmer air temperatures, the rate of mixing slows, because warm surface water sinks more slowly than cool water. It takes a long time for the heat to work its way down into the deepest ocean depths. Thus, when Earth is cooling, it takes less time for the oceans to reflect this trend. In contrast, when the planet heats up because of greenhouse gases, it takes the surface layers of the oceans about three decades to absorb heat from the atmosphere, and a thousand years or more for this heat to reach the ocean depths—all of which means that, from the perspective of global warming, the oceans are still working on absorbing the atmosphere from the 1970s.

There is nothing we can do to prevent this slow transfer of heat from the atmosphere to the ocean, which is bad news, because the heat absorbed by the ocean causes the sea level to rise in two ways. The first way is subtle. Much of the sea rise that has occurred over the past century has come from an expansion of the oceans, because warm water occupies more space than cold. This "thermal expansion," which happens at a slow creep, is expected to raise sea levels by 20 to 80 inches over the next 500 years.

The second way that ocean heat causes the sea level to rise is by melting ice. In a positive-feedback loop, warmer oceans melt ice and heat the air, which in turn melts more ice. Fifteen thousand years ago, the oceans stood at least 300 feet (91.4 meters) lower than they do today. At that time, the North

American continent was a veritable empire of ice, exceeding even the Antarctic in the volume of frozen water it held. As the great American ice caps melted, they released enough water to raise global sea levels by 243 feet (74 meters). The sea rose, at times so fast as to change the coastline from year to year, until around 8,000 years ago, when it reached its present level and conditions stabilized. Today, even a modest sea-level rise would be disastrous, given the number of people who live along coastlines. In Bangladesh alone, more than 10 million people live within 3 feet of sea level.

Some countries are preparing for rising sea levels. The Netherlands, two-fifths of which lies below sea level, is already planning for the construction of a super dike to save it from the encroaching ocean. In England, the Thames River barrier is to be strengthened. But countless millions of others live beside the sea and have no protection.

As it did in the past, melting ice will have a major effect on future sea levels. The Greenland ice sheet, the sea ice of the Arctic Ocean, and a few continental glaciers are all that remain of the great Northern Hemisphere ice caps of 15,000 years ago. But there are signs that even these remnants are beginning to melt away. Alaska's spectacular Columbia Glacier has retreated 7 miles (11 kilometers) over the last twenty years. Scientists estimate that Glacier National Park, in Montana, will be glacierless within a few decades if the current rate of melting continues. Glaciers such as those in Alaska and Montana contain only enough water to alter the sea level by a matter of centimeters.

Fortunately, air temperatures remain cold over the highest parts of the Greenland and Antarctic ice sheets—indeed, they are cooling. These are the only places on Earth where significant negative temperature trends are occurring. This is comforting, because a recent study has concluded that should the Greenland ice cap ever melt, it would be impossible to regenerate it, even if our planet's atmospheric CO_2 returned to preindustrial levels.

There are three major types of ice, the melting of which has different consequences for sea levels: sea ice, ice shelves (thick slabs of ice that extend into the sea while remaining attached to land), and land ice (including ice caps, ice sheets, and glaciers). Ice shelves and sea ice contain huge amounts of frozen water, but surprisingly, when they melt, they don't make the sea level rise. The reason is that the ice condenses into water in precisely the same proportion as when it projected as a shelf over the sea or existed as floating sea ice. Prove it to yourself with a simple experiment. Fill a glass with water and a few ice cubes. Put a piece of tape on the glass to mark the water level. Let the ice melt. You'll find that the water level remains the same even after the ice has melted. In contrast, if you'd filled the glass with water and marked the water level *before* you added ice cubes, you would have noticed that the water level rose. Only ice that has melted *on land* and then runs into the sea—from a glacier or a pile of snow, for example—makes the sea level rise.

The largest amount of Earth's ice, by far, is locked up in three ice sheets—two in the Southern Hemisphere and one in the Northern—that could wreak havoc on the sea level if they were ever to melt. Two vast ice sheets cover Antarctica, together containing 90 percent of the world's ice and 70 percent of the world's freshwater. The East Antarctic Ice Sheet, the largest in the world, covers the bedrock core of the continent and is about 2.5 miles (4 kilometers) thick. It contains enough ice to raise the sea level by more than 164 feet (50 meters), were it to melt completely. During the years spanning 1992 to 2003, Curt Davis, a scientist at Missouri University, and his colleagues used satellites to measure minute changes in elevation across the surface of the East Antarctic Ice Sheet. They found that an increase in precipitation has brought more snow and ice to the interior of the ice sheet. This increase, which equals about 45 billion tons per year, appears to have slowed the sea-level rise by about 0.004 inches (0.12 millimeters) per year. This may help compensate for some of the ice being lost at the continent's margins. But most scientists don't believe the additional snow and ice is enough to offset the total amount of ice that is melting along the edges of the ice sheet.

Antarctica's other ice sheet, the West Antarctic Ice Sheet, rests on the rocky floor of what was once a shallow sea basin. Parts of the ice sheet are as much as 8,200 feet (2,500 meters) below sea level. Although the sheet is stable now, that could change. Scientists are concerned about ice that is melting along the edges of the ice sheet. The meltwater could seep down between the rock and the ice sheet and spread beneath the sheet. The layer of water beneath the sheet might be enough to make the ice sheet begin to float. Right now, the ice sheet is considered land ice, because it touches the bottom of the former sea basin. Once it starts floating, it's like adding extra ice cubes to a glass of water, but with catastrophic consequences. It would cause the sea level to rise 6 to 20 inches by 2100. Should more melting occur, enough to cause the West Antarctic Ice Sheet to break apart, the glaciers feeding into the ice sheet would accelerate their flow into the ocean, adding much more ice to the sea. Together, the 0.9 million cubic miles (3.8 million cubic kilometers) of glacial ice contained in and held back by the West Antarctic Ice Sheet contain enough water to raise global sea levels by 20 to 23 feet. There's nothing subtle about a sea-level rise of that magnitude—it's enough to completely flood the world's major coastal cities.

Earth's third ice sheet is the Greenland Ice Sheet. Mountains along the continent's coast surround an inland plateau that is covered by the ice sheet, and glaciers make their way to the ocean along valleys between the mountains. Jakobshavn Isbræ, Greenland's largest glacier, is challenging scientists to explain the cause of its surprising change in speed during the years 2000 to 2005: the glacier's normal pace of about a foot a day ratcheted up to an amazing 113 feet (34.4 meters) per day. Greenland's temperatures have risen 0.8°F to 3.6°F (0.4°C to 2°C) over the past fifteen years, and the winter temperature has risen by 11°F (6°C). The warming trend is increasing the amount of meltwater on the glaciers. It's also accelerated the glacier flows. Indeed, a study conducted by Eric Rignot, from the National Aeronautics and Space Administration's (NASA) Jet Propulsion Laboratory, provides evidence that the amount of ice discharged into the Atlantic Ocean by Greenland's glaciers has doubled in the last ten years.

The Greenland Ice Sheet, sometimes referred to as an ice cap, contains enough water to raise sea levels globally by around 23 feet (7 meters). In the summer of 2002, it, along with the Arctic ice cap (which is sea ice), shrank by a record 400,000 square miles—the largest decrease ever recorded.

Clearly, if Earth's three ice sheets and all of Earth's glaciers were to melt completely, an overwhelming rise in sea level—about 230 feet (70 meters)—would occur, bringing about a catastrophe of unimaginable proportions with respect to human civilization.

Ice shelves and sea ice are kind of like a buffer zone between the oceans and inland ice sheets, and in recent years, Antarctica has provided disturbing news of ice-shelf breakups and melting sea ice. The first dramatic indication that all was not well came in February 2002, when the Larsen B Ice Shelf—about the size of Luxembourg—broke up over a matter of weeks. Although scientists knew that the Antarctic Peninsula, where Larsen B is located, was warming more rapidly than almost any other place on Earth, the speed and abruptness of Larsen B's collapse shocked many. In its wake, scientists learned that there was an important and hitherto-overlooked exception to the rule that melting sea ice does not affect sea levels.

Almost immediately after the breakup of Larsen B, the inland ice sheets and glaciers that fed into the now-fragmented ice shelf began to flow more rapidly. Glaciers, of course, flow much more slowly than rivers. Yet they do flow, and the collapse of Larsen B demonstrated forcefully that one of the most important features determining a glacier's speed is the extent of ice at its terminus, or end. A thick ice shelf acts much like a dam, slowing the flow of inland glacial ice to the sea, thereby restricting its rate of melting. Remove the ice shelf, and movement of the ice covering the land surface speeds up.

The fate of Larsen B soon had researchers looking at the details of its demise and at other ice shelves in the region. In 2003, a study summarizing a decade of satellite data revealed the ultimate cause of Larsen's collapse. Summer melting at both the top and the bottom of the ice shelf, brought about by warming of both the atmosphere and the ocean, had so thinned it and riven it with crevasses that its destruction was inevitable. But melting of the ice from below was the most important factor. While the Weddell Sea's deep waters, which flow past the ice, were still cold enough to kill a person in minutes, they had warmed by 0.58°F (0.32°C) since 1972, and this change was enough to initiate the melting.

Scientists are convinced that sometime this century the rest of the Larsen ice shelf will break up, but by then our attention will be gripped by the fate of far greater ice masses. The first to enter our consciousness is likely to be the Amundsen ice plain, a flat area of sea ice just off the coast of West Antarctica that flows onto the Amundsen Ice Shelf. (The base of an ice plain still touches the bedrock, but it's almost to the point where it's ready to go afloat.) In late 2002, a team of scientists led by NASA researchers discovered that this ice plain was thinning rapidly. In their study, published in October 2004, the researchers reported that large sections of the ice plain had become so thin that they were nearing a point that could allow them to float free of their "anchors" on the ocean bed and collapse like Larsen B. Since then the team has made further observations that concern them. In 2006 to 2007, the glacier's flow sped up more than it has during the past thirty years. In 2008, according to team member Eric Rignot, "The glacier is currently edging on a knoll but thinning more rapidly than ever before. . . . A large part of the ice plain is now near floatation . . . and we are maintaining predictions that the glacier could double or triple its speed in the coming years . . . as it retreats into deeper grounds." The researchers ventured that the fatal moment for the Amundsen ice plain could be as little as two to five years off.

When scientists surveyed the Amundsen ice plain, they noticed that the glaciers feeding into the Amundsen had increased their rate of discharge to around 60 cubic miles (250 cubic kilometers) of ice per year—enough to raise sea levels globally by 0.01 of an inch (0.25 millimeters) per year.

There is enough ice in the glaciers feeding into the Amundsen Sea to raise global sea levels by 4.3 feet (1.3 meters). Their increasing rate of flow, and the incipient breakup of their ice plain "brake," should be of concern to everyone.

The situation in the Northern Hemisphere isn't looking much better. The greatest extent of sea ice in the Northern Hemisphere is that covering the polar sea, and since 1979 its extent in summer has contracted by 20 percent. Furthermore, the remaining ice has greatly thinned. Measurements taken from submarines traveling beneath the ice reveal that the sea ice is only 60 percent as thick as it was four decades earlier. Scientists believe climate change is a major factor in its thinning.

In 2005, a dramatic change occurred on the Ayles Ice Shelf, which extended from the coast of Canada's Ellesmere Island, located about 500 miles from the North Pole. Satellite images revealed that on August 13, a 25-square-mile section of the ice shelf had cracked free of Ellesmere Island. It now rests, held by frozen seawater, several miles offshore. "We think that the Ayles broke up because there was record warming and record minimum sea ice holding it in," states Warwick Vincent, a biology professor at Laval University, in Canada, who says that each year for the last two decades, sea ice in the Arctic has reached a record low. Climatologists' concerns that the breakup of the Ayles Ice Shelf might herald similar Arctic ice-shelf breakups in the future were proved valid in August 2008, when the Markham Ice Shelf broke off the coast of Ellesmere Island. The new ice "island," which is about the size of Manhattan, is now adrift in the Arctic Ocean. Over the past century, more than 90 percent of Canada's ice shelves have disappeared.

The indirect effects of an ice shelf's breakup can also affect the polar regions. After an ice shelf cracks apart, if it and any other sea ice melt, they will significantly change the Earth's albedo. Remember, one-third of the sun's rays falling on Earth are reflected back to space. Ice, particularly at the poles, is responsible for a lot of that albedo, because it reflects 90 percent of the sunlight hitting it back into space. Water, in contrast, is a poor reflector. Replacing Arctic ice with a dark ocean will result in a lot more of the sun's rays being absorbed at Earth's surface. These will reradiate as heat and create local warming, which, in classic positive-feedback-loop fashion, will hasten the melting of the remaining continental ice. A new scientific projection indicates that the Arctic ice cap may almost completely disappear in the summer by 2040. If it does, that will further warm the ocean, which will in turn warm the air. And rising air temperatures will speed the melting of inland ice.

With ever-increasing frequency, scientific reports make clear that a great domino effect—wherein the breaking up of one ice field leads to the destruction of a neighbor—may be playing itself out at Earth's polar regions. Because ever-larger expanses of ice are being affected, it is becoming evident that rapidly melting polar ice could be a huge contributor to a rising sea in coming decades. The jury is still out on whether the increase in precipitation recorded on the interior sections of the East Antarctic and Greenland ice sheets can compensate sufficiently for the ice being lost at the continent's margins, though just how much compensation this will bring, and for how long, is currently unknown.

So swift have been the changes in ice-plain science, and so great is the inertia of the oceanic juggernaut, that climate scientists are now debating whether humans have already tripped the switch that will create an ice-free Earth. If so, we have already committed our planet and ourselves to a rise in the level of the sea of around 220 feet. The next great question would be, how long will it take for the ice to melt? Many scientists think that, regardless of the amount of melting in store, the bulk of the sea-level rises will occur after 2050, and it will take millennia for all of the ice to melt. Still, some scientists are predicting a rise in sea levels of 10 to 20 feet over a century or two.

CALL TO ACTION

Is Your Home Adequately Insulated?

Save fossil fuel by adequately insulating your home. Insulation saves energy loss during both the heating and cooling seasons.

Ask your parents how well insulated your home is. If they don't know, take a look in your attic or crawl space and find out what's there. Insulation may be in the form of batting or in small paperlike particles. The attic, exterior walls, and any crawl spaces under the house should be insulated. If they are not, make plans to add some. Insulation makes a huge difference in heating and air-conditioning bills, and your home will feel more comfortable.

The amount of insulation required in each area of the home varies. When installing insulation, it's important to know its R-value. The R-value indicates how effective the insulation is as a barrier to heat loss. For example, attic areas need insulation with a higher R-value, because heat rises.

If you don't know whether there is enough insulation in your home, call your local utility company and ask about an energy audit. Energy-audit inspectors can quickly determine if your home's insulation is sufficient. Also visit the Department of Energy's insulation information website at **http://www.ornl.gov/sci/roofs+walls/insulation/ins_01.html**. The site has an R-value calculator that can help you determine what level of insulation your home needs.

Chapter 15

Leveling the Mountains

For every hundred yards you climb a mountain, the temperature drops about 1°F (0.55°C), a difference in temperature that permits mountain ecosystems to develop unique flora and fauna. Without this cooling, mountains would be nothing more than topographically challenged versions of the lowlands that surround them. It's in this sense that climate change, in the form of rising temperatures, can level the world's mountains.

Because of rising temperatures, every habitat—from alpine herb fields to elfin woodlands and mossy mid-montane forests—each of which has its own unique species, is climbing upward. Nothing in predictive climate science is more certain than the extinction of many of the world's mountain-dwelling species. We can even foretell which will be the first to go. This high degree of scientific certainty comes from three factors. First, the effect of rising temperatures on mountain habitats is easily calculated, and past adjustments in response to warming are well documented. Second, the conditions that many mountain-dwelling species can tolerate are known. And finally, as the climate warms, mountain species have nowhere to go but up, and the height of mountain peaks worldwide has been precisely ascertained. Given the rate of warming, we can calculate the time to extinction of most mountain-dwelling species.

The last time the world warmed rapidly—at the end of the last ice age—mountain-dwelling species rapidly retreated to higher, cooler regions. On the island of New Guinea, alpine herb fields initially grew as low as 7,000 feet. Today they have retreated to elevations above the tree line—the elevation above which trees do not grow—at 13,000 feet. This mile-high retreat reduced their range by nine-tenths. Now the alpine herb fields can be found only on the summits of the island's highest mountains—secluded jewels in an otherwise forested landscape. The reason for their ascent is the increase in global surface temperature of around 9°F (5°C) over 7,000 years.

We know that our planet will heat by 2°F (1.1°C) this century, come what may. If we stay on our present energy course, the temperature may rise 5°F (2.7°C). The very highest peak in New Guinea—Puncak Jaya—is a little more than 16,000 feet, which means that, taking past changes as a guide, even a rise of 5°F (2.7°C) would push the last of New Guinea's alpine habitat off its summit. Indeed, given such extreme changes, there are few mountains anywhere on Earth high enough to provide an alpine refuge.

Like Puncak Jaya, every high mountain on Earth has an equivalent alpine habitat that is rich in biodiversity, and below it are mountain forests that are even richer in life. Indeed, the world's mountain ranges nurture a staggering variety of life—from iconic species such as pandas and mountain gorillas to tiny lichens and insects. On the global scale, the importance of mountain habitats is illustrated by diversity in the alpine zone—the area lying between the tree line and the perpetual snow of the mountaintops. Although alpine habitats make up a mere 3 percent of the surface of Earth, they are home to more than 10,000 plant species, along with countless insects and larger animals.

The study that identified the global "fingerprint" of climate change found that, over the course of the twentieth century, mountain-dwelling species have withdrawn upward on average 20 feet (6.1 meters) each decade. The creatures and plants did this because conditions at the lower margins of their distributions became intolerable—too hot or dry—or because of newly arrived species with which they could not compete. This may seem a small amount of movement, but we must remember that our planet has not been warmer than it is now for millions of years, a situation that has left many ancient species clinging to the last few hundred yards of mountain peaks around the world.

Few studies of the impacts of climate change on specific mountain regions have been completed. So far, some of the most detailed are those undertaken by biologist Steve Williams of Australia's James Cook University and his colleagues, which deal with the impact of climate change on the rain-forest-clad mountains of northeast Queensland, Australia.

These mountain ranges are arguably the most important habitat in all of Australia, because they are home to an archaic assemblage of plants and animals—survivors from the period when Australia's climate was cooler and moister, about 20 million years ago. The significance of this region to the world as a whole was recognized in 1988, when the rain forests were listed as Australia's first World Heritage Area.

High up in the tallest trees, lemurlike ringtail possums leap from branch to branch. They are living fossils—remnants of the lineage that gave rise to the majestic yard-long greater glider of the eucalypt forests. Ringtail possums lack a gliding membrane but are extraordinary leapers whose noisy crashing through the canopy is one of the most constant noises at night. Lower down in the trees, green ringtail possums forage for food. So selective are they in their diet that in order to learn which leaves are best, the young stays with its mother until it's almost adult-size. The reason that such creatures haunt the mountain summits is clear. Just four to five hours spent in temperatures of 86°F (30°C) or above will kill them, and such temperatures are an almost-daily event in the surrounding lowlands.

Sixty-five species of birds, mammals, frogs, and reptiles are unique to the region, and none can tolerate warmer conditions. They include the golden bowerbird, the Bloomfield nursery frog, and Lumholtz's tree kangaroo. It's not widely known outside of Australia that some kangaroos inhabit the treetops of tropical rain forests. At one time such creatures were widespread; their fossils have been found as far south as the state of Victoria. As Australia's climate changed, becoming warmer and drier, the cool rain forests shrank to the east coast. Ice ages further shrank the tree kangaroo's habitat. Today Australia's tree kangaroos survive only in the rain forests of northeast Queensland.

Steve Williams's study indicates that rising temperatures and increasing periods of extreme heat will directly affect creatures such as the green ringtail, which need to stay cool. Higher CO_2 levels will also impact plant growth. Plants grown experimentally in CO_2-enriched environments tend to have reduced nutritional value and tougher leaves. These changes alone are predicted to reduce possum numbers. As species retreat to higher elevations, the poor soils that dominate on the summits will further reduce the nutritional value of their food. To make matters worse, rainfall variability is likely to increase, with droughts becoming more pronounced, while the cloud layer, which now provides 40 percent of the water that nourishes the mountain forests, will rise, exposing the forests to more sunlight and thus evaporation. All of this adds up to a catastrophic impact.

The 2°F (1.1°C) temperature increase we are already committed to will cause the extinction of the Thornton Peak nursery frog, a frog so recently discovered that it hasn't yet received a scientific name. With a 3.6°F (2°C) increase, the wet tropic ecosystems will begin to unravel. At a 6.3°F (3.5°C) increase, around half of the sixty-five species of animals unique to the wet tropics will have vanished, while the rest will become restricted to tenuous habitats of less than 10 percent of their original distribution. In effect, their populations will be nonviable, their extinction only a matter of time.

The sixty-five species of larger creatures unique to the wet tropics constitute just the tip of a mountain full of biodiversity. Plant species abound but are threatened as well. Two species of native pines with fernlike leaves and glorious red or blue fruit are restricted to the summits of the ranges. The bunya pine—a relative of the monkey puzzle tree and the oldest species in an ancient lineage—is restricted to two mountain ranges. This species, or something like it, has been living on Earth for 230 million years. Tens of thousands of species of invertebrates—worms, beetles, and other flying and crawling things—are threatened by the loss of their homes. The impending destruction of Australia's rain forests—indeed, rain forests everywhere—is a biological disaster on the horizon.

Throughout the world, every continent and many islands have mountain ranges that are the last refuge of species

CALL TO ACTION

The Phantom in Your House

Do you: leave your cell-phone charger plugged in, even when the phone is not connected to it? How about the printer, scanner, speakers, or other peripheral devices connected to your computer? These devices are electricity phantoms in your home. They are drawing power from the grid and wasting it.

Stop burning up your money. Plug those devices into a power strip. Turn the power strip off when you are not using your computer.

How often is a television set left on in your home while no one is watching it? Get in the habit of turning off the set when you are finished watching. Using a television as white noise is just wasting energy.

Another television energy waster is watching the same program on more than one TV set. Many families have more than one television. If two people in your home are watching the same show, turn one set off and watch the show together.

of remarkable beauty and diversity. And we stand to lose it all, from gorillas to pandas, from trees to beautiful orchids. No rescue effort could ever be comprehensive enough to establish captive colonies of even one-tenth of 1 percent of the species under threat. There is only one way to save them. We must act to stop the problem at its cause—the emission of CO_2 and other greenhouse gases.

There is, surprisingly, one group of species that will benefit enormously from an increase of CO_2 and other greenhouse gases that lead to climate changes including warmer temperatures and an increase of rainfall in some areas. This group is the parasites that cause the four strains of malaria. From Mexico City to Papua New Guinea's Mount Hagen, the mountain valleys of the world support human populations in high densities. Today, malaria is rare at these elevations. Just below these communities—in the case of New Guinea at around 4,500 feet—are great forests where no one lives. This is because of malaria, which is so prevalent in parts of the tropics—including these forests—that it controls human populations. As temperatures warm and rainfall increases, the mosquito that carries the parasite, the *Anopheles* mosquito, will spread into those high mountain valleys. The malarial season will lengthen, and the disease will proliferate among tens of thousands of people without any resistance to the disease.

PART 3

What's to Come?

Chapter 16
Model Worlds

Today, with the establishment of the United Nations World Meteorological Organization, scientific activity relating to climate and weather is coordinated on a global scale. One hundred and eighty-five countries participate in this program, and among them they monitor 10,000 land-based observation stations, 7,000 ship-based ones, and ten satellites. The data from all these sources, particularly satellite surveillance data that records changes at the surface of our planet, plus the improved capabilities of modern computers and a firm grasp of Earth systems such as the carbon cycle, have enabled scientists to build virtual worlds—models—to see the approximate shape of things to come and how things might stand if we change our ways. These virtual crystal balls—referred to as global circulation models (GCMs)—have much to tell us about our climatic future over coming decades.

Today there are around ten different GCMs seeking to simulate the way the atmosphere behaves and to predict how it will behave in the future. The most sophisticated models are at the Hadley Center in England, the Lawrence Livermore National Laboratory in California, and the Max Planck Institute for Meteorology in Germany. All three centers are able to reproduce the general trends in temperature Earth has experienced over the twentieth century.

At the Hadley Center for Climate Prediction and Research, more than 120 researchers strive to reduce the uncertainty of predictions by producing ever more sophisticated models that mimic the real world. If our planet were a uniform black sphere, the Hadley people would have an easy task, because doubling the parts per million of CO_2 in the atmosphere would have an equal effect on all areas of Earth. But Earth is not black, nor is its surface uniform. Instead, mountains and valleys create varying surfaces. Oceans, deserts, vegetation, ice, and clouds reflect light and absorb CO_2 in widely differing amounts. While our knowledge of ice and its effect on climate is increasing, clouds still continue to give the climate modelers headaches. Clouds cloud the issue, so to speak, because no one has yet developed a theory of cloud formation and dissipation. That can affect a GCM because clouds both trap heat and reflect sunlight back into space, which can, depending on the circumstances, powerfully heat or cool the atmosphere.

So how good are models, such as those generated by the Hadley Center's cloudy, computerized crystal ball, at predicting Earth's future? There are four major tests that any GCM must pass before its predictions can be deemed credible:

- Is the physical basis of the model consistent with the laws of physics—the conservation of mass, heat, moisture, and so on?
- Can the model accurately simulate the present climate?
- Can it simulate the day-to-day evolution of the weather systems that make up our climate?
- Can the model simulate what is known of past climates?

Computer models such as those run at the Hadley Center pass all of these tests with a reasonable degree of accuracy. But if models are to remain accurate and effective, they must be able to incorporate new data as new discoveries are made in the real world.

Climatologist Nathan Gillett and his colleagues have recently documented how human-induced climate change is altering air pressure at sea level. Areas with high air pressure usually have clear skies; areas with low pressure are subject to cloudy skies. Gillett found that in the Arctic, the air pressure at sea level has decreased, while the air pressure in the subtropic areas of the Northern Hemisphere has increased. It appears that 50 percent of Eurasia's winter warming trend, 60 percent of the rainfall increase in Scotland, and 60 percent of the rainfall decrease in Spain during the past three decades are associated with these air-pressure changes. This is the first clear evidence of greenhouse gases directly affecting a meteorological factor other than temperature. However, increases in sea-level pressure had not previously been incorporated in GCMs. Gillett believes not doing so has led to an underestimation of the impact of climate change on storms in the North Atlantic.

All computer models draw from evidence and incorporate as much empirical, or observed, data as possible to build testable hypotheses about future change. However, they are not perfect, and there are climatologists who are skeptical of the models' predictions. In the years between 1940 and 1970, Earth's average surface temperature declined despite increasing greenhouse gases in the atmosphere. Early computer models predicted that Earth should have warmed twice as much as it did, given the amount of CO_2 that was being pumped into the atmosphere. It turned out that the prediction was flawed because a crucial factor in climate change had been omitted: the presence of aerosols, minuscule particles that drift in the atmosphere.

Aerosols can be anything from dust ejected by volcanoes to the fine soil and sand particles found in desert landscapes. The smokestacks of coal-fired power stations churn out a cocktail of deadly aerosol particles, including mercury and sulfur, and diesel engines, tire rubber, and fires are additional sources of aerosols. Early computer models did not include aerosols in their calculations, in part because no one fully appreciated the extent to which human activities were increasing their number. We now know that between one-quarter and one-half of all the aerosols in our atmosphere today are put there by human activity.

Aerosols can be very damaging to human health. They were the cause of significant mortality in seventeenth-century London as people turned to coal for heating fuel after timber became scarce. Today, even with technologies that help clean the coal, aerosols generated by burning coal kill around 60,000 people annually in the United States. Part of the reason is that coal acts like a sponge, soaking up mercury, uranium, and other harmful minerals that are released when it is burned. The state of South Australia is home to the world's largest uranium mine, yet its largest single-point source of radiation is not the mine but a coal-fired power plant at Port Augusta. It's no real surprise that lung cancers commonly result from burning coal. In Australia's Hunter Valley, where coal-fired power generation is concentrated, lung cancer rates are a third higher than in nearby Sydney, despite the pollution levels in the metropolis.

Sulfur dioxide is released when low-quality coal is burned, and by the 1960s lakes and forests at high latitudes in the Northern Hemisphere were dying. Evergreen trees were losing their needles, while the lakes were becoming crystal clear and emptied of life. The cause was acid rain resulting from the sulfur dioxide emissions of coal-burning power stations. This realization prompted legislation to enforce the use of "scrubbers" on coal-burning power plants in the industrialized world. These have been used since the 1970s and have dramatically reduced sulfur dioxide emissions.

There was, however, an unintended consequence of this improvement. Sulfate aerosols are very effective at reflecting sunlight back into space. In effect, they helped cool the planet. Scientists now think that the temperature decline of the 1940s to 1970s was caused by aerosols, particularly sulfur dioxide. Because most aerosols last just a few weeks in the atmosphere (with sulfur dioxide degrading at the rate of 1 to 2 percent per hour at normal humidity), the newly installed scrubbers had an immediate effect. As the air cleared, global temperatures, driven by CO_2 released from those same power stations, resumed their upward creep. The experience was the perfect example of how Earth's systems interconnect with one another.

The 1991 eruption of Mount Pinatubo, in the Philippines, provided an exceptional test of the new global circulation models' capacity to predict the influence of aerosols. The volcanic blast ejected 20 million tons of sulfur dioxide into the atmosphere. Scientist James Hansen works at NASA's Goddard Institute for Space Studies. He and his colleagues forecast that the blast's result would be around 0.5°F (0.3°C) of global cooling—and this figure is *exactly* what was seen in the real world.

Among the most important and best supported of these models' predictions are that the poles will warm more rapidly than the rest of the Earth; temperatures over the land will rise more rapidly than the global average; there will be more rain; and extreme-weather events will increase in both frequency and intensity. Changes will also be evident in the rhythms of the day—nights will be warmer relative to days, because nighttime is when Earth loses heat through the atmosphere to space. There will also be a trend toward the development of semi-permanent El Niño–like conditions.

The answers to two key questions still remain uncertain in all models: Will a doubling of CO_2 lead to an increase in warming of 3.6°F (2°C) (the threshold beyond which change is considered dangerous) or 9°F (5°C) (the generally accepted uper limit)? And will the models be able to answer this question with more certainty than they do now? This is a critical issue, not least because some governments, including the U.S. government, have been dragging their feet, unwilling to reconsider climate-change policy until there is more certainty. Given that almost thirty years of hard work and astonishing technological advances have failed to reduce the degree of uncertainty, we may not be able to expect much more precision than we have now. That said, many people would argue that we already know enough: even 3.6°F (2°C) of warming would be catastrophic for large segments of humanity.

The largest study of climate change was published in early 2005 by a team from Oxford University. It was conducted by using the processing capacities of more than 90,000 personal computers whose owners volunteered their use for the project. The study focused on the temperature implications of doubling CO_2 in the atmosphere. The average result indicated that this would lead to 6.1°F (3.4°C) of warming. Overall, however, there was an astonishingly wide range of possibilities—from between 3.4°F and 20.2°F (1.9°C and 11.2°C) of warming, the higher end of which had not been predicted earlier. The project is still ongoing, with more than 95,000 computers participating as of 2008.

This wide range of potential temperature increases brings up a puzzling anomaly. At the end of the last ice age, CO_2 levels increased by 100 parts per million, and Earth's average surface temperature rose by 9°F (5°C). Yet in most computer models, a CO_2 increase almost three times as large (doubling the pre-industrial level) predicts a temperature rise of only about 5.4°F (3°C). Why would a bigger CO_2 increase forecast a smaller rise in temperature?

Scientists working on aerosols think that they might have the answer. Direct measurement of the strength of sunlight at ground level and worldwide records of evaporation rates (which are influenced primarily by sunlight) indicate that the amount of sunlight reaching the Earth's surface has declined significantly (up to 22 percent in some areas) over the last three decades. It is as if something has been filtering out some of the visible light as it passed through the atmosphere.

The scientists believe that the phenomenon known as global dimming—the same thing that appears to have contributed to the climate changes that led to the Sahelian drought in Africa—may be filtering out visible light. Here's what they think happens: First, aerosols such as soot increase the amount of light that clouds reflect. This is because soot particles foster the formation of many tiny water droplets rather than fewer, larger ones, and these tiny water droplets allow clouds to reflect far more sunlight back into space than do larger drops.

Second, the contrails—streaks of condensed water vapor—left by jet aircraft at high altitudes create a persistent cloud cover. In 2001, in the three days following the September 11 attack on the World Trade Center and the Pentagon, the entire U.S. jet fleet was grounded, and contrails were noticeably absent for those days. During that time climatologists noted an unprecedented increase in daytime temperatures relative to nighttime temperatures. They believe this resulted from the additional sunlight reaching the ground in the absence of contrails from the more than 87,000 flights that normally cross over the United States every day.

If 100 parts per million of CO_2 really can raise the surface temperature by 9°F (5°C), and if aerosols and contrails have counterbalanced this effect so that we have experienced only 1.13°F (0.63°C) of warming, then aerosols' influence on climate must be enormously powerful. It is as if two great forces—unleashed from the world's smokestacks and jet engines—are tugging the climate in opposite directions, except that CO_2 is slightly more powerful.

This leaves us with a grave problem, because particle pollution lasts only days or weeks, while CO_2 is difficult to clean up and lasts a century or more. So what does a 3.6°F (2°C) or a 9°F (5°C) rise in temperature mean—on the ground—to various peoples and ecosystems? These are questions to which we will return, but for now, this much can be said: If our understanding of global dimming is correct, then we have only one option. We *must* start extracting CO_2 from the atmosphere. And at this moment, we don't know how to do that effectively.

While computer models are helpful, there are questions that they can't answer. The first questions we tend to ask about climate change—or any change, for that matter—are "What

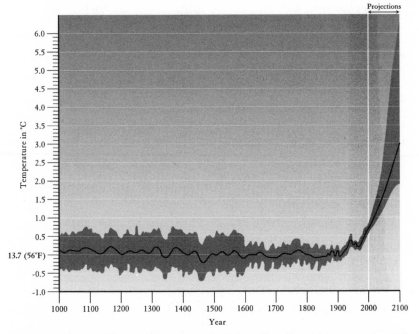

Corals, ice cores, and tree rings can supply information about the temperature of the environments in which they form. Using this data, climatologist Michael Mann created a graph that shows trends in the average surface temperature of Earth (56°F) that occurred during the past 1,000 years. The gray area conveys uncertainty, which is reduced in 1850, when the thermometer grid was established. The projections beyond 2000 give a range of probable temperature increases to 2100. Because of its shape, this graph is often called the hockey stick graph.

caused it?" and "How is it going to affect me and the place where I live?" The answer to the first question is that Earth's climate system is so riddled with positive-feedback loops that determining a single cause of a particular change is difficult. For example, while we can say that an increase in atmospheric CO_2 has led to runaway change, we can't always pinpoint all the other factors that come into play.

The answer to the second question is that there is no foolproof way to determine whether you, personally, will be affected by climate change. Global warming is slow—making each decade a little warmer than the one before it—whereas weather varies greatly from day to day and place to place.

A number of climate groups—often at the request of governments needing advice on how to prepare themselves—have produced computer-based projections for various regions of Earth and for timescales as short as a few decades. The following three examples offer a taste of regional changes predicted by various climate models; however, many climatologists question their usefulness.

The Hadley Center has predicted that human effects of the climate in the United Kingdom will have surpassed all natural effects by the year 2050. Such effects, felt during the following three decades, will include a decrease in snow cover by up to 80 percent near the British coast and up to 60 percent in the Scottish Highlands; an increase in winter rainfall by up to 35 percent, with more intense rainfall events; and a decrease in summer rainfall that will result in one summer out of three being "very dry." An event akin to the severe summer of 1995 (which had seventeen days over 77°F (25°C) and four days over 86°F (30°C)) may recur twice per decade, while the great majority of years will be warmer than the record-breaking 1999. The changes felt in Europe will be more extreme than the increase in the global average: indeed, a global rise in surface temperature of just 3.6°F (2°C) would bring a temperature rise to all of Europe, Asia, and the Americas of 8.1°F (4.5°C). For Britain, this means a more Mediterranean-like climate and, as some newspapers put it, "the end of the English garden." More important are the challenges it throws up for matters such as water security, flood control, and the human health response to heat waves.

In 2003 and 2004, two further regional studies by scientists from Stanford University and the University of California at Los Angeles focused on climate impacts for California. They hypothesized that global warming would bring much hotter summers to the state. That would increase the melting rate of the summer snowpack in the mountains, which in turn would threaten water supplies and health. By the end of the century, heat waves in Los Angeles would be two to seven times as deadly as today, snowpacks would decline by half or more, and three-quarters to nine-tenths of all of California's alpine forests would be lost.

The third example focuses on the state of New South Wales, Australia, with predictions made by Australia's leading science research body, the Commonwealth Scientific and Industrial Research Organization (CSIRO). Twelve separate climate simulations predict a wide range of possibilities for the thirty-year period. These include temperature increases between 0.4°F and 3.8°F (0.2°C and 2.1°C), which will reduce the number of cold spells and frosts. The number of very hot days (above 104°F (40°C)) will increase, as may winter and spring droughts, extreme rainfall events, and wind speeds, and there will be changes in wave patterns and possibly the frequency of storm tides.

One thing to remember: The gas that will cause these changes is already in the air, and right now we have no way of getting it out. This means that the course of climate change is set for at least the next several decades. How we may change the course beyond that remains to be seen.

CALL TO ACTION

Computer Conservation

Make your computer more energy efficient.

- First of all, don't leave it on all the time. If you are leaving the room for an hour or so, turn the computer and the monitor off. Doing this in "the olden days" shortened the life of a computer, but that's not true anymore.

- Put your computer to bed. Set the controls to go into "sleep" mode after the computer sits idle for ten minutes. You can find instructions for doing this by exploring the "control panel" and "power options" in your computer's menu options. A sleeping computer lowers its energy consumption by as much as 90 percent.

- Don't use a screen saver. Keeping the screen lit up just wastes energy.

Chapter 17
A Dangerous Commitment

The full impact of the greenhouse gases already in the atmosphere will not be felt until around 2050. That means that if we stopped all greenhouse-gas emissions right now, Earth would reach a new stable state, with a new climate, around 2050. However, because we lack a way to take greenhouse gases *out* of the atmosphere, we have already made what researchers call "the commitment": we are bound to a future climate change that we can't yet feel but can't prevent from occurring.

Carbon dioxide has a long life in the atmosphere, and much of the CO_2 released into the air by coal-fueled stoves in the aftermath of World War I is still warming our planet today. Most of the damage was done starting in the 1950s, when people cruised around in their fin-tailed Chevrolets and powered their labor-saving household appliances from inefficient coal-burning power stations. But it is the baby-boomer generation, people born between the years 1946 and 1964, that is most culpable: Half of the energy generated since the Industrial Revolution has been consumed in the last twenty years. Their energy "spending" habits have run rampant and are quite likely being imitated by their children—that is, your parents or you!

It's easy to condemn the extravagance that led to the situation in which we now find ourselves, but we must remember that until recently people didn't have the slightest idea that their tailpipe emissions or vacuum cleaners would have an impact on their children and grandchildren. The same cannot be said for us today, because the true cost of our four-wheel-drives, air conditioners, multiple televisions, lawn mowers, clothes dryers, and refrigerators is increasingly evident to all. Moreover, in many developed nations we are three times as affluent on average as your grandparents were at the same stage of life. (Ask your grandparents how many televisions they had in their house when they were growing up or how many cars their family owned.) In many ways, therefore, we can bear the cost of changing our ways.

The climate change already in motion is influenced by several factors:

- the CO_2 we have already released;
- the positive-feedback loops that amplify climate change;
- global dimming; and
- the speed at which human economies can wean themselves from relying on carbon.

Of these, the first—existing greenhouse-gas volumes—is known and gives us our "existing commitment." The second and third—positive-feedback loops and global dimming—are still being explored by scientists. And the fourth—the rate at which we humans can change our emissions—is being argued over right now by governments and in company boardrooms around the world. It is the only impact over which we have control.

Scientists say that a 70 percent reduction in CO_2 emissions from 1990 levels by the middle of the twenty-first century is required to stabilize Earth's climate. This would result in an atmosphere with 450 parts per million CO_2 (recall that the current level is around 387 ppm). At that rate, our global climate would stabilize by around 2100 at a temperature at least 2°F (1.1°C) higher than the present, with some regions warming by as much as 9°F (5°C).

The European nations are talking of emissions cuts on this scale. But the coal industry and some governments, including that of the United States, are resistant to changes of this magnitude for cost and profit reasons, so it may be unachievable as a global target. A more realistic scenario may be stabilization of atmospheric CO_2 at 550 parts per million—double the preindustrial level. This would result in climatic stabilization centuries from now and an increase in global temperature of around 5.4°F (3°C) this century. Even this depends on good luck, because despite our best efforts, the level of greenhouse gases already in the atmosphere may trigger positive-feedback loops that could cause change that we can't control.

Left unchecked, greenhouse gases could raise temperatures until they reach a tipping point that pushes Earth over a threshold that would result in changes catastrophic to life. If we are to avoid crossing such a threshold, we must have some idea of what it might be. In other words, what rates of climate change are dangerous, and do we have time to adapt to them?

A widely accepted view places the limit at around 3.6°F (2°C) of warming. As 1.13°F (0.63°C) of warming has already occurred, this leaves us "wiggle room" of around 2.3°F (1.3°C) of temperature increase. But while some species, including humans, are flexible and can adapt to a moderate change in temperature, others, like the golden toad, have already become extinct due to global warming. So the question of what constitutes dangerous climate change raises another question: Dangerous to whom? Some humans are already being affected. The Inuit, whose primary food sources of caribou and seal are now difficult to find as a result of climate change, have already crossed an economically and culturally damaging threshold.

It's too late to avoid changing our world, but there is still time, if we implement good policy, to avoid disaster. The question remains: Will we do it?

CALL TO ACTION

Use Recycled Paper

The next time you buy writing paper or paper for your printer, buy recycled paper. Each pad or ream of paper you buy cuts back on CO_2 emissions by reducing the transportation of newly cut timber to the factories and the CO_2 produced as the wood pulp is converted into paper. Buy rolls of paper towels and toilet paper that are made with recycled paper. Look for the phrase "100% post-consumer recycled paper" on the package. "Post-consumer" means that the product was made from paper that people already recycled.

Whenever possible, try to buy printed paper that's been produced with soy-based ink. Other inks may contain petrochemicals.

Chapter 18

Fleeing Climate Change

Researchers Camille Parmesan and Gary Yohe defined the "global fingerprint" of climate change. But what will that fingerprint look like after 2°F (1.1°C) or even the predicted average 5.4°F (3°C) of warming?

Species have survived past shifts of climate because mountains have been tall enough, continents extensive enough, and the change gradual enough for them to migrate. Sometimes the distances traveled have been enormous. Just 14,000 years ago, for example, the deciduous forests that now grow around Montreal, Canada, could be seen only in northern Florida. The climatic changes that prompted that migration, although far slower, were on a scale similar to those projected to occur this century. This tells us that the key to survival in the twenty-first century will be to keep on moving. But how will species manage such long-distance movements in the modern world, with its 6.3 billion humans? Today, most biodiversity in the United States is restricted to national parks and forests that are often surrounded by a landscape profoundly modified by humans.

If temperatures in Australia rise by the predicted 5.4°F (3°C) this century, half of the genus *Eucalyptus* tree species—a koala's favorite food—would end up growing in a climate that is too warm to support them. To survive, the trees would have to migrate. Unfortunately, the Southern Ocean and human-modified landscapes stand in their way.

William Hare, on behalf of the Potsdam Institute, has written a global view of the impacts likely to be seen in the world's natural systems as a result of shifting climate. Looking at his results, it's clear that there is not an ecosystem on Earth that will be unaffected by climate change. South Africa's succulent karoo flora, the richest arid-zone flora on Earth, comprise some 2,500 species of plants found nowhere else. The karoo flora region is renowned for the beauty of its spring flowers, which depend on marginal winter rainfall. As the climate changes, this vegetation simply has no room to migrate. To the south and east—the direction that climate change will drive it—lie the Cape Fold Mountains, whose topography and soils are unsuitable for karoo plants. Computer models forecast that by 2050, 99 percent of the succulent karoo will have vanished.

Also in Africa, south of the Cape Fold Mountains, grows the fabulous fynbos, one of six floral kingdoms on Earth, and the most diverse plant community to be found outside the rain forests. The plants are little more than knee high, but their form is extraordinary. Rushes bear brilliant bell-shaped flowers, whose nectar is sipped by brightly colored "humming flies" with three-quarter-inch-long siphons that reach deep into the bells. Rocky slopes are adorned with bushy shrubs studded with saucer-size pink star flowers, while the profusion of pea flowers, daisy-like flowers, and iris relatives seems endless. Hemmed in by ocean at the southern tip of the continent, the fynbos is a natural paradise. But as the Earth warms, the lovely blue sea prevents vegetation from the fynbos from migrating. Its range will be reduced by more than 50 percent by 2050.

The winter habitat for migratory shorebirds in the United States will be significantly reduced because of drying trends, rising sea levels, and increased storm surges like those caused by hurricanes. Warmer summers, higher evaporation rates, and more variable weather dictate that the breeding habitat of waterfowl living in regions such as the Prairie Potholes will suffer. Remnants of the most recent ice age, the Potholes are wetlands studded with small lakes and marshes found primarily in the states of North Dakota, South Dakota, Minnesota, and Wisconsin. Among the most important wetlands in the world, the Prairie Potholes are home to more than 50 percent of North America's waterfowl, including many species of ducks and geese.

In states such as Alaska and Washington, warming stream water will diminish salmon populations. By 2006, British Columbia's Fraser River, one of the world's most important salmon spawning streams, had been fatally hot for salmon during six of the prior fifteen years. In the North Atlantic, commercially valuable fish are already following the cold water downward and northward.

In Mexico, the fauna will be squeezed by heat, drying, and extreme-weather events, resulting in many extinctions. These same factors have led botanists to declare that one-third of Europe's plant species face severe risks.

On islands, the situation is even more critical. Many Pacific island birds will be pushed beyond their limits. And without room to migrate, it is virtually certain that extinctions will occur to many forms of life, from island trees to unique insects.

Imagine the world's climate zones changing dramatically over your lifetime—so that New York City's climate is more akin to that of Georgia today, or a summer in Chicago is more like that of eastern Texas. Try to think of what it means for the trees, birds, and other animals of the region where you live.

While you're thinking about the bigger picture, don't forget about oceans, which are critical to Earth's climate. Consider the polar regions, where the icy water of the deep ocean comes to the surface. Richard Feely of the Pacific Marine Environmental Laboratory and his colleagues have investigated what might happen in these regions as more CO_2 is absorbed. Remember that oceans absorb CO_2 from the atmosphere, and as they do, the seawater undergoes acidification. The increased acidity "eats up" the neutralizing carbonate that is present in seawater. If the level of carbonate drops too low, there may not be enough of it for shell-forming animals to make their shells. After that point is reached, the corrosive seawater dissolves the creatures' shells, making it impossible for them to maintain their protective covers. If you want your great-grandchildren to know the taste of oysters, we need to limit CO_2 emissions now.

The ocean depths are home to many marvelous creatures, some of which we never knew existed until fairly recent times. Such was the case with the megamouth shark and the giant squid. If such large creatures escaped our knowledge, imagine how many smaller creatures there are waiting to be discovered. Life in the depths subjects its residents to cold, dark, and high pressure. Studying its inhabitants is sure to enlighten us as to how to survive at the extreme limits of habitability.

The ocean deep is not just another of life's zones; it is almost a parallel universe brimming with evolutionary possibilities. This region is so far from human reach that you might wonder what possible threat we could pose to such a world. While the threat is not immediate, lessons from the past indicate that even this vast realm may fall victim to climate change.

Fifty-five million years ago, when an eruption of methane that had been locked in clathrates warmed our planet, the ocean depths became nearly as warm as its surface, and life in the deep ocean was almost annihilated. We have no remains of deep-sea fishes surviving from this time (indeed, we have almost no fossils of them at all), but the surviving evidence in the rocks speaks eloquently of the mass extinction of the smaller creatures that shared their habitat.

Greenhouse gases clearly have the power to change ecosystems both on land and in the sea. One way to understand how climate change is affecting the planet's ecosystems is by looking at groups of species and their response over time to climate change. We can mass together the available data, which involves observations of more than 1,000 species such as trees, crustaceans, and mammals, to see what they say statistically as a whole. This was the approach taken by a group of researchers led by Chris Thomas of the University of Leeds, England, who published their findings in the journal *Nature* in 2004.

The project examined the fate of 1,103 species of plants and animals, from small shrubs to primates, in the face of climate change to 2050. The locations were drawn from regions covering 20 percent of the Earth's surface, including Mexico, South Africa, Europe, South America, and Australia.

Thomas and his colleagues found that at the low range of predicted temperature rises (between 1.4°F and 3°F (0.77°C and 1.66°C)), around 18 percent of the species sampled appear to be doomed, while at the high range (over 3.6°F (2°C)), more than a third of the species will become extinct. Believe it or not, this is the best-case scenario. Thomas's predictions assume that the species can migrate. But if they live in areas where migration is impossible, the likelihood of extinction is roughly doubled.

We must remember, however, that if we act now, it lies within our power to save *two* species for every one that is currently doomed. To do it, we must reduce greenhouse-gas emissions. If we carry on with business as usual, in all likelihood three out of every five species will not be with us at the dawn of the next century. Your decisions affecting greenhouse-gas emissions can help save animals and plants from extinction.

CALL TO ACTION

Stop the Junk Mail

If your family is like most, junk mail makes up the largest percentage of the mail delivered to your home. According to the Native Forest Network, each adult receives about 560 pieces of junk mail each year. Annually, we produce almost 4.5 million tons of junk mail. About 100 million trees are ground up each year to produce junk mail, most of which ends up in the trash, unopened and unread. Talk about waste.

Help reduce junk mail:

- Send a postcard that includes your name, address, and signature to the Direct Marketing Association at Mail Preference Service, Direct Marketing Association, P.O. Box 643, Carmel, New York 10512. You may also visit their website at **http://www. dmachoice.org** and follow the Consumer Guide prompts for more information. This will eliminate about 70 percent of the junk mail that comes to your home.
- To remove your name from credit-card companies and their preapproved offers, call 1-888-567-8688.

Visit the Native Forest Network at **http://native forest.org** for more junk-mail facts and for information about ongoing forest-conservation issues.

Chapter 19

Three Tipping Points

Some climate changes are slow and steady. Others, like those caused when clathrates were belched forth 55 million years ago, cause sudden snaps in Earth's systems. At such times, a new world order is suddenly created, to which the survivors must adapt or perish.

There are three main "tipping points" that scientists feel could cause Earth's systems to undergo rapid change: a slowing or collapse of the Gulf Stream, the death of the Amazon rain forests, and the release of clathrates from the seafloor. All three occur on occasion in the virtual worlds created by global circulation models, and there is some geological evidence for all having happened in Earth's history. So what leads to these sudden shifts, what are the warning signs, and if they occur, how might they affect us? The following scenarios are only scenarios—for now. We still have the time and power to change them.

SCENARIO ONE:
The Collapse of the Gulf Stream

The importance of the Gulf Stream to the Atlantic rim countries is enormous. In 2004, the Hollywood disaster movie *The Day After Tomorrow* imagined the consequences of a possible shutdown of the Gulf Stream. In the movie, runaway ice sheets essentially buried the Northern Hemisphere. For dramatic effect, the timelines for the collapse were greatly compressed. Scientists have been working at understanding the consequences of a Gulf Stream collapse for biodiversity as a whole, and they *are* catastrophic. Biological productivity in the North Atlantic will fall by 50 percent, and oceanic productivity worldwide will plummet by more than 20 percent. So what are the chances of the Gulf Stream shutting down this century? Under what conditions might it occur, and what would be the warning signs?

Sailors have known of the Gulf Stream since the time of Columbus, but the first map of the current was not produced until Benjamin Franklin printed one in 1770. Today we know that the Gulf Stream is the fastest ocean current in the world, spreading into a series of whirls and subcurrents as its waters flow northward. The volume of water in its flow is stupendous. Recall that ocean currents are measured in Sverdrups. Overall, the Gulf Stream's flow rate is around 100 Sverdrups, which is 100 times as great as that of the Amazon River. As the warm waters of the Gulf Stream flow north, they release their heat to the air, warming Europe's climate by an amount equivalent to a third of the continent's sunlight. As the waters yield their heat, they sink, like a great underwater waterfall. This waterfall is the powerhouse of the ocean currents of the entire planet. However, it is also their Achilles' heel, because it is vulnerable to interruption, as shown throughout history.

As the Earth's climate shifted from full icehouse mode 20,000 years ago to the mild climate of today, the Gulf Stream was repeatedly destabilized. The first time was about 12,700 to 11,700 years ago; the second, between 8,200 and 7,800 years ago; and the third, 4,200 to 3,900 years ago. On at least two of the occasions, the disruption seems to have been caused by massive amounts of freshwater flowing into the North Atlantic, which diluted its salinity. When the Gulf Stream water becomes diluted with fresh water, it will not sink when it cools because fresh water is less dense than salt water. If this circulation stops, then no warm water would be drawn northward, putting an end to the Gulf Stream and, with a dominolike effect, the circulation of the oceans worldwide.

If most of the Arctic ice melted and the rainfall increased in the northern Atlantic regions, the quantity of freshwater produced would probably be enough to disrupt the Gulf Stream's flow.

How likely is this to happen? Researcher Ruth Curry of Woods Hole Oceanographic Institution and her colleagues carried out an intensive study that examined the salinity of the Atlantic Ocean from pole to pole over two fourteen-year periods, 1955 to 1969 and 1985 to 1999. They discovered that at all depths the tropical Atlantic is becoming saltier, while the north and south polar Atlantic are becoming fresher. The change, they believe, is due to increased evaporation near the equator and enhanced rainfall near the poles. When they found similar changes in other oceans, they realized that something—most probably climate change—had accelerated the world's evaporation and precipitation rates by 5 to 10 percent.

This remarkable discovery has even greater potential impact on the Gulf Stream. The increasing tropical saltiness, the researchers suggest, will lead to a temporary speeding up of the Gulf Stream that will ironically signal a shutdown. This will occur because the extra heat transferred to the poles will melt more ice and thus freshen the North Atlantic, producing enough Sverdrups of freshwater to collapse the currents.

If the Gulf Stream were to fail, how fast might it happen? Ice cores from Greenland indicate that, as the Gulf Stream slowed in the past, the island experienced a massive 18°F (10°C) drop in temperature in as little as a decade. Presumably, similarly rapid changes were also felt over Europe, although no sediment record of climate change has survived to tell of it. It is possible that extreme changes could be felt over Europe and North America within a couple of winters if the Gulf Stream were to slow.

When is such an event likely to happen? Scientists don't agree on a time frame. In fact, not all scientists agree that a collapse or even a slowing of the Gulf Stream is imminent. Scientists at the Hadley Center in England rate the chance of major disruption to the Gulf Stream this century at 5 percent or less. Their main concern is a potentially even more catastrophic event—the collapse of the Amazon rain forest.

SCENARIO TWO:
The Collapse of the Amazon Rain Forest

The reserve of carbon in the rain forest soil is a potential source of CO_2 so enormous that it dwarfs the amount stored in living vegetation. The carbon in this reserve is finely balanced, with only a small change in temperature needed to turn a soil from a CO_2 absorber to a large-scale emitter. This change is brought about by bacterial decomposition. At lower temperatures, decomposition is slow, allowing carbon to accumulate, but as the soil warms, decomposition accelerates and CO_2 is released in large amounts. This is a good example of a positive-feedback loop: increasing temperature (from increased CO_2

emissions) leads directly to emission of even more CO_2 into the atmosphere.

The Hadley Center created a vegetation computer model that predicts that as the concentration of atmospheric CO_2 in the virtual world increases, the plants—particularly in the Amazon—will start behaving in unusual ways.

Transpiration is the process by which plants release water vapor into the atmosphere. In the Amazonian rain forest, the large volume of transpired water vapor forms clouds whose moisture falls as rain. It turns out that CO_2 affects transpiration. Plants open the stomata in their leaves to gain CO_2 from the atmosphere. But when the stomata are open, plants lose water vapor, so they keep their stomata open only as long as required. As CO_2 levels in the atmosphere increase, the plants of the Amazonian rain forest keep their stomata open for a shorter amount of time (because they take in more CO_2), and transpiration is reduced. With less transpiration there will be less rain.

The Hadley Center vegetation model indicates that by around 2100, levels of CO_2 will have increased to the point that Amazonian rainfall will reduce dramatically, with 20 percent of that decline attributable to closed stomata. The rest of the decline, the model predicts, will be due to a persistent El Niño–like climate—including droughts—that will develop as our globe warms.

The cumulative impact of these changes will reduce rainfall from the current Amazon basin-wide average of 0.2 inches (0.5 cm) per day to 0.08 inches (0.2 cm) per day by 2100. In northeastern Amazonia, it will fall to almost zero. These conditions, combined with a basin-wide rise in temperature of 10°F

(5.6°C) will, the model indicates, stress plants to the point that collapse of the Amazonian rain forest will become inevitable. With the loss of the rain-forest canopy, soils will heat and decompose more rapidly, leading to the release of yet more CO_2. This constitutes a massive disruption of the carbon cycle, reducing the storage of carbon in living vegetation by 35 gigatons and in soil by 150 gigatons. These are huge figures—totaling around 8 percent of all carbon stored in the world's vegetation and soils.

The ultimate outcome of this series of positive-feedback loops is that by 2100 the Earth's atmosphere will have close to 1,000 parts per million of CO_2, nearly triple our current level of 387 parts per million, as opposed to the 710 predicted in earlier models.

When might all of this happen? If the model is correct, we could start to see signs of rain-forest collapse around 2040, and the process should be complete during this century, by which time rain-forest cover will have been reduced from its present 80 percent to less than 10 percent. Half of the deforested region will turn to grass, while the other half turns to desert. The time to stop the CO_2 increase is now!

SCENARIO THREE:
Methane Release from the Seafloor

The Arctic Ocean is where manifestations of the third possible great tipping point may first appear. In this particular scenario, the cause is something that has not yet figured largely in the workings of climate modelers but which prehistory teaches us should be given serious attention: a sudden unleashing of clathrates.

Clathrate comes from the Latin term for "caged," and it refers to the structure in which ice crystals trap molecules of methane. Clathrates contain lots of gas under high pressure, which is why pieces of the icy substance hiss, pop, and, if lighted, burn when brought to the surface. Because of this, they are also known as the "ice that burns."

Massive volumes of clathrates are buried in the seabed around the world—perhaps twice as much in energy terms as all other fossil fuels combined—where ocean water is more than 1,300 feet (396 meters) deep and bottom temperatures are below 34°F to 35°F (1.1°C to 1.6°C). The material is kept solid only by the pressure of the overlying water and the cold. There are large volumes of clathrates in the Arctic Ocean at shallower depths, because there temperatures are sufficiently low, even near the surface, to keep them stable.

Scientists estimate that there are between 13,100 and 55,020 trillion cubic yards of clathrates scattered around the ocean floor. Compare that with the 482 trillion cubic yards of recoverable natural gas in the world, and it's not surprising that the fossil-fuel industry can see a future in this unusual material.

If pressure on the clathrates was ever relieved or the temperature of the deep oceans was to increase, colossal amounts of methane could be released. Paleontologists are now beginning to suspect that the unleashing of clathrates may have been responsible for the biggest extinction event of all time. Two hundred and forty-five million years ago, around nine out of ten species living on Earth became extinct. Known as the Permo-Triassic extinction event (after the geologic time periods it straddles), it killed off early mammal-like creatures, in turn opening the way for the age of the dinosaurs.

The cause of the extinction is thought to be one of two

things: the collision of an asteroid with Earth or a massive out-pouring from volcanoes in the region now called Siberia. These eruptions released up to 0.5 million cubic miles (2 million cubic kilometers) of lava and billions of tons of CO_2 and sulfur dioxide. It's this second hypothesis that is gaining strength, and these gases are thought to have interacted with clathrates.

So vast was the input of greenhouse gas to the atmosphere that it is thought to have led to an initial rise in global average temperature of about 11°F (6.1°C). At the same time, widespread acid rain, caused by the sulfur dioxide, released yet more carbon. The total impact of the increasing temperature triggered melting followed by the release of huge volumes of methane from the tundra and clathrates on the seafloor—more than enough to cause rapid climate change.

Clathrates are important structural elements in seafloor stability, and their sudden sublimation could lead to "slumping," or collapse of the seafloor, and the generation of tsunamis of unprecedented power. Indeed, a slump off the Carolina coast 15,000 years ago is thought to have released enough methane to increase atmospheric concentrations by 4 percent. It's a sobering thought to ponder that there could be an unstable clathrate time bomb off a beach near you.

Both the Amazon rain-forest dieback and the release of clathrates are positive-feedback loops, where changes build on one another to produce even greater global warming. Of the three tipping points presented, the release of the clathrates is the least likely to occur this century. Only a truly massive warming event could trigger it.

There's one other positive-feedback loop that is worth discussing, because it directly concerns us and may be the trigger for further change. Throughout our history we have engaged in a constant battle to make ourselves comfortable with respect to temperature. Think about it: How many times a day do you change your body position to make yourself feel warmer or cooler? How often do you put on or take off a sweater? What about raising or lowering the thermostat in your house? Today we use fossil fuels to heat and cool our homes, schools, stores, and offices, an enterprise costly in terms of both energy use and the environment. In the United States, 55 percent of the total domestic energy budget is devoted to home heating and air-conditioning—while home heating alone costs Americans $44 billion per year.

As our world becomes more uncomfortable courtesy of climate change, it is inconceivable that the demand for air-conditioning will lessen. In fact, during heat waves it could mean the difference between life and death. But unless we change our ways, that demand will be met by burning fossil fuels, and this represents a powerful positive-feedback loop. An insatiable demand for air conditioners is already evident in countries such as the United States and Australia, where, until recently, construction codes for houses have been appallingly lax regarding energy use. Wouldn't it be awful if in our quest to cool our homes, we end up cooking our planet?

CALL TO ACTION

Celebrate Arbor Day

The first Arbor Day was held in Nebraska, the result of a tree-planting holiday proposed by Nebraska pioneer J. Sterling Morton. He and other settlers recognized the importance of using trees to anchor soil on the flat prairies. The trees would also serve as windbreaks, as well as creating shade and a pretty landscape. On April 10, 1872, Nebraskans planted more than a million trees.

Get permission to plant a tree on your school property for Arbor Day, which is usually celebrated the last Friday in April. Volunteer to plant trees in other areas of your city. Call the city hall and ask what Arbor Day activities are planned and how you can participate.

The Arbor Day Foundation has a website: **http://www.arborday.org.** Visit it for more ideas on ways to take action.

Chapter 20

Civilization: Big City versus Small Town

Our civilization is built on two foundations: our ability to grow enough food to support a large number of people who are engaged in tasks other than growing food, and our ability to live in groups large enough to support great institutions, such as businesses, schools, and governments. These clusters of people are known as cities, and it is from their citizens that the word *civilization* is derived.

Today, very large cities lie at the heart of our global society, and our most valued institutions are found in them. Yet they are fragile entities vulnerable to the stresses brought about by climate change, because the people living in cities rely on others to supply them with food, water, and energy. Imagine if you woke up tomorrow and no one in the town where you live had water running from the faucets in their home. No toilets would flush, no showers or baths would be available, you couldn't wash dishes or clothes, and if you wanted a drink of water, you would be out of luck. Then imagine that gasoline supplies came to a halt. Food could not be delivered, garbage wouldn't be removed, and people couldn't get to school or work. Could climate change threaten the resources that you and your neighbors who live in your town need to survive?

Past civilizations have collapsed as a result of climate change. The Anasazi people lived in the area that is now northern New Mexico and southern Colorado beginning around the year 1200 BC. For many hundreds of years, their civilization was a bustling center, densely populated with people living in multistoried pueblo homes and cliff dwellings. The climate, mostly desert, barely supported the demands the Anasazi made on it for agriculture. But they did survive. By the year AD 1300, however, the civilization had vanished.

Scientists believe that tree rings may partially hold the answer for the Anasazis' disappearance. Tree-ring studies indicate that during the years AD 1125 and 1180, rainfall in the area decreased, stressing the crops and the people. After a brief return to normal rainfall, a severe drought dried the land, this time for four years. A season of normal rainfall, in AD 1274, gave the Anasazi a glimpse of hope, but that was soon dashed as yet another drought began in 1275—one that lasted fourteen years. The droughts made it difficult to grow enough food to feed the population, especially as lowland fields dried out. At the same time, a climate-cooling trend at higher elevation made the soil unsuitable for growing certain crops. Disputes over water access between the Anasazi and nearby peoples may have caused stress too.

Another theory, also surmised from tree rings, is that climate change altered the pattern of rainfall. Perhaps the precipitation still fell, but at the wrong time of year to benefit crops growing in the summer season. While other causes likely factored into the situation, the droughts and altered rainfall patterns certainly didn't help matters. The surviving Anasazi left the area and joined people living in other regions.

If Earth's climate were to change rapidly, it could put a

similar kind of stress on many communities. People would have to turn to other locations for their water and food supply. And if the volume they needed was very large, that might stress the resources of the community they "borrowed" from. If people had to abandon their homes entirely, as the Anasazi did, sufficient housing could be a problem in the locations they move to.

The threat posed by increased climate variability is a very real one. A good example of the relationship between climate variability and human population size is provided by Australia. It is unique among the larger nations in consisting of either very small settlements or large cities, for the middle-size towns that predominate in the United States and elsewhere in the world are almost entirely absent. This is a consequence of the cycle of drought and flood that has characterized Australia's land from the first settlement.

Small regional population centers have survived because they can batten down the hatches and endure drought, and large cities have also survived because they are integrated into the global economy. The resource networks of towns, however, are smaller than the region affected by climate variability, making them vulnerable to swings in income, which can mean loss of jobs. Typically, what happens is that, as a drought progresses, the farm machinery dealership and automotive dealership close down. Then, with everyone feeling the pinch, the pharmacist, the bookseller, and the banks leave. When the drought finally breaks and people have cash again, these businesses do not return, and instead people travel to larger centers to buy what they need, and in time end up moving there.

The Australian example shows that climate variability has in fact encouraged the formation of cities: today it is the most urbanized nation on Earth. But the only reason that Australia's cities are refuges from climate variability is that they draw their resources from a region broader than that affected by the continent's droughts and floods.

With climate change, however, we are talking of a global phenomenon. Water will be the first critical resource to be affected. Water is heavy and people don't want to pay much for it, and so it is unprofitable to transport long distances. This means that most cities source their water supply locally, in areas small enough for mild climate change to have an impact. On the other hand, food such as grain is easily transported and is often sourced from afar, which means that only truly global disruptions would cause shortages of food in the world's cities.

For the past ten years, droughts and unusually hot summers have caused world grain yields to fall or stagnate, while the number of extra mouths humanity must feed has grown by around 800 million. But so far, we have been able to cope with what have been relatively small-scale drops in food supply.

One of the arguments made by people who dismiss global warming as a threat is that increasing levels of CO_2 will "fertilize" the world's crop plants, providing a solution to world hunger. In fact, a video called *The Greening of Planet Earth* promotes the idea that "fertilizing" the world with CO_2 will boost crop yields by 30 to 60 percent. Beware of this claim. Many experiments in which plants have been fed artificially high levels of CO_2 have now been completed, and botanists Elizabeth Ainsworth and Stephen Long have analyzed some of the results.

It turns out that trees benefit far more than shrubs or grasses from increases in CO_2, and that the species that benefit least are grasses belonging to a group that includes our most important crops. Rice, for example, showed an increase in yield of only

6 percent in response to a doubling of CO_2, while wheat yields rose by only 8 percent. In the future, crops will be stressed by higher temperature, more ozone at ground level, and changes in soil moisture, all of which will decrease yields. Thus, rather than an agricultural paradise, a CO_2-rich world promises to be one in which crop production is lower than today.

When it comes to climate change, cities are more like plants than animals, because they can't just pick up and move when threatened by climate change. Instead, a city must weather whatever troubles climate change throws its way. These may include repeated battering by extreme-weather events, rising seas and storm surges, extreme cold or heat, water deprivation or flood, or even disease.

So could the day ever come when the taps run dry, or when power, food, or fuel is no longer available in many of the world's cities? That depends on the amplitude of climatic change that increased greenhouse gases bring: if it exceeds the extent of a city's resource procurement network, then collapse is inevitable. As yet, we have no figures as to what degree of warming could trigger such a collapse, but we do know that 1.1°F (0.6°C) of warming has inflicted acute distress on large regions such as the Sahel, the Arctic, and subantarctic waters. Five degrees Fahrenheit of warming (3°C)—five times as much as has been experienced thus far—will have more wide-reaching impacts, enough perhaps to destabilize continent-size regions. At the highest end of the scale—20°F (11°C) of warming—the impacts are unimaginable and would threaten our species as a whole.

If we were to experience an abrupt climate shift, it is possible that a near-eternal, dreary winter would descend on the cities of Europe and eastern North America, killing crops and freezing ports, roads, and human bodies as well. Or perhaps extreme heat, brought on by a vast outpouring of CO_2 or methane, would destroy the productivity of oceans and land. Neither situation offers a rosy prospect for our cities.

Humanity, of course, would survive such a collapse, because people will persist in smaller, more robust communities such as villages and farms. Just as temperate forests (unlike rain forests) have relatively few species, small towns have relatively few people, and the inhabitants of both are hardy and multiskilled. These characteristics mean that both the temperate forest and the small town can withstand periods of shortage that would destroy a rain forest or city.

For a small town, a drought may be a worry, but because whatever rain falls on a nonporous roof could be captured in a water tank, it could benefit from even the briefest shower. In contrast, dams, which create large reservoirs that supply whole cities, require substantial rain to create flows, because a lot of the water behind the dam soaks into the soil. Likewise, while a late fuel delivery or failure of power supply would be annoying to those in small communities, the impact on them is nothing compared with that on the inhabitants of a city's many-storied apartment buildings. In the long term, however, even medium-size towns lack the know-how to keep their complex infrastructure—such as medical services and machinery—working. They are ultimately just as dependent on our civilization as are the city dwellers, meaning that a major shift in climate change will ultimately affect them too.

Scientists began expressing concern about global warming in the 1970s. We have known for some decades that the climate change we have been creating for the twenty-first century is of a similar magnitude to that seen at the end of the last ice age, only it's occurring thirty times faster. We have known that the

Gulf Stream shut down on at least three occasions at the end of the last ice age, causing sea levels to rise by at least 300 feet (90 meters). We have plenty of evidence to prove that the Earth's biosphere was profoundly reorganized by these events. We know that sudden climate change will disrupt agriculture and cause extinctions. So why have we done so little about global warming?

CALL TO ACTION

Stop Pouring Energy Down the Drain

According the U.S. Department of Energy, heating water for baths, showers, dishwashing, and laundry may consume 14 to 25 percent of a home's energy budget. A few changes will make a big difference in your energy consumption and save you money.

- Check the water heater in your home. If it's twelve or more years old, chances are it's not energy efficient. Ask your parents to buy an Energy Star water heater when it's time to replace the unit.
- If you are replacing a water heater, consider looking into a tankless, on-demand water heater. These heaters heat water as it is used rather than keeping a stored tank of hot water, which requires constant heating, on hand. Depending on your hot-water needs, an on-demand water heater might work for you.
- If the water heater isn't an energy-saving heater, buy an insulating jacket made especially for water heaters.
- Insulate the first 6 feet of pipes that are connected to the water heater, both hot and cold.

- Check the temperature of the hot water from one or two of your faucets. If it's hotter than 120°F, lower the water heater's thermostat until it reaches that temperature.
- Don't start a load of dishes or clothes until the washers are fully loaded.
- Time yourself when you take a shower. The next time you shower, reduce the length of time. Even a minute or two less will make a difference.
- Take showers rather than baths. A bath uses 15 to 20 gallons of hot water; a shower uses about half that amount.
- Ask your parents to install a water-saving shower head. The flow should be 2.5 gallons or less per minute.
- Don't let the water keep running while you are brushing your teeth, washing your hands, shaving, etc.

Chapter 21

The Ozone Hole: A Success Story

At some point, you've probably slathered sunscreen on yourself—maybe at the beach or during a summer sporting event. The reason, of course, is to protect your skin from overexposure to the sun's ultraviolet (UV) rays, which can cause health problems. The ozone layer in Earth's atmosphere is like a chemical sunscreen: it protects all living organisms from UV rays. We're lucky it's there. Without ozone's very high sun-protection factor, UV radiation would kill you fast, by tearing apart your DNA and breaking other chemical bonds within your cells.

Ozone was discovered in the laboratory in the 1830s, and by 1850 it was detected occurring naturally in the atmosphere. Throughout the nineteenth century, measurements at ground level were being undertaken around Europe. By the 1920s, Oxford University's Gordon Dobson and his collaborator F. A. Lindeman realized that ozone played an important role in the stratosphere, and to this day the amount of ozone in the atmosphere is measured in Dobson units. Then in 1957—a year referred to as the International Geophysical Year, when governments around the world spent a billion dollars on scientific explorations that would help us to better understand Earth processes—a sustained effort to measure ozone began.

The first signs of a problem arose in the 1970s, when readings of ozone concentration in the stratosphere above the Antarctic began to look decidedly odd. The instruments were reporting ozone loss at a phenomenal rate: In 1955, the air over the Antarctic held 320 Dobson units. In 1975, there were 280 Dobson units, and by 1995, only 90. Given the relative stability of ozone levels being reported elsewhere, the readings seemed so bizarre that for ten years they were put down to some sort of instrumental error. Yet as early as 1974, three scientists—Paul Crutzen, F. Sherwood Rowland, and Mario Molina—were arguing that the depletion was real, that there was a hole in Earth's ozone layer, and that man-made chemicals had caused it. In 1995, the three were awarded the Nobel Prize in chemistry for this pioneering work.

A "hole" in the ozone layer is defined as an area of atmosphere with less than 220 Dobson units of ozone. By 2000, the hole had become a chasm spanning 11 million square miles, and a halo of thinned ozone spread around it, covering most of the globe below the latitude of 40°S. By the 1990s a second hole had appeared, this time over the Arctic. Even over the tropics, ozone concentration was reduced by around 7 percent. (For reasons outlined below, ozone holes form most readily over the polar regions.)

The destruction of the ozone layer began long before anyone was aware of it. Chlorofluorocarbons (CFCs) and hydrofluorocarbons (HFCs) had been invented by industrial chemists in 1928 and were found to be very useful for refrigeration, in making Styrofoam, as propellants in spray cans, and in air-conditioning units. CFCs and HFCs contain atoms of the element chlorine. Because they don't react with other substances, people were confident that there would be few environmental side effects, so they were embraced by industry.

By 1975 spray cans alone were spewing 500,000 tons of the stuff into the atmosphere. By 1985 global use of the main types of CFCs stood at 1.8 million tons. Ironically, their stability, which had made them so attractive, was a key factor in the damage they caused, because they lasted a very long time in the atmosphere.

CFCs evaporate easily, and once they are released into the atmosphere, it takes about five years for air currents to waft them into the stratosphere. Once there, UV radiation slowly breaks them down chemically, causing the release of their chlorine atom. It is the chlorine in CFCs that is so destructive to ozone—just a single atom can destroy 100,000 ozone molecules. Its destructive capacities are maximized at temperatures below –45°F (–43°C). This is why the ozone hole first appeared over the South Pole, where the stratosphere is a frigid –80°F (–62°C).

It was Mario Molina who discovered that CFCs had elevated chlorine levels in the stratosphere to five times their background level. As a result of the hole they punched in the ozone layer, people living south of 40°S are experiencing a spectacular rise in the incidence of skin cancer.

At 53°S, Punta Arenas in Chile is the southernmost town on Earth. Since 1994 skin-cancer rates there have soared by 66 percent. Even nearer to the equator—and closer to the great centers of human population—shifts in cancer rates are evident. In the United States, for example, the chance of getting melanoma was one in 250 just twenty-five years ago. Today it is one in 84, which is partly due to ozone depletion.

Ultraviolet radiation also causes eye damage, and its incidence is also rising. Researchers estimate that humans—and any other organisms with eyes—will experience a 0.5 percent increase in cataracts for every 1 percent decrease in ozone concentration. Cataracts cause the lens of the eye to become cloudy, causing partial or complete blindness. Because 20 percent of cataracts are due to UV damage, wearing sunglasses is important for reasons other than looking cool.

A third major impact on human health comes from the capacity of UV to damage the immune system. This will manifest itself as a general sickening in the stricken communities. Among vulnerable groups such as the Inuit, these impacts are already being felt.

Indeed, the impacts of increasing UV will be felt throughout the ecosystem. The microscopic single-celled plants that form the base of the ocean's food chain are severely affected by it, as are the larvae of many fish, from anchovies to mackerel. In fact, anything that spawns in the open is at risk. So vulnerable are many marine species that without stratospheric ozone they would go into a swift decline, precipitating a collapse of the oceans' ecosystems. Agriculture can also succumb to UV overexposure. The yield of crops such as peas and beans, for example, decreases 1 percent for every extra percent of UV radiation received.

For a decade after Crutzen and his team published their paper linking CFCs to ozone decline, the problem kept getting worse, yet scientists were unable to marshal proof positive that the scientists' hunch was right. So disastrous were the implications of ozone depletion, however, that color images of the ozone hole shown on television screens around the world convinced thousands of people that action needed to be taken, even if only as a precaution. People bombarded politicians with letters requesting that the chemicals be banned. The DuPont Company, one of the world's largest makers of chemical products, was the company responsible for most of the CFCs' manufacture, and in retaliation it and other chemical producers launched a massive public relations campaign aimed at discrediting the then-tenuous link between their products and the problem. They had a point, because science was still unable to provide conclusive proof of CFCs' damaging impact.

Still, public concern and protest continued. In 1987, despite the companies' objections about cost, representatives from a number of nations met in Montreal, Canada, and signed the Montreal Protocol, a treaty in which the use of CFCs was phased out. Later that year, scientific proof of the link between CFCs and ozone depletion was announced.

Today we know just how important approving the Montreal Protocol was. Had it not been enacted, by 2050 the middle latitudes of the Northern Hemisphere (where most humans live) would have lost half of their UV protection, while equivalent latitudes in the Southern Hemisphere would have lost 70 percent. As it was, by 2001, the Protocol had limited real damage to around a tenth of that.

Not all countries were initially bound by the Montreal Protocol. Indeed, China continues to produce CFCs and may well go on polluting until 2010, when under the treaty it must cease. Despite such exceptions, the Montreal Protocol marks a groundbreaking moment, because it represents the first-ever victory by humanity over a global pollution problem. In 2004, the ozone hole over the Antarctic had reduced by 20 percent. Because the size of the hole waxes and wanes from year to year, we cannot be certain that this decrease signals the end of the problem. Nevertheless, scientists are optimistic that in fifty years' time the ozone layer will be returned to its former strength.

One would think that such a stunning all-around success would motivate the nations of the world to jump at the chance to address climate change using a similar type of agreement. And at first there was great enthusiasm for an international treaty to limit emissions of greenhouse gases. And then the momentum stalled.

CALL TO ACTION

Make Your Voice Heard—Make Your Vote Count

If you are concerned about global warming, get the names and addresses of your state's governor, your state senator, your congressional representative, and your U.S. senators, and write them a letter. A handwritten letter holds the most clout, followed by a faxed message. While e-mail is convenient, it's the easiest to disregard and delete. For an online directory of your U.S. senators and representatives, see **http://www.senate.gov** and **http://www. house.gov.**

So pick up your pen and write. Here's an example to get you started:

Dear Governor/Senator/Congressperson _____,

I am concerned about global warming and the environment. What are you doing to enact laws that will reduce the level of greenhouse gases in Earth's atmosphere? What have you done to encourage the utilization of renewable energy sources, such as solar and wind power?

I would like our state to be a national role model, leading the way in the reduction of fossil-fuel consumption and the development of alternative energy sources.

Soon I will be a registered voter. When I am, I will vote for men and women who actively work to reduce carbon dioxide emissions.

I'll look forward to hearing what actions you are taking on these important issues.

Sincerely,

Chapter 22

The Kyoto Protocol

Reducing greenhouse-gas emissions is going to take a concerted global commitment and will require the participation of essentially all nations if it is to succeed. To assure that all parties "toe the line," a treaty is necessary. Toward this end, representatives from more than 160 countries attended a series of conferences from 1992 through December 1997 in Kyoto, Japan, during which they drafted a treaty known as the Kyoto Protocol.

The first objective of the Protocol was to set a limit on global CO_2 emissions. Industrialized countries, such as the United States, Canada, Australia, Russia, and the European countries, would agree to adopt measures that would drop human-made emissions of greenhouse gases by an average of 5.2 percent below 1990 levels during the years 2008 to 2012. Developing nations, such as China and India, were exempt from the limits. But they would agree to institute programs that would lessen their effects on climate change. With all countries signed to the agreement, only ratification, or formal approval, was required to bring it into effect.

The treaty, however, could not be ratified until countries accounting for a combined 55 percent of the CO_2 emissions had agreed to it. That proved to be a major stumbling block, especially after the United States—which at that time accounted for almost 25 percent of global CO_2 emissions—withdrew from negotiations in 2001. On February 16, 2005, however, ninety days after Russia ratified (bringing the number of ratifying nations to fifty-five, accounting for a proportion of emissions above 55 percent), the Protocol came into force. As of 2008, the United States is the only developed nation that has not ratified the Protocol. It seems clear that the Kyoto Protocol will influence all nations for decades to come.

Why did the United States choose not to ratify the Protocol? Many members of the U.S. government felt it was unfair that developing countries such as China and India were not required to have target limits. Some believed that developing countries were being given a "free ride" and that their exclusion from limits would give them an unfair economic advantage. While it is true that the emissions of many developing nations were not limited, it is only fair to note that "transitional" nations such as Ukraine, the Czech Republic, Bulgaria, and Romania were assigned limits. On July 25, 1997, the U.S. Senate passed a resolution—ninety-five to zero—declaring that it would reject any treaty that did not require "new specific scheduled commitments to limit or reduce greenhouse gas emissions for Developing Country Parties within the same compliance period."

So are the developing nations really "free riders"? Some experts believe that there are valid reasons for excluding the developing nations from the first round. Foremost is the principle of natural justice: the developed world has largely created the problem to date, so it should carry the bulk of the burden. There is also the example of the Montreal Protocol's success with CFCs. Developing nations initially were not bound by it either.

One of the principal fears (particularly expressed in the United States and Australia) of exempting developing nations from carbon limits was that domestic jobs would go offshore—that rather than pay the costs to reduce emissions, companies would pull up stakes and shift their plants to countries where emission standards weren't required.

Another criticism of the Kyoto Protocol concerns the carbon emission limits that it sets for participating countries. Each country has its own target limit. For example, the target limit for the United States was a reduction in emissions to 7 percent below those we produced in 1990. When setting the limits, the Protocol took into account the economy of each ratifying country. For example, the eastern European countries formerly part of the Soviet Union have suffered economic ruin since 1990. Because they no longer produce goods at the rate they did before then, they are also producing 25 percent less CO_2 than they did in 1990. With their Kyoto carbon-target limit set at 8 percent less than their 1990 level, they have valuable carbon credits to trade: under the treaty, the difference between the percentage of emissions they produce today and the 8 percent limit set by the Kyoto Protocol may be traded to other countries that plan to use them to augment their own carbon-target limits. Globally, carbon-credit trading is valued at more than $10 billion—not a sum to sneeze at. Indeed, the World Bank thinks that carbon trading could be a way for the poorest countries to financially sustain their development.

How does trading carbon credits work? First, the Protocol permits developed (industrialized) countries to trade with one another; for example, the eastern European countries can trade their credits to other developed countries.

The second way credits can be traded is by participating in

projects that offset emissions. For example, a developed country can finance a project—such as planting a forest or dismantling an industrial plant—based in either a developing country or another developed country that has carbon credits to trade, and it will receive those credits in return.

Projects financed by carbon-credit trading require trust between nations. We must trust that the recipient of the traded carbon credit will do what is required; there's no real guarantee that forests will be planted and cared for or that an industrial plant that pollutes will actually be dismantled after the sale of carbon credits. Even with goodwill on all sides, such schemes may fail because nations such as Russia do not have the legal and regulatory institutions in place to ensure compliance.

The essential problem with trading credits is that they do little or nothing to diminish climate change, because after the trade occurs, the country that receives the credits uses them as a way to avoid reducing its own emissions (and the costs involved in doing so). In other words, it's like paying for the right to pollute.

Another problem is that a country can have a target limit *greater* than its 1990 emission level. Australia, for example, has a carbon limit 8 percent greater than its emissions produced in 1990. How did that come about? The Australian delegation to Kyoto argued that Australia's special circumstances—including a heavy dependence on fossil fuels, special transport needs (being a large, sparsely populated continent), and an energy-intensive export sector—placed a heavy financial burden on them and that concessions were needed. The delegation made its case effectively, and the country was given a higher target limit of emissions. In 2007, after ratifying the Kyoto Protocol, Australia's government announced that it had revised its long-term target for greenhouse gases. Australia now hopes to cut carbon emissions by 60 percent of 2000 levels by 2050.

Perhaps the most severe criticism of Kyoto is that it is a toothless tiger. That is indisputably true, because the momentum of climate change is now so great that Kyoto's target of reducing CO_2 emissions by 5.2 percent is simply nowhere near enough. Stabilizing our climate will require emission cuts of at least 70 percent by 2050 just to keep atmospheric CO_2 at double the preindustrial level. The Protocol's advocates, however, know how difficult it has been to get even a toothless treaty signed, and they believe that pushing for deeper cuts at this stage would prove fatal to the wide yet fragile consensus. For now, Kyoto has begun a dialogue among nations that, with time and effort, can be transformed into something truly meaningful.

It is of utmost importance to understand that the Kyoto Protocol is the only international treaty in existence created to combat climate change. For those who urge abandonment or who criticize Kyoto, there are two questions: What do you propose to replace Kyoto with, and how do you propose to secure international agreement for your alternative?

In addition to the reasons already mentioned, the government of the United States has stated that it refuses to ratify Kyoto because the changes it requires are prohibitively expensive. A strong economy, the government has said, offers the best insurance against all future shocks, and it is hesitant to do anything that might slow economic growth.

Economic experts disagree widely about what the costs of meeting Protocol limits might be. William Lash from the Center for the Study of American Business says ratification would mean that pay raises would come less often and domestic energy costs would skyrocket. Also, he thinks ratification would require a 25 percent reduction in the domestic consumption of fossil fuels—the equivalent of stopping all road, rail, air, and sea traffic permanently—and an increase in farm-production costs of $10 to $20 billion.

On the other side there are those—including a coalition of public-interest groups—who argue that there may be a positive economic benefit in ratification. They posit that the United States could comply and still see domestic energy bills decline by $530 per household per year.

Two economists, Yale University's William Nordhaus and Harvard's Dale Jorgenson, argue that the emission decreases required to meet the first round of Kyoto targets (to 2012) will be modest—certainly not so high that the nation will become bankrupt. In the long run, it may even benefit the country's economy by directing investment into new infrastructure.

However, the cost of compliance is only half of the equation. To make a truly informed decision about Kyoto—or more radical proposals—we need to know the cost of doing nothing. What kinds of costs have been piling up in the United States due to extreme-weather-related events?

The National Climatic Data Center, part of the National Oceanic and Atmospheric Administration, maintains a list of severe weather events that cost a billion or more dollars in damages. They include droughts, floods, wildfires, tropical storms, hailstorms, tornadoes, heat waves, ice storms, and hurricanes. From the years 2000 to 2006, these disasters cost Americans more than $251 billion; the most expensive, at a cost of $125 billion, was Hurricane Katrina in 2006. And in 2008, the damage from Hurricanes Ike and Gustav combined exceeded

$32 billion. As extreme-weather events increase in severity, damage costs will only go higher. Failing to include these costs in the price tag for maintaining business as usual is misleading.

Over the last four decades, the insurance industry has been reeling under the burden of losses as a result of natural disasters. The effects of the 1998 El Niño offer a fine example. Paul Epstein of Harvard Medical School calculated that, in the first eleven months of that year alone, weather-related losses totaled $89 billion, while 32,000 people died and 300 million were made homeless. This was more than the total losses experienced in the entire decade of the 1980s.

Since the 1970s, insurance losses have risen at an annual rate of around 10 percent, reaching $100 billion by 1999. Losses at this scale threaten the very fabric of our economic system, because an annual increase in the damage bill of 10 percent means that the total bill doubles every seven or eight years. Such a rate of increase implies that by 2065 or soon thereafter, the damage bill resulting from climate change may equal the total value of everything that humanity produced in the course of a year.

You may wonder how hurricanes along the eastern coast of the United States could affect your pocketbook if you live in Iowa or Illinois. Here's how it works: If you own a home, you have homeowners' insurance, which protects the property if it gets damaged or destroyed. With extreme-weather events on the increase, a Florida homeowner now pays the extraordinary deductible (the amount he or she pays before the insurance company "kicks in" with its share) of around $100,000. Both insurance-industry and climatic trends suggest that homeowners elsewhere whose weather-related deductibles are now only in the hundreds of dollars may soon be facing deductibles in the thousands or tens of thousands of dollars. Why? To remain in business, insurance companies raise their rates—and your deductible—to offset the losses they have to pay to hurricane victims in Florida. Similar escalations apply to extreme events as diverse as hurricanes, wildfires, floods, and heat waves. With all projected to increase, the rapid escalation of insurance bills is unavoidable.

If scientists were predicting the imminent return of the ice age, would we be reacting differently? "Global warming" creates an illusion of a warm, cozy future that is deeply appealing, because we are an essentially tropical species that has spread into all corners of our globe, and cold has long been our greatest enemy. From the beginning we have associated cold with discomfort, illness, and death, while warmth is the essence of everything good—love, comfort, and life itself. Left unchecked, however, global warming will prove that too much of "a good thing" will cause us plenty of trouble.

CALL TO ACTION

Can It!

Drinking soda from an aluminum can? Think carefully before tossing your empty into the trash: recycling just one aluminum can saves enough energy to run a television for three hours or a 100-watt incandescent bulb for four hours! Aluminum cans are made with an ore called bauxite. Four pounds of bauxite are saved for every pound of aluminum that is recycled. Recycling aluminum cans saves 95 percent of the energy that must be used to manufacture cans from the ore.

If your school doesn't already recycle cans, start a program to do so. Try to get 100 percent commitment of the student body. According to the Can Manufacturers Institute, recycling aluminum cans is definitely worth your time, because:

- an aluminum can that is recycled can be back on the shelf in sixty days.

- each aluminum can is worth about a penny. You can sell them to recycling centers.
- Recycling one ton of aluminum saves the equivalent in energy of 2,350 gallons of gasoline. This is equivalent to the amount of electricity used by the typical home over a period of ten years.

Some states offer a cash refund for cans and bottles that are returned to the stores where they were purchased. See if your state offers this deposit refund alternative. Also, some charities, such as Shriners Hospitals and Ronald McDonald House, collect the tabs from aluminum cans, which can be taken to recycling centers for cash rebates.

Chapter 23
What to Believe?

In the 1970s, the United States was a world leader and innovator in energy conservation, photovoltaics, and wind technology. Today, however, the United States still relies mainly on traditional sources of energy—fossil fuels. While advocates of wind power are taking steps to promote weaning ourselves from oil dependency, wind still generates only about 1 percent of the electricity used here. Other countries have made serious strides in using wind to generate electricity. In Denmark, for example, wind supplies 20 percent of the energy needed to generate electricity. What's slowing down the pace of innovation in the United States?

During the past eight years, the fossil-fuel lobby in Washington, D.C., has become very powerful. In June 2005, the *New York Times* ran a story revealing one of the ways that lobbyists are affecting government policy. Philip A. Cooney, a government aide and an oil-industry lobbyist fighting against the regulation of greenhouse gases, removed or adjusted descriptions of climate research in reports that government scientists and their supervisors had already approved. Many of Cooney's changes appeared in the final reports, and their overall effect was to minimize concern about climate change. Other climate-change studies, by the National Academy of Sciences, the

**BUILDING A PORTABLE,
ECO-FRIENDLY HOUSE**

In the fall of 2008, Elizabeth Turnbull decided she would live at home when she began her graduate studies at Yale University, in New Haven, Connecticut. But she did it with a highly unusual twist: she brought the house with her. Elizabeth spent the months before she left for Yale building her own portable, eco-friendly house on a flatbed trailer.

After completing an undergraduate major in Environmental Policy and Economics, Elizabeth Turnbull turned her attention toward graduate studies that would permit her to further explore how science, economics, and government interact. She firmly believes that business success and ecological responsibility are not mutually exclusive. "The environment has to be part of a good business strategy in the same way that accounting does. And I'm inspired by that," Turnbull declared. "Increasingly, you are seeing companies that are really kicking butt in the marketplace and doing well because they are a step ahead of their competitors on the environmental front."

Fond of hiking and camping, Elizabeth has always been concerned about how her actions affect the environment. As she prepared for graduate work, she also became concerned about her budget. That's when she started to think "outside the box." Influenced by small houses she'd seen that were designed by a company called Tumbleweed Tiny House Company, Elizabeth determined she could build her own little house that would fit within the constraints of her housing budget and reduce her carbon footprint at the same time.

The house, which Elizabeth calls her Tiny House, measures 8 by 18 feet. It is constructed of wood that was certified by the Forest Stewardship Council, a guarantee that the wood came from a certified well-managed forest. She designed the house to be passively solar, so one side is loaded with windows. Some of the windows are recycled from other houses; others she bought because of their ability to prevent heat loss. Because the house is on a flat-bed trailer, "in the wintertime, the heavily windowed side can be turned toward the south," Turnbull explained. That will help to heat the house.

An insulation company that makes spray-in-place insulation donated the insulation for the Tiny House's construction to support Turnbull's project. The insulation is a soy-based product, made from the soybean oil left over from the production of cosmetics and foodstuffs, and contains no HFCs or CFCs. Insulation, in effect, cocoons the Tiny House; even the roof is insulated. While Turnbull had hoped to avoid using fossil fuel, she did install a small propane stove as a backup heat source in case she needs it on super-cold days.

The Tiny House is also outfitted with three solar panels that generate enough electricity to run her laptop, recharge her cell phone, and operate a couple of small appliances. The panels are fastened to a glorified sawhorse, which sits on the ground outside the house. This gives her the flexibility to turn them so that they can catch the most sunlight regardless of how the house is positioned now and on future sites.

Someday, when she owns her own land, Turnbull hopes to outfit her Tiny House with a composting toilet. Composting toilets use heat and bacteria to break down human waste until it essentially becomes a compost that can be used in most areas of a garden. Due to zoning laws, Turnbull won't be able to take that step while the house is located near Yale. But she has roughed in the area for her bathroom—3 feet by 3 feet, about the size of a boat's bathroom—in anticipation of the future. The same laws don't permit her to have running water at this time. The host site where the house is located lets her use their bathroom and water supply. Yale University supports Turnbull's mission, and the Tiny House is designated as a site for learning and demonstration, where it is open to the public in a site-appropriate way.

Although she's already made an environmental difference, Elizabeth Turnbull continues to look toward the future. She is already thinking about what her career choice might be after she finishes graduate school. "Every single business is dependent in a very fundamental way on natural resources. There are ways that businesses can improve their use of the environment, and I'm excited to explore that," she said. Her dream job will allow her to work with businesses in ways that will help them treat the environment and use Earth's natural resources wisely. And someday, if she should build a bigger house, Turnbull said, laughing, "It will definitely have a solar hot-water system. That's the biggest bang for your green dollar. It will be insulated very well, with a smart balance of insulation and ventilation. And I'll use a product like soy-based insulation, or maybe even a cotton insulation that's made of, believe it or not, blue jeans that have been shredded and processed into insulation bats. Last, I'll get really smart and use all low-E-value double-insulation windows." (A low-E value window is one that has been coated with a substance that reduces the amount of heat lost through the glass.) In the meantime, we'll have to wait to see what happens the next time Elizabeth Turnbull decides to "think outside the box." ✱

National Oceanic and Atmospheric Administration, and NASA, received the same kinds of alterations. In September 2002, the White House released the Environmental Protection Agency's annual report with the entire section dealing with climate change deleted. Apparently these kinds of changes had been occurring for many years. Where's the stimulus for innovation if you don't know a problem exists?

In 2007, the Intergovernmental Panel on Climate Change (IPCC) published its fourth report on global warming and climate change. (The others were published in 1990, 1995, and 2001.) The IPCC is not an industry or lobby group. A joint subsidiary body of the United Nations Environment Programme and the World Meteorological Organization, its membership includes scientists, other experts, and government representatives from more than 100 nations. Although the fossil-fuel industry itself is not directly represented, it gains an effective voice through the government appointees of fossil-fuel-dependent nations such as Middle Eastern states and the United States. The reports issued by the panel are written by consensus, so every party involved has a direct influence on the language used and the statements made. Because they present a consensus view, the panel's pronouncements, issued roughly every five years, carry weight with the media and governments.

The IPCC's 2007 report notes that warming of the climate is unequivocal. Scientific evidence from all continents and oceans supports this statement. Greenhouse gases have risen, and the net effect of human activities since the Industrial Revolution has contributed to the warming trend. If continued at the present rate or increased, greenhouse-gas production by human activity is, at the very least, likely to affect the global sea level, animals, and plants.

Are industries beginning to take notice? Some industries in the fossil-fuel sector are playing an active role in combating climate change by altering "business as usual." British Petroleum (BP) is now one of the world's largest producers of photovoltaic cells. BP has moved "beyond petroleum," as its advertisements proclaim, making a 20 percent cut in its own CO_2 emissions while earning a profit.

Even so, BP came under fire in 2007 and 2008 for the emissions at its refinery in Whiting, Indiana, located about fifteen miles southeast of Chicago. The plant had already been upgraded for emission controls. However, on July 13, 2008, the *Chicago Tribune* reported, "Even with those upgrades, the refinery is the fourth-largest source of industrial air pollution in the Chicago area, according to a *Tribune* review of federal records. The 333 tons of airborne chemicals and heavy metals released by the refinery in 2006, the last year for which figures are available, included several toxic byproducts of turning crude oil into gasoline, including benzene, ammonia and mercury." Residents and lawmakers in the area have expressed concern that the permit that allows the refinery's flares to burn "relies on fuzzy math that enables BP, one of the largest sources of air pollution in the region, to avoid deeper cuts required under the Clean Air Act."

What—or whom—to believe? The issue of global warming is complicated. You should learn all you can about it from books, newspapers, and the Internet (see the Call to Action at the end of this chapter for some suggested resources). Check the source from which any information comes, and question the evidence on which it is based. As members of Earth's global community, we all have a responsibility to understand this threat to our planet.

CALL TO ACTION

Read, Learn, Decide

The best way to help yourself decide what to believe is to seek sources that require rigorous scientific evidence to support the information they are providing. There are many magazines that are reputable in this regard. *Earth* (formerly titled *Geotimes*) is a publication of the American Geological Institute. You can find more information about it at **http://www.earthmagazine.com.** *Scientific American, National Geographic, Science News,* and *Popular Science* regularly feature articles about environmental and climate issues. Most public libraries have subscriptions to them, or they can be readily found at magazine stands and bookstores. Find out if your school subscribes to the science-related magazine *Science World,* published by Scholastic.

On the Internet, you can visit the RealClimate website at **http://www.realclimate.org.** At this website, working climate scientists comment on developing news stories and try to provide the scientific context for the stories that are being reported. The format is a comment/blog style.

Chapter 24
Engineering Solutions

By the 1980s, the problem of global warming loomed so large that industry and scientists began casting about for engineering solutions in order to change the carbon balance on a planetary scale. All would agree that we are facing a dire crisis that may require heroic actions to overcome. Yet initial attempts at some of the more ambitious proposals—such as "fertilizing" the ocean with iron filings to stimulate the growth of plankton, which captures CO_2, or pumping compressed CO_2 directly into the ocean depths—yielded disappointing results, making these solutions appear to be at best ineffectual and at worst dangerous to ocean life. With many programs still in the testing or theoretical stage, the most we can do is examine progress to date.

As the prospects of dumping CO_2 into the sea have dimmed, the coal industry has been developing procedures to pump it underground. The process, known as geosequestration, is simple in its approach: the industry would simply rebury the carbon that it had dug up. After all, oil and gas companies have been pumping CO_2 underground for years, with the Sleipner oil field in the North Sea the example most frequently cited. A large volume of CO_2 comes up with the other material as oil is extracted from the soil and rock, and the Norwegian government placed a heavy tax—$40 per ton—on those CO_2 emissions. To reduce the tax, the industry separates the CO_2 that comes up with oil, concentrates it, and pumps it back into the rocks. At a few other oil wells around the world (but not at Sleipner), the CO_2 is pumped back into the oil reserve, helping to maintain head pressure, which assists with the recovery of oil and gas, making the entire operation more profitable. Reputedly, "most" of the CO_2 stays underground. Applying this model to the coal industry, however, is not straightforward.

The problems for coal commence at the smokestack. The stream of CO_2 emitted there is relatively dilute, making CO_2 capture unrealistic. Because of this, the coal industry has staked its future on a new process known as coal gasification, in which water and oxygen are mixed with the coal to create carbon monoxide and hydrogen. The hydrogen is used as a fuel source, while the carbon monoxide is converted to a concentrated stream of CO_2. The plants that have this technology are not cheap to run: around one-quarter of the energy they produce is consumed just in keeping them operating. All indications suggest that building them on a commercial scale will be expensive and that it will take decades for them to make a significant contribution to power production.

There are other problems associated with the coal gasification procedure. Let's assume that some plants are built and their CO_2 emissions are captured. For every ton of anthracite burned, around four tons of CO_2 are generated. If the captured gas could be pumped back into the ground below the power station, it would not pose an issue. Unfortunately, coal-bearing rocks crack apart easily, and since the gas could leak out, the rocks are not useful for storing CO_2; that means the captured gas must be transported elsewhere. In the case of Australia's Hunter Valley coal mines, for example, it needs to be conveyed over Australia's Great Dividing Range and hundreds of miles to the west.

Once the CO_2 arrives at its destination, it must be compressed into a liquid so that it can be injected into the ground. This step typically consumes 20 percent of the energy yielded by burning coal in the first place. Then a hole about two-thirds of a mile (a kilometer) deep must be drilled and the liquid CO_2 injected into it. From that day on, the geological formation must be closely monitored; should the gas escape, it has the potential to kill. In the old days, miners called concentrated CO_2 "chokedamp," which is an appropriate name, for it instantaneously smothers its victims.

The largest recent disaster caused by CO_2 occurred in 1986 in Cameroon, Central Africa. A volcanic-crater lake known as Lake Nyos released volumes of the gas into the still night air. The gas settled around the lake's shore, where it killed nearly 1,800 people and countless thousands of animals, both wild and domesticated. Obviously no one is suggesting sequestering CO_2 in volcanic regions such as Lake Nyos, so the CO_2 dumps created by industry are unlikely to cause a similar disaster. Still, Earth's crust is not a purpose-built vessel for holding our CO_2 wastes, and the storage must last thousands of years, so the risk of a leak must be taken seriously. Currently the debate about where and whether these dumps should be established is held between government officials and industry behind closed doors. But these negotiations must be opened up to the people who live near such dumps, who, after all, must assume the risks involved and need to know who will bear the costs of any disaster that might occur.

If geosequestration were to be practiced on the scale needed to offset all the emissions from coal, the world would quickly run out of high-quality storage reservoirs near power stations. Moreover, there are enough other fossil-fuel reserves on planet Earth to create 5,000 billion tons of CO_2, a volume impossible to bury. All of this suggests that the best-case scenario for geosequestration is that it will play a small role (at most perhaps 10 percent by 2050) in the world's energy future.

There are other forms of sequestration that are vital for the future of the planet and carry no risk. Earth's vegetation and soils are reservoirs for huge volumes of carbon, and they are critical elements in the carbon cycle. So far, agriculture's role has largely been one of using up this resource, with the result that the world today is mostly deforested and its soils exhausted. But sustainable agricultural and animal husbandry practices can help preserve the soil's ability to hold carbon, because they increase the vegetable mold (which is mostly carbon) in the soil. Lots of carbon—around 1,200 gigatons—is currently stored this way. That's more than twice the amount that is stored in living vegetation, and increasing this storage seems both simple and desirable. A vast range of initiatives, from organic-market gardening to sustainable rangelands management, are beginning to be seen at the grassroots level worldwide. And a grassroots movement is one that you can participate in.

Some industries are pursuing means to store carbon in forests and long-lived forest products. This involves either planting forests or not cutting them down (so that carbon is not released). The Costa Rican government's program to save around 1.2 million acres of tropical rain forest from logging brought its carbon credits equivalent to the amount of CO_2 that would have entered the atmosphere if the forests had been disturbed.

Another example is BP's initiative to fund the planting of 62,000 acres of pine trees in western Australia to offset emissions from BP's refinery near the city of Perth.

Although forestry plantations are destined to be cut and used, they can be a good short-term store for carbon because the furniture and housing they produce are long-lived, and because the roots of the felled trees (along with their carbon) stay in the ground. But researchers question the potential of storing carbon in roots, where carbon turnover has proved to take much longer than once imagined, making sequestration by this means less efficient than thought.

But there is a more important concern about storing carbon from fossil fuels in forests or soil. The carbon in coal has been safely locked away for hundreds of millions of years and would remain so for millions more if we weren't digging it up for fuel. Yet carbon locked away in forests or the soil is unlikely to remain out of circulation for more than a few centuries.

It's clear that some of these engineering solutions to the carbon problem have proved to be neither as straightforward nor as cost effective as industry would like, and the obstacles are so many that an effective solution is unlikely before 2050. Yet scientists continue to work on the problem of safe, secure storage for carbon. Meanwhile, the competition from less carbon-dense fuels is looking simpler and cheaper by the day.

CALL TO ACTION

Bag That Bag!

How many plastic bags did your family use the last time you shopped at a grocery or department store? Americans throw away an estimated 100 billion plastic bags each year. Plastic bags are made of polyethylene, a material derived from petroleum—it takes about 12 million barrels of oil to make the number of bags we *throw away* each year. Not only are plastic bags produced from a nonrenewable energy source, but also their production creates greenhouse-gas emissions.

Unlike paper bags, plastic bags are not biodegradable. Instead, they photodegrade, or break down into smaller and smaller bits of plastic. It can take 1,000 years before they completely disappear. In the meantime, they pose a threat to wildlife, especially marine animals that mistake them for food. Plastic bags take up space in landfills and create unsightly litter. Start noticing how many plastic bags you see littering the roadsides. While some stores offer recycling bins to shoppers who wish to bring bags back, the fact is that less than 1 percent of plastic bags and wraps are recycled. But those that are recycled do make a difference: eleven barrels of oil are saved for every ton of plastic bags that are recycled or reused.

IKEA, a chain of home furnishing stores, has taken a strong environmental stand. In 2006, the IKEA stores in the United Kingdom started charging customers for each plastic bag. Consumption of bags dropped 95 percent.

In 2007, IKEA instituted a similar program in the United States. The five-cent charge collected for bags during the establishment of the program was donated to American Forests, a not-for-profit conservation organization that plants trees to offset carbon emissions.

Paper bags aren't much better. It takes four times more energy to make paper bags as it does to make plastic bags. When trees are cut, Earth loses a carbon absorber. When they are processed to make paper, greenhouse gases are produced. The only positive aspect of paper bags is that they are made from a renewable resource.

It's time to take action: At the very least, bring the plastic or paper bags back to the store and reuse them for new purchases. Better yet, use cloth or string bags that you bring with you to a store when you shop. They last a very long time and make a considerable environmental impact. Reusable bags are available in lots of places. Check on the Internet or in nearby stores. Each one has the potential to eliminate hundreds, maybe thousands, of plastic and paper bags.

Also, the store's cost to buy plastic bags is typically five cents a bag. Start a campaign to get your local stores to lower your bill by five cents for each reusable bag that you fill with new purchases. Some stores, such as Whole Foods Market, already offer customers a rebate of five to ten cents per bag when they bring their own bags.

Chapter 25

So What's the Story with Fuel?

The fossil-fuel industry's answer to climate change is to promote a gradual transition through an ever-diminishing reliance on carbon. Yesterday, the industry argument goes, the most widely used fossil fuel was coal, today it is oil, and tomorrow it will be methane, also called natural gas. Eventually, the argument continues, we will reach the best possible fuel of all, when the global economy makes the transition to hydrogen—a fuel that contains no carbon at all.

The transition from oil to gas is now well under way. But for many years the oil companies regarded natural gas as a volatile waste product. It was either burned off or pumped back underground to increase oil pressure at the well head, which would then pump oil out of the ground faster. Because gas contains more hydrogen than oil, it burns hotter and cleaner than oil and was thus always considered valuable, but we didn't have the technology to transport it safely and cheaply.

One of gas's drawbacks is that it has a low density, which makes it bulky and prone to leaking. It takes a house-size volume of gas to yield the same energy as a barrel of oil, so barrels of gas—and even tankers—were never an option for its transport Pipelines were the obvious solution, but suitable pipelines cost around a million dollars for each mile laid, so,until recently, the profit to be made on gas wasn't high enough.

But technological advances in handling gas, high oil prices, a looming lack of oil, and the demand for a cleaner fuel to replace coal have all combined to change the economics of gas, and today it is big business. The most important technical advance involved the refrigeration of gas so that it becomes a supercooled liquid. In this form it can be cheaply transported, in specially built ships, over large distances. With an international trade in shipping developed, and with the larger corporations willing to invest the billions of dollars required for gas pipelines, gas appears to be the fuel of choice for the twenty-first century.

Although gas is a more expensive fuel than coal, it has many benefits that make it ideal for producing electricity. Gas-fired power plants cost half as much to build as coal-fired models, and they can be built in a variety of sizes. Instead of having one massive, distant generator of electricity, as with coal, a series of small gas-fired generators can be dotted about, which saves money. They can be fired up and shut down quickly, which makes them ideal for complementing intermittent sources of energy generation such as wind and solar.

More than 90 percent of new power generation in the United States today is gas-fired, and around the world it is fast becoming the favored fuel. Despite this, gas is not without its problems, including safety issues and the possibility of terrorist attacks on large plants or pipelines. And because methane is a powerful greenhouse gas, its potential to leak must be addressed: parts of the gas infrastructure—such as the old iron pipes used for reticulating gas throughout cities—are decidedly leaky.

Unfortunately, even if all the coal-fired power stations on Earth were replaced with gas-fired ones, global carbon emissions would be cut by only 30 percent. So despite these savings, we would still face massive climate change. Given this scenario, the transition from gas to hydrogen—the argument continues—is imperative. But how likely is it? Hydrogen as the magical "fix" has its problems.

The power source of the hydrogen economy is the hydrogen fuel cell, which, put simply, takes in hydrogen and oxygen and puts out water and electricity. The first hydrogen fuel cell, known as a "gaseous voltaic battery," was built by Sir William Grove in the 1830s. His cell resembled a standard lead-acid battery in that it used sulfuric acid, but instead of lead, it used platinum to drive the reaction of hydrogen and oxygen that generates electricity. Use of this expensive material slowed the technology's development, but today there are several kinds of fuel cells that use cheaper materials. Whatever their composition, hydrogen fuel cells can be divided into two types: stationary cells used to produce electricity, and those used in transport.

The most promising hydrogen cells for the stationary production of electricity are known as *molten carbonate fuel cells.* They operate at a temperature of around 1,202°F (650°C) and, although highly efficient (having 50 percent efficiency at producing electricity), take a long time to reach working temperature. That wastes energy. They are also very large—a 250-kilowatt model is the size of a train car—making them unsuitable for use in motor vehicles.

What about hydrogen as a transport fuel? A number of car manufacturers, including Ford and BMW, are planning to introduce hydrogen-fueled, internal-combustion-engine cars to the marketplace. And the U.S. government plans to invest

$1.7 billion to build the hydrogen-powered FreedomCAR. At the moment, however, the use of hydrogen as a transport fuel is at a far more rudimentary stage of development than the technology using stationary cells.

The fuel-cell type best suited for transport purposes is known as a *proton-exchange membrane fuel cell*. This much smaller cell operates at around 150°F (65°C) and thus would be ready for action soon after turning the ignition. These cells, however, require very pure hydrogen. In current prototypes this is supplied from a built-in "reformer" that converts natural gas or gasoline to hydrogen, which again means that, from a climate perspective, we would be better off burning these fuels directly to drive the engine. The best energy efficiency obtained by proton-exchange membrane fuel cells is 35 to 40 percent—about the same as a standard internal combustion engine.

Vehicle manufacturers hope to do away with the onboard reformer required by the prototypes. They envision fueling the vehicles from hydrogen "pumps" at fueling stations. There are several ways that this could be done. One closely resembles the way gasoline is supplied now: the hydrogen would be produced at a remote central point (the way gasoline is produced today) and then delivered to fueling stations. It's here that the difficulties involved in moving hydrogen, which is a low-density fuel, become evident.

The ideal way to transport it is in tanker trucks carrying liquefied hydrogen, but because liquefaction occurs at −423°F (−253°C), refrigerating the gas sufficiently to achieve this is an economic nightmare. Using hydrogen energy to liquefy a gallon of hydrogen consumes 40 percent of the value of the fuel. Using the U.S. power grid to do so takes 12 to 15 kilowatt-hours of electricity, and this would release almost 22 pounds of CO_2 into the atmosphere. Around a gallon of gasoline holds the equivalent energy of a kilogram of hydrogen. Burning it releases around the same amount of CO_2 as using the grid to liquefy the hydrogen, so the climate-change consequences of transporting and using liquefied hydrogen are as bad as driving a standard car.

One solution may be to pressurize the hydrogen only partially, which reduces the fuel value consumed to 15 percent, and the canisters used for transport can be less specialized. But even using improved, high-pressure canisters, a 40-ton truck could deliver only 100 gallons of compressed hydrogen, meaning that it would take fifteen such trucks to deliver the same fuel-energy value as is now delivered by a 26-ton gasoline tanker. And if these 40-ton trucks carried the hydrogen 300 miles, the energy cost of the transport would consume around 40 percent of the fuel carried.

Pipelines are another option for transporting hydrogen, but as with gas, they are expensive—they must be large and built from materials resistant to hydrogen, which makes some materials, steel, for example, become very brittle. The pipeline segments must be well connected, because hydrogen leaks so easily. Even if the preexisting gas-pipeline network could be reconfigured to transport hydrogen, the cost of providing a network running from central producing units to the world's fueling stations would be astronomical.

Perhaps hydrogen could be produced from natural gas at the fueling station. This would do away with the difficulties of transporting it. However, the processes used to convert natural gas to hydrogen fuel would produce 50 percent more CO_2 than using the gas to fuel the vehicle in the first place. Hydrogen could also theoretically be generated at home using power from the electricity grid. But the price of electricity for domestic use, and the high cost of hydrogen generation and purification units, would make it prohibitively expensive. Furthermore, the electricity in the grid in places such as the United States is largely derived from burning fossil fuels, so home generation of hydrogen under current circumstances would result in a massive increase in CO_2 emissions.

And there is another danger with home-brewing hydrogen. The gas is odorless, leak prone, and highly combustible, and it burns with an invisible flame. Certain things we do, such as making a call on a cell phone or sliding across the seat in a car, generate small charges of electricity, and thunderstorms generate much larger amounts of electricity. Could an electrical spark generated by any of these situations cause the fuel tank to ignite?

Even if hydrogen is made safe to use, we are still left with a colossal CO_2 pollution issue, which was exactly the opposite of what we set out to do. The only way that the hydrogen economy can help combat climate change is if the electricity grid is powered entirely from carbon-free sources. And this means acceptance of and investment in a series of technologies ranging from solar to nuclear.

CALL TO ACTION

Time to Hang Out

How many loads of laundry does your family wash in a week? Three, four, more? And how do you dry the clothes? Most people don't even think about it: they just toss the wet clothes into a clothes dryer, then use fossil fuels, either gas or electricity, to dry them, both of which add CO_2 emissions to the atmosphere.

Years ago, people hung their clothes out to dry on a clothesline. It's time to hang out again and let the sun and the wind dry your laundry! If you live in a housing subdivision where outdoor lines are banned for aesthetic reasons, start lobbying to get that changed. Or maybe ask for the ban to be lifted on a certain day or days during the week. Another option is to string a clothesline in the basement or some other convenient spot inside. Many discount stores sell wooden clothes-drying racks that are collapsible for storage in a closet or behind a door when they're not in use. By choosing these alternatives, you'll be helping the environment and saving money too!

Chapter 26

Soar with the Wind— Bask in the Sun

Transportation and supplying electricity to homes and busi-nesses are the biggest culprits when it comes to carbon emissions. We must address both issues if we are to make signif-icant reductions in greenhouse gases and bring climate change caused by human activity under control. Decarbonizing the power grid—the means by which fossil fuels currently supply energy to our homes—is crucial, because if we can do that, we can use the renewable power thus generated to decarbonize transportation.

Researchers Steven Pacala and Robert Socolow from Prince-ton University investigated whether we could make deep cuts in CO_2 emissions while still providing a large-scale, reliable electricity network similar to what we now enjoy. They identi-fied fifteen basic kinds of technologies, ranging from sequestra-tion to wind, solar, and nuclear power, that could play a vital role in the next fifty years. It certainly seems apparent that we have sufficient technologies. Indeed, many governments and corporations around the world have slashed emissions (by more than 70 percent in the case of some British local governments) while at the same time experiencing strong economic growth— one of the major concerns often cited when discussing carbon emission reductions. In other words, it can be done without losing money.

The technologies fall into two groups: those that supply power intermittently and those that provide a continuous output of power. Of all the sources of intermittent power, wind is the most mature and economically competitive, and Denmark is an energy role model when it comes to the modern wind industry.

The Danes decided to back wind-powered electricity at a time when its cost was many times greater than electricity powered by fossil fuels. The Danish government, however, saw wind's potential and supported the industry until costs came down. Today Denmark leads the world in both wind-power production and the building of wind turbines. One interesting aspect of Denmark's wind-energy industry is that the power literally lies in the hands of the people: individuals and wind cooperatives own about 85 percent of the business.

In several countries wind power is already cheaper than electricity generated from fossil fuel, which helps account for the industry's phenomenal growth rate of 22 percent per year. It has been estimated that wind power could provide 20 percent of the energy needs of the United States. Over the next few years the unit price of wind energy is expected to drop a further 20 to 30 percent, which will make it even more cost effective.

Naysayers point out that wind power is unreliable, because the wind doesn't always blow. But while it's true that wind does not blow at the same location with consistent strength, if you take a regional approach, it is fairly certain that the wind will be blowing somewhere. Thus, the more widely dispersed wind turbines are, the more they come to resemble the old standby providers like coal. There is a fair amount of redundancy in wind power: sometimes several turbines are idle for each one working at capacity, and this is often pointed to by wind-power skeptics as a major disadvantage. In the United Kingdom, for example, the average wind turbine generates power at only 28 percent of its capacity over the course of a year. But all forms of power generation have some degree of redundancy. In the UK, nuclear power works at around 76 percent, gas turbines at 60 percent, and coal at 50 percent of capacity. And wind's high redundancy is somewhat offset by its high reliability: wind turbines break down less frequently and are cheaper to maintain than coal-fired power plants.

Wind power, unfortunately, has been beset with bad press, including allegations that wind turbines kill birds and are noisy and unsightly. The truth is, any tall structure represents a potential hazard to birds, and early wind towers did increase that risk. They had a latticework design that enabled birds to nest in them, but that design has now been replaced by smooth-sided models. Another issue arose when certain wind farms were built in areas along migratory flight paths. Greater care in site location has been taken to avoid this problem. Moreover, all risks need to be measured against one another. Cats kill far more birds in the United States than do wind farms. That said, another wildlife-mortality issue has recently been raised: bats are flying into the turbines. Scientists are trying to figure out why this happens. It's possible that bats confuse the rotating rotors with flying insects. Perhaps the turbine muddles a bat's sonar system. Clearly, the issue needs further investigation. On the other hand, if we continue to burn coal, how many birds and bats will die as a consequence of climate change? As to noise pollution, you can have a conversation at the base of a tower without having to raise your voice, and the newest models reduce the sound even further. Wind turbines can be placed on property that can also be used for other purposes. In Illinois, for example, turbines are placed among fields where corn and soybeans are growing. They can be placed offshore in the water. In terms of their alleged unsightliness, beauty is surely in the eye of the beholder. Which is more unsightly—the spinning blades of a windmill, a barren land surface stripped by coal mining, or the massive structure of a power plant? Which one has the least impact on the area where it is located?

Another crucial alternative to the use of fossil fuels is solar energy. The sun's power is limitless, and three technologies directly exploit this power. These are solar hot-water systems, solar thermal devices, and photovoltaic cells. Solar hot water is the simplest and, in many circumstances, the most cost-effective method of using the sun's power for household purposes, making it the best way to achieve large, easy savings in most household power bills. Solar hot-water systems rest on a south-facing (in the Southern Hemisphere, north-facing) roof and trap the sun's rays, which are then used to heat water. They require no maintenance, and to ensure that hot water is available whenever you need it, they include a gas- or electric-heat booster.

Solar thermal power stations, also called concentrating solar power (CSP) plants, produce large amounts of electricity—far more than one household could ever use—and they work by concentrating the sun's rays onto small, highly efficient solar collectors. Their name comes from the fact that they produce both electricity and heat. There are many designs in the marketplace at present, and they are rapidly becoming more affordable. In the future, solar thermal power plants can be expected to compete with wind for a slice of the power grid. In fact, since June 2007, the CSP plant Nevada Solar One, located 40 miles (64 kilometers) from Las Vegas, has been producing enough energy to provide power for 14,000 households annually. Nevada Solar One is the first CSP plant built in the United States in seventeen years and the third largest CSP in the world. And the plant's CO_2 emissions are near zero. What's more, solar and wind energies make perfect partners, because if the wind isn't blowing, there's a good chance that the sun will be shining.

Finally, there is the technology that most people recognize as true "solar" power—photovoltaic cells. Once you've bought your own equipment, generating your own electricity with photovoltaics frees you from dependence on large power companies. It is also simple and maintenance free.

There are several types of photovoltaic cells, but all use the sunlight that falls on them to generate electricity. The electricity is then transformed into an alternating current of the correct voltage for your area using an inverter. If you are on the grid, all you need are these two items and a power socket, and you can generate power. The average home requires around 1.4 kilowatts (1,400 watts) of power to run, and the average size of photovoltaic panels is 80 or 160 watts. Ten of the larger size should do the job.

Photovoltaics operate best in summer, when extra power for air-conditioning is needed. In some places, the owner of a photovoltaic system can actually make money during the summer: In Japan, for example, you can sell excess power to the grid for as much as $50 per month. Similar plans exist in fifteen other countries. The cost of photovoltaics is falling so rapidly that electricity generated by this means is expected to be cost effective as early as 2010. While the installation of photo-voltaics requires an up-front cash outlay that may seem large, once the system is installed, your electric energy is free from that point on.

There are, of course, many kinds of power generation not discussed here, including solar chimneys and tidal and wave power, and in certain locations all of these options are now, or soon will be, producing renewable power. In fact, hydropower, a non-fossil-fuel-burning, renewable way to make electricity, already generates close to 9 percent of the United States' electricity. While hydropower is carbon free, it is not without drawbacks. Usually it's necessary to build large dams to hold back a river. Periodically releasing water from behind the dam creates the water-flow velocity needed to generate electricity. However, fluctuations in the water level behind a dam affect ecosystems and their organisms. They must adapt to the changes or move elsewhere.

Renewable energy sources that best suit the areas where we live are viable choices for cutting our carbon emissions. By choosing these options, we can put ourselves well on the path toward reducing CO_2 emissions by 70 percent by 2050, the goal recommended by the IPCC in its 2007 report.

CALL TO ACTION

A Tip from Down Under

One Hour . . . One World . . . Together

On March 31, 2007, the city of Sydney, Australia, held its first-ever Earth Hour. In an effort to reduce the impact of carbon emissions generated by the use of electricity, many of Sydney's residents and businesses voluntarily turned off their electric lights from 7:30 to 8:30 p.m. For that hour, people relaxed over candlelit suppers or by chatting outdoors with family and friends. And the night sky was dazzling! You'd be surprised how many more stars you can see when the glare from electric lights is dimmed. The idea caught on: In 2008, Earth Hour went global and fifty million people worldwide participated. In 2009, 88 countries and 4,000 cities joined in the fun. People in Toronto, Canada, lowered their electric consumption by about 15 percent during the hour; the residents of Christchurch, New Zealand, lowered theirs by 13 percent.

This type of event is free and easy to organize. How about starting a grassroots campaign for an Earth Hour in your town? Participate in sixty minutes of action in Earth's behalf. See the Earth Hour website at **http://www. earthhour.org/home/** for more information.

Chapter 27
What about Nuclear?

We are living in a time when our demand for energy just keeps getting bigger. In the 1970s, nuclear power was often considered the energy of the future. Nuclear power plants were constructed and began generating electricity. But after witnessing two nuclear disasters, maintenance concerns that cropped up at several reactors, and the inherent risks involved in handling nuclear materials, many people became leery about its use. In light of climate change, however, the role of nuclear power is being reassessed, and what was until recently a dying technology may yet make a comeback.

All power grids need reliable "base load" generation—the minimum amount of electricity needed on hand to maintain the grid. Some people question whether renewable technologies, such as wind and solar power, have the capacity to provide a reliable base load. But nuclear power already provides 18 percent of the world's electricity, with no CO_2 emissions. France supplies nearly 80 percent of its power from nuclear sources, while Sweden provides half, and the United Kingdom one quarter. Nuclear reactors generate about 20 percent of the electricity used in the United States.

A nuclear power plant creates electricity by using nuclear fission, a process in which atoms split, thereby giving off heat, inside a reactor. The heat is used to boil water, forming steam, which is then used to turn turbine blades that generate electricity when they spin.

As with coal, nuclear power stations are very large—around 1,700 megawatts—and with a starting price of around $2 billion apiece, they are expensive to build. Because they are large and many factors relating to safety must be considered, the permitting process for a nuclear power station can take up to a decade, with construction taking around five years. With a fifteen-year period before any power is generated, nuclear energy is no immediate fix to the carbon-emission problem. In addition, people who supply money to build power plants don't find nuclear plants particularly appealing for that very reason: it takes too long for them to make any money on the project. These issues explain in part why no new nuclear reactors have been built for twenty years in either the United States or the United Kingdom. According to the Energy Information Administration, as of 2005 the United States had 104 commercially operating nuclear power plants. No new commercial reactor has become operational in the United States since May 1996, and no U.S. commercial builder has applied for a construction permit to build a new plant.

The other major obstacle is safety concerns. Three factors loom large in the public mind whenever nuclear power is mentioned—accidents, disposal of waste, and bombs. The 1986 Chernobyl disaster in Ukraine was a catastrophe of stupendous proportions whose consequences, two decades after the accident, just keep growing. Some 7 percent (3.3 million people) of the Ukrainian population have suffered illness as a result of the meltdown. In neighboring Belarus, which received 70 percent of the fallout, the situation is even worse. Only 1 percent of the country is *free* from contamination, with 25 percent of its farmland having had to be put permanently out of production.

In the United States and Europe, safer reactor types predominate, but as the 1979 core meltdown at Three Mile Island, Pennsylvania, showed, no one is immune to accident, or to sabotage. With several nuclear reactors in the United States located near large cities, there are real concerns for a possible terrorist attack.

Managing radioactive waste is another concern. The nuclear industry in the United States has long looked to the proposed high-level radioactive waste dump at Yucca Mountain, Nevada, as a solution. But the waste stream has now reached such proportions that even if Yucca Mountain were opened tomorrow (estimates indicate that the earliest opening date is likely to be 2020), it would be filled at once and another dump would be needed. In reality, the plan to use Yucca Mountain as a waste dump may be eliminated. In 2009, President Obama announced that his administration is seeking another solution for nuclear waste disposal, one that does not include storing it beneath Yucca Mountain. And the problem of what to do with old and obsolete nuclear power plants is almost as intractable. The United States' 104 nuclear plants were originally licensed to operate for thirty years but are now slated to grind on for double that time. No reactor has ever yet been successfully dismantled, perhaps because the cost is estimated to be around $500 million a pop.

The majority of new nuclear power plants are being built in the developing world. China will commission two new nuclear power stations per year for the next twenty years. From a global perspective this is highly desirable, because 80 percent of China's power now comes from coal. India, Russia, Japan, and Canada also have reactors under construction, while approvals are in place for thirty-seven more in Brazil, Iran, India, Pakistan, South Korea, Finland, and Japan. Providing the uranium necessary to fuel these reactors will be a challenge, as world uranium reserves are not large. At the moment, around a quarter of the world's demand is being met by reprocessing nuclear weapons; this raises the issue of such weapons getting into the wrong hands. Anyone who possesses enriched uranium has the potential to create a bomb, and as reactors proliferate, there is an increasing likelihood that nuclear weapons will be available to those who want them.

The nuclear industry hopes that technological developments will lead to foolproof reactor types that produce electricity at a cost equivalent to coal. New reactor types include pebble bed reactors. The "pebbles" in these reactors are not stones. They are made of a material called pyrolytic carbon, which is similar to the form of carbon called graphite. The billiard-ball-size pebbles contain flecks of uranium. Each pebble acts like a tiny reactor and drives the nuclear fission. An inert gas—helium, for example—flows around the pebbles as a coolant. Conventional reactors are cooled by water that flows inside pipes. Since pebble bed reactors don't require complex piping schemes, they can be built on a smaller scale than conventional plants. Also, the melting point of the pebbles is higher than the hottest temperature generated by the reactor, so a meltdown, like the one that occurred in Chernobyl, can't happen. The elimination of brittle pipes and a lower level of radioactivity in the coolant seems to indicate that pebble bed reactors may be safer than conventional plants. Indeed, China already has a pebble bed reactor under construction and the two per year it plans to build until 2020 will be pebble bed types.

What role might nuclear power play in averting the climate-change disaster? China and India are likely to pursue the nuclear option with vigor, as there is currently no inexpensive, large-scale alternative available to them. In the developed world, though, any major expansion of nuclear power will depend upon the viability of new, safer reactor types.

There is one other option for the continuous production of power. Geothermal energy uses Earth's heat to generate power. In general, for every 328 feet (100 meters) of depth, the temperature of the rock beneath Earth's surface rises about 5.4°F (3°C). By the time you drill 10,000 feet down, the temperature is hot enough to boil water, which may then be pumped into turbines that generate electricity. In areas where there is volcanic activity, the rock temperature rises even faster. Geothermal power plants in many of the contiguous western United States plus Alaska and Hawaii are producing electricity for many homes and businesses. Geothermal energy can be used in greenhouses, for aquaculture (fish farms), to supply heat for homes and businesses as well as pools and spas, and to generate electricity in power plants. Power plants at the Geysers geothermal field near Santa Rosa, California, have been supplying electricity to towns, including San Francisco, since the 1960s. However, despite the considerable amount of heat lying between our feet and our planet's molten mantle, geothermal technologies provide a mere 10,000 megawatts of power worldwide.

This may soon change, because we are discovering new sources of geothermal heat around the globe. Previously, geothermal power has come exclusively from volcanic regions. But in Basel, Switzerland, and in the deserts of South Australia, companies have found commercially usable heat in the form of "hot dry rock" geothermal sources in places previously not considered for geothermal energy. In both places, engineers drilled beneath the surface—in the case of Australia, almost 2.5 miles (4 kilometers) deep—into a large body of a crystalline igneous rock called granite. In Australia the temperature inside the granite was found to be around 482°F (250°C)—the hottest near-surface, nonvolcanic rock ever discovered.

The granite's heat, created by its natural radioactivity, had been kept in place by layers of sediment. What really excited the Australian geologists was that the granite was in a region not where the Earth's crust was being torn apart, but where it was being compressed. This led to horizontal rather than vertical fracturing of the rock. The horizontal fracturing meant that water that was pumped into the rock could be recycled, because it didn't sink farther down inside the Earth.

This one rock body in South Australia is estimated to contain enough heat to supply all of Australia's power needs for seventy-five years, at a cost equivalent to that of brown coal, without the CO_2 emissions. So vast is the resource that distance to market is no object, because power can be pumped down the power line in such volume as to overcome any transmission losses.

In Australia, trial wells have been up and running, but technical difficulties, such as a blockage in one of the wells, have caused some temporary setbacks. Nonetheless the Cooper Basin project expects to be operational in 2009 and able to generate 500 megawatts of power by 2015. The energy project in Switzerland has also run into a snag. Engineers began injecting water into the rock in the beginning of December 2006. On December 8 and 9, a series of small earthquakes shook the area and caused minor damage to some buildings. Drilling work has been stopped pending investigation and analysis of the situation. Australian geologists report that the area where they are working has a much lower risk of earthquake activity. While hot dry rock geothermal energy may have an exciting future, clearly there are concerns that must be addressed before it can be widely used.

The power technologies we have discussed place humanity at a great crossroads. Trillions of dollars will need to be invested to make the transition to a carbon-free economy, and once a certain path of investment is embarked upon, it will gather such momentum that it will be difficult to change direction. In the hydrogen and nuclear economies, the production and distribution of energy is likely to be centralized, which would mean that energy ownership lies in the hands of big corporations. Pursuing wind and solar technologies, on the other hand, opens the possibility that people can generate most of their own power, transportation fuel, and even water (by condensing it from the air). In other words, energy would be generated by the individuals who are using it—you and your family, neighbors, and friends.

CALL TO ACTION

The Virgin Earth Challenge: $25 Million Prize

The challenge: Submit a commercially viable design to achieve the net removal of significant volumes of anthropogenic atmospheric greenhouse gases each year for at least ten years without countervailing harmful effects. The removal must have long-term benefits (over, say, 1,000 years) and must contribute materially to the stability of the Earth's climate.

The individual or group producing a design that best fulfills this challenge will win a $25-million-dollar prize.

The prize is sponsored by Sir Richard Branson, a British entrepreneur whose business ventures, many of which operate under the Virgin name, include various entertainment/recording companies, airlines, Virgin Galactic (a company that ultimately hopes to offer space flights to the public), and his new venture, Virgin Fuel—a company seeking to produce an alternative, clean fuel that would be used in cars, trucks, trains, and possibly jet airplanes.

The projects submitted for consideration will be judged by a panel of five experts highly respected for their knowledge on global warming and climate change. To read more about the Virgin Earth Challenge, see **http://www.virginearth.com**. The closing date for entries is February 8, 2010.

Chapter 28
Hybrids, MiniCATS, and Contrails

Wind, solar, and nuclear power are several ways we can decarbonize the power grid. But transportation is responsible for a large percentage of our CO_2 emissions. And the Annual Energy Outlook 2008, published by the U.S. Energy Information Administration, predicts that all forms of transportation used for travel will continue to increase until 2030 (the final year for the report's predictions). What can we do to decarbonize our transportation systems?

Among nations pursuing renewable energy sources for transportation, the Brazilians have the lead. Their domestic vehicle fleet runs largely on ethanol derived from sugar cane—which grows very well in Brazil. Ethanol is a clear, colorless, flammable liquid produced when the sugars in agricultural crops or the cellulosic residues from wood chips or switchgrass are fermented. In the United States, ethanol is largely derived from corn. But the amount of fossil fuel needed to grow the crop means that the use of corn-derived ethanol in transportation provides little in the way of carbon savings—only about 25 percent more energy than growing the corn required. Switchgrass, a native perennial grass that can be grown in most states, is a highly efficient source of ethanol. Raising this fast-growing grass requires less fossil-fuel input than raising corn, and it yields three to five times as many gallons of ethanol per acre as corn. Burning cellulosic ethanol also generates less CO_2 than burning ethanol derived from corn. Unfortunately, producing cellulosic ethanol with today's technologies is too costly for general use. But it's encouraging to know that this is likely to change within the next ten years. Whether we could grow a sufficient quantity of crops to supply all our ethanol fuel needs is another consideration. The crops would have to make up 20 percent of all productivity on land to power the world's cars, ships, and aircraft. Humans are already consuming more of the planet's resources than is sustainable, so providing this extra biological productivity will be hard indeed.

A final concern with ethanol fuels is that they have to be delivered to fueling stations in trucks, the way gasoline is delivered. Trucks, of course, add CO_2 emissions.

Despite such problems, technological advances in manufacturing vehicles are so rapid that ways forward can be glimpsed. While some U.S. automakers were focusing on hydrogen fuel-cell cars (Ford, for example, has the Edge HySeries hydrogen hybrid, which at this point is only a concept car that costs $2 million to manufacture), Japanese carmakers Toyota and Honda brought a revolutionary new technology to market that halves fuel consumption and has opened the way to astonishing future developments. Known as hybrid-fuel vehicles, these automobiles pair a gasoline-driven engine with an electric motor.

The first thing you notice when traveling in a Toyota Prius is silence. There is no roaring or hum of an idling engine. Instead, when slowing down or stopped in traffic, the 1.6-quart (1.5-liter) gas engine shuts down. It doesn't start operating again until speed has been built up. While the gas engine is off, the silent electric motor takes over. This motor is partly powered by energy generated from braking—energy wasted in an ordinary vehicle. The Prius can travel almost 600 miles before it needs a gasoline refill, and it cuts CO_2 emissions by 70 percent, the amount scientists say is required of the world economy by 2050 in order to stabilize climate change. If we want to make a real impact on global warming, we shouldn't wait for hydrogen— we should all buy hybrids.

After the Prius's success, several other automakers have followed Toyota's lead: Honda, Saturn, Ford, Chrysler, General Motors, and Lexus all offer hybrid cars. The gas mileage of hybrid cars ranges from 25 to 61 miles per gallon in city driving and 27 to 68 miles per gallon on the highway, depending on the model. Hybrid SUVs have the lower-end mileage rates.

If the grid were to be decarbonized, many other transportation options would become attractive. Outside the United States, electric cars have been on the market for years; France already has a fleet of 10,000 such vehicles. In 2008, General Motors unveiled its electric car called Chevrolet Volt. The Volt is a plug-in hybrid that uses electricity—not gasoline—during the first 40 miles of daily travel. After that, the engine uses gasoline to create more electricity to drive the car about 300 miles. The Volt is expected to go on sale in 2010.

But even more exciting technologies are under development: the possibility of fueling cars with air! In France, experimental cars called the MiniCAT and the CitiCAT (seating three and six people, respectively) run on compressed air. CAT stands for "compressed air technology." A three-minute puff of air from a commercial compressor fills the storage tank inside the car, and the compressed air is then injected into a small chamber within the engine. The compressed air expands as it enters the chamber, pushing down the engine's pistons, which cause the crankshaft to turn and thus power the car. With a top speed of 75 miles per hour, the cars aren't sluggish and can travel about 200 miles at 30 miles per hour. The cost of refueling: $2.50.

Electricity is used to generate the compressed air, so while the car has zero gas emissions, its production is not completely carbon free. But imagine what the CitiCAT might mean for a family living in Denmark. They may well own a share in a wind generator that powers their home and could also be used to compress air for their car's fuel. This family's energy consumption would be both climate friendly and self-reliant.

One of the foulest pollutants on Earth is the fuel oil that powers shipping. Over the past few years, the volume of international shipping has grown by 50 percent, meaning that cargo ships have become a leading source of air pollution. The matter that powers these vessels is the leftovers from the production of other fuels. It is so thick and full of contaminants that it must be heated before it will even flow through a ship's pipes.

Satellite surveillance reveals that many of the world's shipping lanes are blanketed in semipermanent clouds that result from the particulate emissions from ships' smokestacks. Solving this problem is potentially easy through modern solar and wind technologies. Combining these renewable energy sources with energy-efficient engines could make shipping cargo by sea a carbon-free venture.

Air travel requires large amounts of high-density fuel of a type that, given today's technology, can only be provided by fossil fuels, and it is increasing in volume every year. In 1992 air travel was the source of 2 percent of CO_2 emissions. In the

United States, where air traffic already accounts for 10 percent of fuel use, the number of passengers transported is expected to double between 1997 and 2017, making air transport the fastest-growing source of CO_2 and nitrous oxide emissions in the country.

The cocktail of chemicals that constitute aircraft emissions works in somewhat opposite ways. Because most modern jets cruise near the troposphere, the water vapor, nitrous oxide, and sulfur dioxides they emit have particular impacts. The nitrous oxide emitted by aircraft may enhance ozone in the troposphere and lower stratosphere yet deplete it further in the upper stratosphere; sulfur dioxide has a cooling effect.

But what is becoming a surprisingly important emission is water vapor from jets, which you can see as aircraft contrails. Under certain conditions contrails give rise to cirrus clouds. These clouds cover around 30 percent of the planet, to which aircraft may be contributing as much as 1 percent. As we saw in chapter 16, this may have a significant impact on climate by masking the impacts of warming caused by CO_2.

Transportation accounts for around a third of global CO_2 emissions. Land and sea transport can easily be powered in ways that emit less, with technologies that either already exist or are on the horizon. Air transport, however, is fast growing and not likely to be fueled by anything but fossil fuels. Since jet contrails contribute to global dimming, it may be just as well that the jets keep flying long after wind- and solar-powered ships and compressed-air cars transform surface transport.

CALL TO ACTION

Your First Set of Wheels

If you wish to make a real contribution to combating climate change, don't hurry out to buy your "first set of wheels" as soon as you get your driver's license. Keep saving your money and think about buying a hybrid-fuel car. Or encourage your parents to do so the next time they replace the family car. Help Earth and your wallet by choosing wisely—even if it means waiting a few more months before buying the car. Remember while making your choice that each gallon of gasoline your car burns releases 20 pounds of CO_2, and cars are responsible for 25 percent of the greenhouses gases produced in the United States. According to the U.S. Energy Information Administration, 390 million gallons of gasoline were used for transportation every day in 2007. Here are some smart guidelines when buying a car:

- Although hybrids are the best environmental choice, they are expensive. Try to look into buying a used hybrid. It may be hard to find, but it's worth a shot.
- Buy the smallest car that you feel you can safely drive. Smaller cars usually get better gas mileage (a four-cylinder engine gets better mileage than a six- or eight-cylinder one), and cars with manual transmissions get better mileage than those with automatic transmissions.
- Visit the U.S. Department of Energy website at **http://www.fueleconomy.gov** for an up-to-date analysis of the fuel-efficiency ratings of a wide variety of cars.

Chapter 29

We Took Action

Good citizens and smart consumers can control their carbon impact on Earth's environment. The Calls to Action throughout this book will get you started on your personal carbon-emission-reduction program and will make a difference. Even something as easy as switching to a fluorescent bulb makes a difference. You can, in a few months rather than the fifty years allowed by some governments, make inroads toward attaining the 70 percent reduction in greenhouse-gas emissions necessary to stabilize our effect on Earth's climate. You won't be alone in making changes. In fact, many people and organizations have already done so.

ALASKA YOUTH FOR ENVIRONMENTAL ACTION

In 1998, six teenagers in Alaska founded Alaska Youth for Environmental Action (AYEA), an organization sponsored by the National Wildlife Federation and committed to educating other young people about  environmental issues affecting the community on both state and local levels. Today AYEA has more than 1,200 participants who are *very* involved.

In 2006, AYEA's members collected 5,000 signatures from teens across Alaska on a petition urging their U.S. representatives to take action on global warming. AYEA then went to Washington, D.C., to present the petition to Alaska's Senator Lisa Murkowski. The project was selected by the U.S. Environmental Protection Agency as the region's winner of the President's Environmental Youth Awards, an annual competition among youth organizations to promote environmental awareness.

Not content to rest on its laurels, AYEA began a new project in 2007: the 3-2-1 Efficiency! Pledge, a simple and effective plan to reduce a person's carbon footprint. The plan was simple: those pledging agreed to replace three incandescent bulbs with compact fluorescents, to lower their home's thermostat by two degrees in the winter, and to unplug one household appliance when it wasn't in use.

High-school student Wiley Cason has served as a publicity intern at AYEA and has been an active member of the organization since eighth grade. "I started hearing about global warming and met people who were passionate about the subject. They converted me to trying to take action," he recalled. Cason was present at the inception of the 3-2-1 Efficiency! Pledge. "We were at the AYEA summer get-together, and someone mentioned they had participated in a 3-2-1 pledge-type campaign at a church. We took the idea and, as a group, modified it for our purposes," Cason explained.

During the course of the pledge campaign, Cason and other AYEA members brought compact fluorescent bulbs to the doorsteps of families in Alaska, explaining the environmental impact each bulb can have. "We're trying to expand the statewide support and the statewide effort on climate change. We want to bring the message of AYEA and the effects of 3-2-1 to other youth who might not have been exposed to it," he said. He called the public's support of the initiative encouraging. "A lot of people want to do something. They realize there is a problem — they've read about it in the newspaper — but they don't know what to do. They felt a sense of completion after taking the pledge, that they'd actually done something." And they had. By the end of the 3-2-1 campaign, more than 3,500 individuals had pledged.

Alaska is on the frontline of global warming and climate change. Cason, who lives in Anchorage, noted, "Up north, where they're on top of permafrost and where ice packs surround the coast all the time, they're really feeling climate change. There has been increased snowmelt."

Many members of AYEA have personally witnessed evidence of global warming. In 2005, AYEA teens did an exercise in which they listed all the impacts they had seen in their communities. Polly Carr, the former branch manager of AYEA, concluded, "The list is long." Some of the impacts included spotting a great white shark off the coast of Yakutat Bay, changing migration patterns of snow geese and caribou that are making hunting more difficult, increasing numbers of salmon on the Yukon River infected with "ick" (a disease that makes their meat inedible), higher water levels, and the sinking of three homes in one youth's village due to coastal erosion in Norton Sound. "The graveyard in her community actually was flooded, and some coffins went tumbling down the beach," Carr said.

AYEA members are involved with recycling programs, letter-writing campaigns, and educational programs. Carr added, "3-2-1 is just the beginning of youth-led solutions to major problems. As AYEA moves into the future, we will be exploring the use of media and art to help teens tell their stories about climate change and other issues. . . . We will be implementing additional projects to involve youth from diverse backgrounds with environmental health and youth empowerment."

For more information about AYEA and lots of good ideas on getting involved in environmental issues, check out their website at http://www.ayea.org. ■

PORTSMOUTH ABBEY SCHOOL

Portsmouth Abbey School in Rhode Island is a boarding school for students in grades nine through twelve. It was founded in 1926 by the English Benedictine Congregation, and a Benedictine monastery is one of the buildings on the campus. With the support of the monastery, the school has gone green in a big way: in 2006, it installed a 660-kilowatt wind turbine that supplies nearly 40 percent of the school's electricity.

With its 500-acre campus sitting on a ridge overlooking Narragansett Bay, the school was a perfect candidate for a wind turbine. "People had been suggesting [wind power], but we had been nervous to try it," stated Brother Joseph, a member of the Abbey's faculty and the school's wind-turbine expert.

Aware that the large turbine would dominate the skyline, Brother Joseph undertook a door-to-door neighborhood campaign to inform people about the wind turbine and to listen to their concerns about its installation and operation. The school also held two community information meetings. "The neighbors were overwhelmingly for it," added Brother Joseph.

Because the school uses about 2.6 million kilowatt-hours per year, they chose a Vestas 660 kW turbine, a tried-and-true workhorse capable of generating more than enough electricity to supply the school. The turbine is securely anchored to a concrete foundation that is 30 feet deep. The turbine's tower stands 164 feet tall; three 77-foot-long blades rotate around its top. The electricity generated is transferred via underground cables to the school's twenty-five buildings, and a meter records the school's electricity production and its rate of consumption.

When operating, the blades rotate at a constant spin of 28.8 rotations per minute. The wind turbine automatically alters their pitch, or tilt, according to the speed of the wind. The turbine always keeps itself faced into the wind, and it generates electricity in winds up to 55 miles per hour, explained Brother Joseph. "The turbine is rated to withstand winds up to 130 miles per hour, and it has a disc brake that can lock the rotors so they don't move at all during a period of excessively high wind."

Because New England has a number of low-wind days—the "dog days" of summer, for example—Portsmouth Abbey remains connected to the main power grid. But when the turbine spins, the meter "at the street" slows as the turbine displaces the electricity the school buys from the grid. On windy days, the meter stops completely as the turbine supplies the school's entire load. A continued supply of wind makes the meter run backward and the turbine actually "feeds" electricity into the electric company's power grid—which the power company has to buy from the school. Portsmouth Abbey is the first school in Rhode Island to get checks from the power company.

Noise is one of the often-cited objections to wind power. At first, the neighborhood response was "We can hear it, but we're getting used to it." But according to Brother Joseph, "You can have a very normal conversation at the base of the turbine. It sounds like the wind through the trees; it's got sort of a rhythm to it. Sometimes it can make a whistling sound, like a jet that's very high up in the sky. But within a week, I was completely used to it." Laughing, he added, "Now I wake up [at night] when I don't hear it turning and wonder if something is wrong."

At times, when the sun is low on the horizon, the rotating

blades create a flickering shadow that, Brother Joseph says, can be disconcerting at first. But as the sun's position in the sky gets higher and clears the blades, the shadow flicker stops. He recalled one night shortly after the turbine was installed. The window in his bedroom overlooks the turbine. At one point in the night, he woke and was startled to see strobelike shadows flickering in the room. Again, he emphasized, this is something that one gets used to and is willing to accommodate knowing that the energy being generated is not harming the environment. To date, the school's turbine has had no accidents with birds or bats.

The school had a total budget of $1.2 million for the project. Part of the money came from a state grant that helps to fund sustainable and renewable energy projects; part was endowed by the monastery with the intent that the school would eventually pay back the funds with savings generated by the turbine. The monks consider themselves the stewards of an incredibly beautiful place that they want to maintain as best they can. Toward that goal, they took a vote and changed the "payback" terms. Instead of receiving the money, they created a fund in the school. The turbine's revenue, until it pays back its investment cost, goes into that fund, where it is used to fund other renewable-energy and environmentally friendly projects at the school. To date, the school has converted to fluorescent lighting, replaced old boilers with high-efficiency ones, replaced old water faucets with energy-saving ones, and added an array of solar panels to its new dorm to supply solar heat and hot water. The school has also bought two futuristic-looking electric vehicles to use on campus.

There's no doubt that the wind turbine at Portsmouth Abbey School is making a difference. In addition to the 40 percent of the school's annual electric demand it provides, the extra revenue from the sale of wholesale electricity and renewable energy credits covers about another 10 percent of electric costs. "The turbine has proved to be a great success in every way," reported Brother Joseph in the fall of 2008. In fact, the local town of Portsmouth, following the school's lead, is now installing a turbine of its own, which is expected to be up in the new year. That's one trend any school can be proud to set. ■

THE SEATTLE PUBLIC LIBRARY

When you walk into the building that houses the Ballard Branch of the Seattle Public Library and the Ballard Neighborhood Service Center, one of the first things you notice is a display case that fea-tures information about the eco-friendly building. The librarians are eager to share the news that the American Institute of Architects and its Committee on the Environment selected their building as one of their 2006 Top Ten Green Projects in the United States. The library is also a recipient of a 2006 American Institute of Architects National Honor Award.

The building is a model of sustainable architecture and includes many design features that enhance and protect the environment. Even before you enter the library, its sloped roof, natural wood eaves and beams, planters overflowing with vegetation, and floor-to-ceiling windows shout, "This is one cool building." Seven skylights reduce the need for artificial light by channeling sunlight directly into the library, giving ample light for reading without creating a harsh glare. According to Sibyl de Haan, the manager of the Ballard Branch from 1990 to 2008, there is fluorescent lighting throughout the building for use on cloudy days and at night. A sensor measures available daylight and dims the lights when appropriate, saving energy when doing so, and the manager's office and study rooms have occupancy sensors, which turn the lights on or off when a person enters or leaves the room.

Before the Ballard Branch was built, a bank and a parking lot occupied the area. One hundred percent of the ground was covered with hardscape, or places where the soil surface has been covered with materials such as brick, concrete, and asphalt. Approximately 76 percent of the new site is planted surface.

Instead of being placed outside the library, the parking lot was built beneath the building. "Locating the [parking] garage below grade represents good land use within the city. Surface land that would have been used for parking was divided from the property and sold. The proceeds helped to pay for the underground parking," stated David Cinamon, an architect with Bohlin Cywinski Jackson, the architectural firm that designed the building.

Instead of a traditional shingled or tarred roof, the building literally has a green roof. More than 18,000 low-water-use plants (more than fifteen different species) are planted in a bed on the building's roof. "In its own small way, the green roof helps to reduce the heat reflected back into the atmosphere from all the hard, reflective surfaces found within the built environment [of large cities]. These hard, reflective, impervious 'heat islands' are a huge contributor to global warming worldwide," Cinamon added. Sibyl de Haan explained that the green roof helps to insulate the building and reduces water runoff during storms. "Plus, it looks nice, and it's fun!" People are not allowed to walk on the roof, but library patrons enjoy using a periscope inside the building, which allows them to look at the plants.

In addition to plants, the roof also supports seventeen solar panels. "The power generated by the solar panels on the roof is equivalent to that needed by an average three-bedroom home in the Seattle area," de Haan stated. "The large windows of the Neighborhood Service Center . . . have a solar film imbedded in the panels to demonstrate that a vertical installation is viable, but it also reduces the heat gain from the southwest exposure. The films acts as a shading device while generating power. This is one of the first installations of this type of window in the United States."

Extending the building's commitment to the environment, the carpeting, glass, ceramic tiles, and ceiling tiles used to finish the interior of the building are made from recycled materials. Environmentally friendly sealants and adhesives were used to install them. The tables and chairs are of a "notch and tab" style designed by Robert Miller of Bohlin Cywinski Jackson: the pieces slide together using no screws, nails, or metal hardware. The furniture is cut from single sheets of laminated wood, which reduces waste.

By choosing an environmentally smart design, the Seattle Public Library has reduced its carbon emissions while increasing the vitality of the Ballard neighborhood. The library's decision benefits everyone in the community—even those living far away. ∎

The transportation motor pool for Northern Illinois University, in DeKalb, Illinois, includes buses, trucks, and cars that are driven by university employees to and from business obligations, such as conferences and presentations

at other universities. As of the spring of 2009, ninety-two of the vehicles were sedans. Although Northern Illinois University's sedan fleet burns gasoline, thirty-seven of the sedans are hybrid cars— the largest number of hybrids owned as a fleet by any Illinois state agency.

Bill Finucane, the manager of transportation services, began incorporating the Prius into the university fleet in 2003, the third year the car was available in the United States. "We'd been looking at ways to cut some of our costs in terms of fuel use. Obviously, everyone is aware that fossil fuels are a finite resource," Finucane said. He was so satisfied with the reduction in fuel demands and the performance of the hybrid car that he approached the chief of the university police and asked if they would be interested in using them too. At the time, the police department used large sedans, gas guzzlers powered by eight-cylinder engines. "The chief agreed to try one Prius for a six-month trial period. After only two months, he was ready to convert all their squad cars to the hybrid," Finucane said with a chuckle. "We added hybrids to the police fleet every year, as the eight-cylinder cars needed replacement. Now, all of the squad cars are hybrids." He was quick to add, however, that while the Prius works well as a university police squad car, it may not work in every situation for a large municipal police department.

"The president of the university is very supportive of our program," Finucane added. That's not surprising. From December 2002, when the first two Priuses were purchased, to December 2006, the gasoline saved by using the hybrid cars, which by then numbered nineteen, amounted to more than 15,757 gallons— equivalent to a cost savings of more than $34,500.

The future of hybrid and alternative-fuel vehicles at Northern Illinois University is bright. The entire university fleet, including SUVs and trucks, numbers 240 vehicles. Four of the SUVs are Ford Escape hybrids. Including the fleet's vans and trucks, two-thirds of the university fleet runs on alternative fuels, such as ethanol blends and biodiesel fuels.

In the years to come, Finucane hopes to add a few electric cars to the university fleet. Electric cars, some of which are commercially available now, are often criticized for their limited range, about 40 miles on a battery charge. But Finucane is certain they could serve the university's needs perfectly. "We are looking at them for the future. They'd be ideal for our parking attendants, who monitor parking conditions and issue tickets. They never go off campus, and they could plug the vehicle in every night."

Northern Illinois University's Transportation Services Department hasn't limited its environmental action to the purchasing of hybrid cars. "We want to do things that are environmentally correct. We're trying to think globally, while acting locally," Finucane declared. The gasoline that fuels the university's cars is a 10 percent ethanol blend, and all of the diesel fuel used in the university's buses and trucks is 20 percent soy biodiesel fuel. That supports the area's farmers, who grow corn and soybeans.

The university's commitment doesn't stop there, according to Finucane. They recycle all their tires, used oil filters, and waste oil, and they make special use out of the 55-gallon metal barrels, called drums, containing the oil they buy. "Most places use the empty barrels as trash containers or send them to the landfill. We do something different with ours," Finucane said. "The School of Music at Northern Illinois University has an award-winning steel drum band." The steel drums played by the musicians are made by cutting and tuning the oil drums. "All of our empty drums go to the shop, here in town, where the band makes their drums. They don't have the cost of buying drums, and we're not dumping the cans. It's really a great hand-in-hand cooperative effort."

Northern Illinois University's actions are saving fuel, reducing carbon emissions, and recycling waste materials. And the music produced by the steel band provides hours of carbon-emissions-free listening pleasure. ■

YOUR TURN

We are the generations fated to live in the most interesting of times, because our energy choices and consumption directly affect how our children and their children will live. What we choose to do affects Earth's climate, and because of that, we are now, in some respects, the weather makers. The future of biodiversity and civilization hangs on our actions. While reports of global warming and climate change seem grim, it's not too late to act. The actions taken by Alaska Youth for Environmental Action, Portsmouth Abbey School, the Seattle Public Library, and Northern Illinois University illustrate the various ways, both big and small, that all of us can make a difference.

Now it's your turn. What will you do to save the planet today?

SOURCE NOTES

CHAPTER 1

pp. 4–5: "Carbon is found . . . is far greater." Archer.

CHAPTER 2

p. 13 : "Nitrogen, the primary component . . . that we breathe." Lutgens and Tarbuck.

p. 14: "For every molecule . . . fifty in the oceans." Weart.

p. 16: "If the CO_2 level . . . boiling point of water." Lovelock.

p. 16: "Water vapor retains . . . greenhouse gases." Kump.

CHAPTER 3

p. 21: "However, laboratory experiments . . . heat it trapped." Weart.

p. 21: "Scientists call this . . . increase its effect." Weart.

p. 21: "about 56 percent . . . all global warming." Kump.

p. 23: "Coal's composition is . . . type of coal." Herman.

p. 23: "Scientists calculate that . . . oxygen in our atmosphere." Dawkins.

p. 24: "In very round figures . . . life on land." Feely et al.

p. 25: "They have absorbed . . . between 1800 and 1994." Sabine et al.

p. 25: "The North Atlantic alone . . . humans since 1800." Sabine et al.

p. 25: "The sea's layering . . . emitted by humans." H. Thomas et al.

p. 26: "In fact, scientists have discovered . . . ocean is decreasing." Sabine et al.

p. 26: "During the 1980s . . . below 1.8 gigatons." Cox et al.

p. 29: "The average American's slice . . . person per day." Zuckerman.

CHAPTER 4

pp. 36–37: "Whether sunspots played . . . affect Earth's temperature." Lutgens and Tarbuck.

CHAPTER 5

p. 42: "We know this . . . volumes of CO_2." Beerling et al.

p. 44: "Until November 2003 . . . planet-altering climatic event." Zachos et al.

p. 45: "Norwegian scientists have . . . gas came from." Svensen et al.

p. 46: "These scientists believe . . . in the ocean floor." Dickens.

p. 46: "The scientists theorize . . . after the explosion." Little and Vrijenhoek.

CHAPTER 6

pp. 50–51: "Tree-ring records . . . on the colonists." Blanton.

pp. 51–52 : "In June 2004 . . . further 13,000 years." EPCA Community Members.

pp. 52–53: "If we pursue . . . century seems inevitable." Jones et al.

p. 53: "While the scale . . . per thousand years." Bush, Silman, and Urrego.

CHAPTER 7

p. 60: "In 2005, the burning . . . gas, 20 percent." U.S. Department of Energy, Energy Information Administration website.

p. 61: "When brown coal . . . emissions than methane." Hamilton.

p. 62: "In 1990, coal-fired . . . 44 percent of global carbon emissions." U.S. Department of Energy, Energy Information Administration website.

p. 62: "Indeed, the dawn . . . drilling for oil." Roberts.

p. 63: "Oil is the product . . . the sunlit surface." Dukes.

p. 64: "In order to use . . . always a concern." World Petroleum Council website.

p. 65: "Every one of . . . over that period." Weart.

pp. 65–66: "Taking into account . . . gallon of gasoline." Dukes.

p. 66: "Since then, we . . . our overspending habits." World Wildlife Fund *Living Planet Report 2004*.

CHAPTER 8

p. 74: "So when scientists . . . back to 1840." Urban, Cole, and Overpeck.

p. 74: "Between 1945 and 1955 . . . been below 77°F (25°C)." Nash.

p. 74: "In 1976, the rise in . . . forty-eight states." Canby.

pp. 74–75: "In modern times . . . very largest beaks." Grant.

p. 78: "However, the normally . . . of the Netherlands." Nash.

p. 78: "Ever since the 1976 . . . two La Niñas." Trenberth and Hoar.

p. 79: "In 2003, researchers . . . from whaling ships . . ." Parmesan and Yohe.

p. 80: "Thirty-five nonmigratory . . . no longer suitable." Parmesan et al.

p. 80: "Costa Rica's lowland . . . 1.2 to 2 days earlier." Walther et al.

p. 81: "Marcel Visser . . . find them everywhere." Visser and Holleman.

p. 82: "Only males are . . . at less than 87.8°F (31°C)." Cogger and Zweifel.

p. 82: "Inevitably, the lake's . . . times as deep." Verburg, Heky, and Kling.

p. 84: "In fact, if every . . . from the roads." Commonwealth Edison/Excelon Corporation website.

p. 85: "They estimate that . . . as 66 percent." Sullivan.

CHAPTER 9

p. 86: "Antarctic hair grass . . . other sheltered spot." Comiso.

p. 87: "since 1976, the krill . . . percent per decade." Atkinson et al.

p. 87: "The emperor penguin . . . by 70 percent." Hoegh-Guldberg.

p. 88: "Over the past . . . America's recorded history." Whitfield.

p. 89: "The Sami people . . . as they migrate." Hassol.

p. 89: "Scientists predict that . . . this century alone." Hassol.

pp. 90–91: Pitseolak Alainga quotations from interview on *The Story with Dick Gordon,* www.thestory.org.

p. 92: "In 1978, an Inuit . . . proves the rule." Lopez.

p. 92: "Like the ringed . . . 2001, and 2002." Hassol.

pp. 92–93: "Research shows that polar . . . for nourishment." Appenzeller and Dimick.

pp. 93–94: "The changes we're . . . very little precipitation." Betts.

p. 94: "However, scientists can estimate that . . . cannot be reversed." Betts.

CHAPTER 10

p. 96: "Most commonly, coral . . . the world's coral." National Oceanic and Atmospheric Administration, National Climatic Data Center, 2006 Annual Report.

p. 97: "Then late in 1997 . . . over the water." Abram et al.

pp. 97–98: "The smog cloud . . . problems for corals." Swing.

p. 98: "Dinoflagellate blooms are . . . dimmer than ever." Swing.

p. 99: "He described Myrmidon . . . did coral survive." Woodford.

p. 100: "In 2002, a panel . . . signs of damage." Hughes et al.

p. 100: "The message was . . . Great Barrier Reef." Pockley.

p. 100: "According to reef . . . 'total devastation.'" Woodford.

p. 100: "Extinctions caused by . . . emblematic of them." Abram et al.

pp. 101–102: "Recent research has . . . grow right now." Baker et al.

p. 102: "Only 50 of . . . the reef's biodiversity." Woodford.

CHAPTER 11

pp. 107–108: "I trudge uphill . . . dark brown mud." "We see a large . . . kitchen sink–sized pool." "Breeding seems to . . . Costa Rica." Crump.

pp. 108–109: "After a long . . . pools in anticipation . . . ?" Crump.

p. 112: "When the first . . . threatened with extinction." Stokstad.

p. 112: "'There's almost no evidence of recovery.'" Stokstad.

p. 112: "One fundamental discovery . . . 80 percent die." Pounds.

CHAPTER 12

p. 116: "The capacity of . . . increase in rainfall." Hadley Center, *Climate Change: Observations and Predictions.*

p. 117: "The area affected . . . rains will return." Zeng.

p. 118: "The true origin . . . 1930 and 2000." Gianni, Saravanan, and Chang.

p. 118: "In the end . . . dramatic climate shift." Zeng.

p. 119: "In 2005, scientists . . . the twenty-first century." Held et al.

p. 119: "The Sahelian climate . . . from the Sahel." Prospero and Lamb.

p. 120: "The Australian climatologist . . . even farther southward." Karoly.

p. 122: "By 2004, the situation . . . species with extinction." Environmental Protection Authority of Western Australia, Water and Rivers Commission.

p. 123: "In response to . . . plant's carbon emissions." SPG Media Limited, Water-techonology.net.

p. 123: "Research shows that . . . than it is today." Cook et al.

p. 123: "This suggests . . . rising ocean temperatures." Hoerling and Kumar.

p. 124: "'it would be . . . from megadrought.'" Overpeck, Cole, and Bartlein.

p. 124: "Over the last . . . flow in half." Service.

p. 125: "With temperatures in . . . is least needed." Service.

p. 126: "Five thousand years . . . big ghost town." Feidel.

CHAPTER 13

p. 128: "In 2003, climate . . . several hundred meters." Santer et al.

pp. 129–130: "The amount of . . . at 50°F (10°C)." Lutgens and Tarbuck.

pp. 132–134: Katherine Hart, telephone interview by Sally M. Walker and e-mails, March 2007.

p. 135: "Since 1974, . . . since the 1990s." Kerr, *"Katrina."*

p. 135: "In the 1960s, . . . 150 million." Blair.

p. 135: "The United Kingdom . . . predicted to continue." Hadley Center, *Climate Change: Observations and Predictions.*

p. 136: "The European summer . . . every 46,000 years." Schar et al.

p. 136: "In the United States . . . causes combined." Lutgens and Tarbuck.

p. 136: "In terms of . . . than anywhere else." Lutgens and Tarbuck.

p. 136: "The National Oceanic . . . twentieth-century mean." National Oceanic and Atmospheric Administration, National Climatic Data Center, 2006 Annual Report.

pp. 136–137: "In India . . . in human lives." Ray and De.

p. 137: "in 2005, . . . in widespread floods." United Nations Environment Programme website.

CHAPTER 14

p. 140: "'The rate has . . . humans are responsible.'" Kenneth Miller, Rutgers University, e-mail message, January 22, 2007.

p. 142: "In Bangladesh alone . . . of sea level." Victor.

pp. 142–143: "This is comforting . . . to preindustrial levels." Toniazzo, Gregory, and Huybrechts.

p. 143: "The largest amount . . . the world's freshwater." British Antarctic Survey, National Environment Research Council website.

pp. 143–144: "The East Antarctic Ice Sheet . . . the ice sheet." Davis et al.

pp. 143–144: Curt H. Davis, Department of Electrical and Computer Engineering, University of Missouri-Columbia, e-mail message, January 23, 2007.

p. 145: "Jakobshavn Isbræ . . . (34.4 meters) per day." *Nova, ScienceNow* website.

p. 145: "Indeed, a study . . . last ten years." Rignot and Kanagaratnam.

p. 145: "In the summer . . . decrease ever recorded." Clarke.

p. 145: "Clearly, if Earth's . . . to human civilization." Chernicoff and Whitney.

pp. 146–147: "In 2003, a study . . . initiate the melting." Shepherd et al.

p. 147: "Scientists are convinced . . . greater ice masses." Kaiser.

p. 147: "In their study, . . . like Larsen B." R. Thomas et al.

p. 147: "In 2008, according . . . into deeper grounds.'" Eric Rignot, National Aeronautics and Space Administration, Jet Propulsion Laboratory, e-mail message, September 24, 2008.

p. 148: "'We think that' . . . shelves have disappeared." Vincent Warwick, Professor of Biology, Laval University, e-mail message, January 22, 2007.

p. 149: "A new scientific . . . summer by 2040." Holland, Bitz, and Tremblay.

p. 150: "Many scientists think . . . century or two." Overpeck, Cole, and Bartlein.

CHAPTER 15

p. 154: "The study that . . . each decade." Parmesan and Yohe.

p. 154: "So far, some . . . northeast Queensland, Australia." Williams, Bolitho, and Fox.

p. 158: "As temperatures warm . . . to the disease." Tanser, Sharp, and le Sueur.

CHAPTER 16

p. 161: "Today there are . . . in the future." Schiermeier.

p. 163: "Climatologist Nathan Gillett . . . air-pressure changes." Gillett.

p. 164: "We now know . . . by human activity." Weart.

p. 164: "Today, even with . . . the United States." Freese.

p. 165: "Scientists now think . . . their upward creep." Kump.

pp. 166–167: "The average result . . . been predicted earlier." Stainforth et al.

p. 167: "The project is . . . as of 2008." http://www.climateprediction.net.

p. 168: "They believe . . . the United States every day." National Air Traffic Controllers Association website.

p. 170: "The Hadley Center . . . record-breaking 1999." Hadley Center, *Climate Change Scenarios for the United Kingdom,* April 2002.

p. 170: "The changes felt . . . of 8.1°F (4.5°C)." Hadley Center, *Climate Change: Observations and Predictions.*

p. 171: "In 2003 and 2004, . . . impacts for California." Bell, Sloan, and Snyder.

p. 171: "Twelve separate climate . . . of storm tides." Hennessey et al.

CHAPTER 18

pp. 178–179: "If temperatures in . . . to support them." Hughes, Cawsley, and Westoby.

p. 179: "William Hare, on . . . of shifting climate." Hare.

p. 180: "By 2006, British Columbia's . . . prior fifteen years." "Formula for Predicting Climate Change Impact on Salmon Stocks Established."

p. 180: "These same factors . . . face severe risks." C. D. Thomas et al.

pp. 180–181: "Imagine the world's . . . of eastern Texas." Union of Concerned Scientists website.

p. 181: "Richard Feely of . . . their protective covers." Richard A. Feely, National Oceanic and Atmospheric Administration, e-mail message, January 2007.

p. 181: "Such was the . . . the giant squid." Owen.

CHAPTER 19

p. 186: "Biological productivity . . . more than 20 percent." Schmittner.

p. 186: "Overall, the Gulf . . . the Amazon River." Sarkisyan.

p. 187: "Researcher Ruth Curry . . . and 1985 to 1999." Curry, Dickson, and Yashayaev.

p. 187: "The increasing tropical . . . collapse the currents." Kerr, "Gas Hydrate."

pp. 187–188: "Ice cores from . . . little as a decade." Swing.

p. 188: "The reserve of . . . into the atmosphere." Jones, Cox, and Huntingford.

pp. 189–190: "The cumulative impact . . . by 150 gigatons." Betts et al.

p. 191: "Scientists estimate that . . . this unusual material." Kerr, "Gas Hydrate."

p. 192: "At the same . . . rapid climate change." Benton.

p. 192: "Clathrates are important . . . by 4 percent." Sloan.

p. 193: "In the United States . . . billion per year." Blumberg.

CHAPTER 20

p. 196: "Scientists believe that . . . living in other regions" Annenberg Media, Learner.org website; Johnson.

pp. 198–199: "Many experiments . . . lower than today." Ainsworth and Long.

CHAPTER 21

p. 205: "By 2000, the . . . over the Arctic." Blatt.

CHAPTER 22

p. 213: "especially after the . . . negotiations in 2001." Sheram and Soubbotina.

p. 213: "On July 25, 1997, . . . 'same compliance period.'" Victor.

pp. 214–215: "First, the Protocol . . . credits in return." United Nations Framework Convention on Climate Change, Kyoto Protocol.

pp. 216–217: "William Lash from . . . $20 billion." Lash.

p. 217: "They posit that . . . per household per year." Alliance to Save Energy, American Council for an Energy-Efficient Economy, Natural Resources Defense Council, Tellus Institute, and the Union of Concerned Scientists.

p. 217: "They include droughts . . . Katrina in 2006." National Oceanic and Atmospheric Administration, National Climatic Data Center, 2006 Annual Report.

p. 217: "And in 2008, . . . exceeded $32 billion." Drye; Williams and Augstums.

p. 218: "Paul Epstein of . . . course of a year." Meyer.

CHAPTER 23

p. 222: "In June 2005, . . . about climate change." Revkin.

pp. 222, 227: "Other climate-change . . . kinds of alterations." Kennedy.

p. 227: "The IPCC's 2007 . . . animals, and plants." Intergovernmental Panel on Climate Change, IPCC Fourth Assessment Report.

p. 228: "'Even with those . . . Clean Air Act.'" Hawthorne.

pp. 223–226: Elizabeth Turnbull, telephone interview by Sally M. Walker, September 13, 2008.

CHAPTER 24

p. 233: "But sustainable agricultural and . . . simple and desirable." Betts et al.

p. 233: "The Costa Rican . . . had been disturbed." Saleska et al.

p. 234: "Another example is . . . city of Perth." Henschke.

p. 234: "carbon turnover . . . efficient than thought." Matamala.

p. 234: "The carbon in . . . up for fuel." Kirschbaum.

p. 235: "But those that . . . recycled or reused." Matsushita.

p. 236: "It takes four . . . make plastic bags." Reusablebags.com.

p. 236: Ashley Hawkins, Customer Service Representative, Whole Foods Market, e-mail message, September 2008.

CHAPTER 25

p. 237: "But for many . . . the ground faster." Roberts.

pp. 237–238: "Pipelines were the . . . wasn't high enough." Roberts.

p. 238: "With an international . . . twenty-first century." Roberts.

p. 240: "At the moment . . . using stationary cells." Romm, *The Hype About Hydrogen*.

CHAPTER 26

p. 244: "Researchers Steven Pacala . . . next fifty years." Pacala and Socolow.

p. 245: "In several countries . . . percent per year." Girardet.

pp. 245–246: "There is a fair . . . coal-fired power plants." Business Council for Sustainable Energy.

p. 246: "Cats kill far . . . do wind farms." Business Council for Sustainable Energy.

p. 246: "bats are flying . . . needs further investigation." Blum.

pp. 247–248: "In fact, since June 2007, . . . are near zero." Acciona Company—Nevada Solar One website.

p. 248: "In Japan, for example . . . fifteen other countries." Girardet.

p. 249: "In fact, hydropower . . . United States' electricity." U.S. Environmental Protection Agency website.

CHAPTER 27

p. 251: "Nuclear reactors generate . . . the United States." Nuclear Energy Institute website.

p. 252: "According to the . . . a new plant." Energy Information Administration website.

p. 253: "In the United States . . . possible terrorist attack." Kennedy.

p.253: "The United States' . . . double that time." Energy Information Administration website.

p. 255: "Power plants at . . . since the 1960s." Calpine Corporation website.

CHAPTER 28

pp. 259–260: "Switchgrass, a native . . . acre as corn." Union of Concerned Scientists website.

p. 260: "Burning cellulosic ethanol . . . next ten years." Kanellos.

p. 262: "Over the past few years, . . . of air pollution." Blatt.

pp. 262–263: "In the United States . . . in the country." Blatt.

p. 263: "But what is . . . aircraft contrails." Penner et al.

CHAPTER 29

pp. 266–268: Wiley Cason, intern, AYEA, interview by Sally M. Walker, April 2008.

pp. 267–268: Polly Carr, Program Manager, AYEA, e-mail message, April 2007.

pp. 269–272: Brother Joseph, Portsmouth Abbey School, telephone interview by Sally M. Walker and e-mails, March 2007–September 2008.

pp. 273–275: Sibyl de Haan, Branch Manager, Ballard Branch, Seattle Public Library, e-mail message, March 22, 2007.

pp. 274–275: David Cinamon, Architectural Associate, Bohlin Cywinski Jackson, e-mail message, March 22, 2007.

pp. 276–278: Bill Finucane, Northern Illinois University, interviews by Sally M. Walker, March 2007 and September 2008.

BIBLIOGRAPHY

BOOKS

Alliance to Save Energy, American Council for an Energy-Efficient Economy, Natural Resources Defense Council, Tellus Institute, and Union of Concerned Scientists. *Energy Innovations: A Prosperous Path to a Clean Environment.* June 1997.

Archer, David. *Global Warming: Understanding the Forecast.* Oxford: Blackwell Publishing Ltd., 2007.

Benton, Michael J. *When Life Nearly Died: The Greatest Mass Extinction of All Time.* London: Thames & Hudson, 2003.

Blair, Tony. Speech on climate change to celebrate the tenth anniversary of HRH the Prince of Wales's Business and the Environment Programme, September 14, 2004.

Blatt, Harvey. *America's Environmental Report Card.* Cambridge, MA: MIT Press, 2005.

Blumberg, Mark S. *Body Heat: Temperature and Life on Earth.* Cambridge, MA: Harvard University Press, 2002.

Chernicoff, Stanley, and Donna Whitney. *Geology.* 4th ed. Saddle River, NJ: Prentice Hall, 2007.

Cogger, H. G., and R. G. Zweifel, eds. *Reptiles and Amphibians.* New York: Southmark Publishers, 1992.

Crump, Marty. *In Search of the Golden Frog.* Chicago: University of Chicago Press, 2000.

Dauncey, Guy, with Patrick Mazza. *Stormy Weather.* British Columbia: New Society Publishers, 2001.

Dawkins, Richard. *The Ancestor's Tale: A Pilgrimage to the Dawn of Evolution.* London: Weidenfeld & Nicolson, 2004.

Feidel, Stuart J. *Prehistory of the Americas.* 2nd ed. Cambridge: Cambridge University Press, 1992.

Flannery, Tim. *The Weather Makers: How Man Is Changing the Climate and What It Means for Life on Earth.* New York: Atlantic Monthly Press, 2005.

Freese, Barbara. *Coal: A Human History.* Cambridge, MA: Perseus Publishing, 2003.

Girardet, Herbert. *Cities People Planet: Liveable Cities for a Sustainable World.* Chichester, England: Wiley Academy, 2004.

Grant, Peter R. *Ecology and Evolution of Darwin's Finches.* Rev. ed. Princeton, NJ: Princeton University Press, 1999.

Hadley Center for Climate Prediction and Research. *Climate Change Scenarios for the United Kingdom.* Devon, England: Met Office, April 2002/ UKCIP02 Report.

———. *Climate Change Scenarios for the United Kingdom.* Devon, England: Met Office, December 2003.

————. *Climate Change: Observations and Predictions.* Devon, England: Met Office, December 2003.

Hamilton, Clive. *Running from the Storm: The Development of Climate Policy in Australia.* Sydney, Australia: UNSW Press, 2001.

Hare, William. *Assessment of Knowledge on Impacts of Climate Change: Contributions to the Specification of Art. 2 of the UNFCCC.* Berlin: WBGU Materialien, 2003.

Hassol, Susan Joy. *Impacts of a Warming Arctic: Arctic Climate Impact Assessment.* Cambridge: Cambridge University Press, 2004.

Hennessey, Kevin, et al. *Climate Change in New South Wales. Part 2: Projected Changes in Climate Extremes.* Consultancy report for the NSW Greenhouse Office. New South Wales, Australia: CSIRO, November 2004.

Henschke, I. "Essays on Global Warming and the World Response." Oxford: Reuters Foundation fellowship paper, 1999.

Herman, Hyman. *Brown Coal.* Melbourne, Australia: State Electricity Commission of Victoria, 1952.

Hoegh-Guldberg, Ove. "Climate Change and Marine Ecosystems." In *Climate Change and Biodiversity,* edited by Thomas E. Lovejoy and Lee Hannah. New Haven, CT: Yale University Press, 2005.

Intergovernmental Panel on Climate Change. IPCC Fourth Assessment Report: Climate Change 2007. http://www.ipcc.ch/ipccreports/assessments-reports.htm (accessed January 2009) .

Kennedy, Robert F. *Crimes against Nature: How George W. Bush and His Corporate Pals Are Plundering the Country and Hijacking Our Democracy.* New York: HarperCollins, 2004.

Lash, William H., III. "A Current View of the Kyoto Climate Change Treaty." Report for the Center for the Study of American Business. St. Louis: Washington University, 1999.

Lopez, Barry. *Arctic Dreams: Imagination and Desire in a Northern Landscape.* New York: Scribner & Sons, 1986.

Lovelock, James. *Gaia: A New Look at Life on Earth.* Oxford: Oxford University Press, 1979.

Lutgens, Frederick K., and Edward J. Tarbuck. *The Atmosphere: An Introduction to Meteorology.* 9th ed. Englewood Cliffs, NJ: Pearson Prentice Hall, 2004.

Meyer, Aubrey. *Contraction & Convergence: The Global Solution to Climate Change.* Schumacher Briefing No. 5. Devon, England: Green Books for the Schumacher Society, 2000.

Nash, J. Madeleine. *El Niño: Unlocking the Secrets of the Master Weather-Maker.* New York: Warner Books, 2002.

National Oceanic and Atmospheric Administration. National Climatic Data Center. "Climate of 2006 — in Historical Perspective: Annual Report." March 9, 2007. http://www.ncdc.noaa.gov/oa/climate/research/2006/ann/ann06.html.

Overpeck, Jonathan, Julia Cole, and Patrick Bartlein. "A 'Palaeoperspective' on Climate Variability and Change." In *Climate Change and Biodiversity,* edited by Thomas E. Lovejoy and Lee Hannah. New Haven, CT: Yale University Press, 2005.

Pearce, Fred. *With Speed and Violence.* Boston: Beacon Press, 2006.

Penner, Joyce E., et al., eds. *Aviation and the Global Atmosphere.* A special report of IPCC working groups 1 and 3, in collaboration with the Scientific Assessment Panel, to the Montreal Protocol on Substances that Deplete the Ozone Layer, 1999. http://www.grida.no/climate/ipcc/aviation/.

Roberts, Paul. *The End of Oil: On the Edge of a Perilous New World.* Boston: Houghton Mifflin, 2004.

Romm, Joseph. *Hell and High Water: Global Warming—The Solution and the Politics—and What We Should Do.* New York: William Morrow, 2007.

———. *The Hype about Hydrogen: Fact and Fiction in the Race to Save the Climate.* Washington, DC: Island Press, 2004.

Ruddiman, William F. *Plows, Plagues, and Petroleum: How Humans Took Control of Climate.* Princeton, NJ: Princeton University Press, 2005.

Steinman, David. *Safe Trip to Eden.* New York: Thunder's Mouth Press, 2007.

Victor, David G. *Climate Change: Debating America's Policy Options.* New York: Council on Foreign Relations/Brookings Institute Press, 2004.

Weart, Spencer R. *The Discovery of Global Warming.* Cambridge, MA: Harvard University Press, 2003.

World Wildlife Fund. *Living Planet Report 2004.* October 9, 2004.

ARTICLES

Abram, Nerlie J., et al. "Coral Reef Death during the 1997 Indian Ocean Dipole Linked to Indonesian Wildfires." *Science* 301 (2003): 952–955.

Ainsworth, Elizabeth A., and Stephen P. Long. "What Have We Learned from 15 Years of Free-Air CO_2 Enrichment (FACE)? A Meta-Analytic Review of the Responses of Photosynthesis, Canopy Properties and Plant Production to Rising CO_2." *New Phytologist* 165 (2005): 351–372.

Appenzeller, T., and D. R. Dimick, with contributions by D. Glick, F. Montaigne, and V. Morell. "The Heat Is On." *National Geographic* 206 (2004): 2–75.

Atkinson, Angus, et al. "Long-Term Decline in Krill Stock and Increase in Salps within the Southern Ocean." *Nature* 432 (2004): 100–103.

Baker, Andrew C., et al. "Corals' Adaptive Response to Climate Change." *Nature* 430 (2004): 741.

Beerling, D. J., et al. "An Atmospheric pCO_2 Reconstruction across the Cretaceous-Tertiary Boundary from Leaf Megafossils." *Proceedings of the National Academy of Sciences of the United States* 99 (2002).

Bell, Jason L., Lisa C. Sloan, and Mark A. Snyder. "Regional Changes in Extreme Climatic Events: A Future Climate Scenario." *Journal of Climate* 17 (2004): 81–87.

Betts, Richard A. "Offset of the Potential Carbon Sink from Boreal Forestation by Decreases in Surface Albedo." *Nature* 408 (2000): 187–190.

Betts, Richard A., et al. "The Role of Ecosystem-Atmospheric Interactions in Simulated Amazonian Precipitation Decrease and Forest Dieback under Global Climate Warming." *Theoretical Applied Climatology* 78 (2004): 157–175.

Blanton, Dennis B. "Drought as a Factor in the Jamestown Colony, 1607–1612." In *Historical Archaeology* 34 2000: 74–81.

Blum, Justin. "Researchers Alarmed by Bat Deaths From Wind Turbines," *Washington Post*, January 1, 2005. http://www.washingtonpost.com/wp-dyn/articles/A39941-2004Dec31.html. (accessed January 2009).

Bush, Mark B., Miles R. Silman, and Dunia H. Urrego. "48,000 Years of Climate and Forest Change in a Biodiversity Hot Spot." *Science* 303 (2004): 827–829.

Business Council for Sustainable Energy. "Dispelling the Myths about Wind." *EcoGeneration* 24 (2004): 8–9.

Canby, Thomas Y. "The Year the Weather Went Wild." *National Geographic* 152 (1977): 799–829.

Clarke, Tom. "Record Melt in Arctic and Greenland." *Nature News,* December 9, 2002.

Comiso, Josefino C. "Warming Trends in the Arctic from Clear Sky Satellite Observations." *Journal of Climate* 16 (2003): 3498–3510.

Cook, Edward R., et al. "Long-Term Aridity Changes in the Western United States." *Science* 306 (2004): 1015–1018.

Cox, Peter M., et al. "Acceleration of Global Warming Due to Carbon-Cycle Feedbacks in a Couple Climate Model." *Nature* 408 (2000): 184–187.

Curry, Ruth, Bob Dickson, and Igor Yashayaev. "A Change in the Freshwater Balance of the Atlantic Ocean over the Past Four Decades." *Nature* 426 (2003): 826–829.

Davis, Curt H., et al. "Snowfall-Driven Growth in East Antarctic Ice Sheet Mitigates Recent Sea-Level Rise." *Science* 308 (2005): 1898–1901.

Dickens, Gerald R. "Global Change: Hydrocarbon-Driven Warming." *Nature* 429 (2004): 513–515.

Drye, Willie. "'Freak' Hurricane Ike Will Cost $22 Billion." *National Geographic News,* September 15, 2008. http://www.news.nationalgeographic.com/news/2008/09/080915-hurricane-ike.html (accessed September 23, 2008).

Dukes, Jeffrey S. "Burning Buried Sunshine: Human Consumption of Ancient Solar Energy." *Climate Change* 61 (2003): 31–44.

Environmental Protection Authority of Western Australia. Water and Rivers Commission. "Environmental Management of Groundwater: Abstraction from the Gnangara Mound." *Western Australian EPA Bulletin* 1139 (2004). http://www.epa.wa.gov.au/docs/1814_B1139.pdf.

EPICA Community Members. "Eight Glacial Cycles from an Antarctic Ice Core." *Nature* 429 (2004): 623–628.

Feely, Richard A., et al. "Impact of Anthropogenic CO_2 on $CaCO_3$ System in the Oceans." *Science* 305 (2004): 362–366.

Feely, Richard A., Christopher L. Sabine, and Victoria J. Fabry. "Carbon Dioxide and Our Ocean Legacy." Brochure, National Environmental

Trust, Washington, DC: 37–42. http://www.pewtrusts.org/Reports/Global_
warming/carbon_dioxide_ocean_legacy.pdf.

"Formula for Predicting Climate Change Impact on Salmon Stocks
Established." *ScienceDaily,* November 21, 2008. http://www.sciencedaily.
com/releases/2008/11/081112124416.htm. (accessed January 3, 2009).

Gianni, A., R. Saravanan, and P. Chang. "Oceanic Forcing of Sahel Rainfall
on Interannual to Interdecadal Timescales." *Science* 302 (2003): 1027–1030.

Gillett, Nathan P. "Climate Modelling: Northern Hemisphere Circulation."
Nature 437 (2005): 496.

Hawthorne, Michael. "BP Refinery's Plan to Add Flares Is Attacked after
Indiana Grants Air Permit." *Chicago Tribune,* July 13, 2008. http://www.
chicagotribune.com/features/lifestyle/green/chi-bpjul14,0,1247804.story
(accessed September 23, 2008).

Held, I. M., et al. "Simulation of Sahel Drought in the 20th and 21st
Centuries." *Proceedings of the National Academy of Sciences of the United States*
102 (2005): 17891–17896. http://www.pnas.org/content/102/50/17891
(accessed September 20, 2008).

Hoerling, Martin, and Arun Kumar. "The Perfect Ocean for Drought."
Science 299 (2003): 691–694.

Holland, Marika M., Cecilia M. Bitz, and Bruno Tremblay. "Future Abrupt
Reductions in the Summer Arctic Sea Ice." *Geophysical Research Letters* 33
(2006).

Hughes, L., E. M. Cawsley, and M. Westoby. "Climatic Range Sizes of
Eucalyptus Species in Relation to Future Climate Change." *Global Ecology and
Biogeography Letters* 5 (1996): 23–29.

Hughes, T. P., et al. "Climate Change, Human Impacts, and the Resilience
of Coral Reefs." *Science* 301 (2003): 929–933.

Johnson, George. "Social Strife May Have Exiled Ancient Indians." *New York
Times,* August 20, 1996. http:www.santafe.edu/~johnson/articles.anasazi.
html (accessed January 2009).

Jones, Chris D., et al. "The Carbon Cycle Response to ENSO: A Coupled
Climate–Carbon Cycle Model Study." *Journal of Climate* 14 (2001):
4113–4129.

Jones, C. D., P. Cox, and C. Huntingford. "Uncertainty in Climate–Carbon
Cycle Projections Associated with the Sensitivity of Soil Respiration to
Temperature." *Tellus 55B* (2003): 642–648.

Kaiser, Jocelyn. "Warmer Ocean Could Threaten Antarctic Ice Shelves."
Science 302 (2003): 759.

Kanellos, Michael. "The Cellulosic Ethanol Road Map from Mascoma's
CEO." CNET News, September 25, 2007. http://www.news.cnet.com/8301-
10784_3-9784515-7.html (accessed January 2009).

Karoly, David J. "Ozone and Climate Change." *Science* 302 (2003): 236–237.

Kerr, Richard A. "Gas Hydrate Resource: Smaller but Sooner." *Science* 303
(2004): 946–947.

———. "Is Katrina a Harbinger of Still More Powerful Hurricanes?"
Science 309 (2005): 1807.

————. "Sea Change in the Atlantic." *Science* 303 (2004): 35.

Kirschbaum, Miko U. F. "Can Trees Buy Time? An Assessment of the Role of Vegetation Sinks as Part of the Global Carbon Cycle." *Climatic Change* 57 (2003): 47–71.

Kump, Lee R. "Reducing Uncertainty about Carbon Dioxide as a Climate Driver." *Nature* 419 (2002): 188–190.

Little, Crispin T. S., and Robert C. Vrijenhoek. "Are Hydrothermal Vent Animals Living Fossils?" *Trends in Ecology & Evolution* 18 (2003): 582–588.

Matamala, Roser, et al. "Impacts of Fine Root Turnover on Forest NPP and Soil C Sequestration Potential." *Science* 302 (2003): 1385–1387.

Matsushita, Elaine. "What's Your Bag — If You're Eco-Conscious?" *Chicago Tribune*, January 28, 2007: 5–6.

Owen, James. "Holy Squid! Photos Offer First Glimpse of Live Deep-Sea Giant." *National Geographic News*, September 27, 2005. http://www.news.nationalgeographic.com/news/2005/09/0927_050927_giant_squid.html (accessed January 2009).

Pacala, S., and R. Socolow. "Stabilization Wedges: Solving the Climate Problem for the Next Fifty Years with Current Technologies." *Science* 305 (2004): 968–972.

Parmesan, Camille, and Gary Yohe. "A Globally Coherent Fingerprint of Climate Change Impacts across Natural Systems." *Nature* 421 (2003): 37–42.

Parmesan, Camille, et al. "Poleward Shifts in Geographical Ranges of Butterfly Species Associated with Regional Warming." *Nature* 399 (1999): 579–584.

Pockley, Peter. "Human Activities Threaten Coral Reefs with 'Dire Effects.'" *Australasian Science*, January–February 2003:29–32.

Pounds, J. Alan. "Climate and Amphibian Declines." *Nature* 410 (2001): 639–640.

Prospero, Joseph H., and Peter J. Lamb. "African Droughts and Dust Transport to the Caribbean: Climate Change Implications." *Science* 302 (2003): 1024–1027.

Ray, K. C. S., and U. S. De. "Climate Change in India as Evidenced from Instrumental Records." *World Meteorological Organization Bulletin* 52 (2003): 53–59.

Revkin, Andrew C. "Bush Aide Softened Greenhouse Gas Links to Global Warming." *New York Times*, June 8, 2005. http://www.nytimes.com/2005/06/08/politics/08climate.html?scp=1&sq=+&st=nyt (accessed September 30, 2008).

Rignot, Eric, and Pannir Kanagaratnam. "Changes in the Velocity Structure of the Greenland Ice Sheet." *Science* 311 (2006): 986–990.

Sabine, Christopher L., et al. "The Oceanic Sink for Anthropogenic CO_2." *Science* 305 (2004): 367–371.

Saleska, Scott R., et al. "Carbon in Amazon Forests: Unexpected Seasonal Fluxes and Disturbance-Induced Loss." *Science* 302 (2003): 1554–1557.

Santer, B. D., et al. "Identification of Anthropogenic Climate Change Using a Second-Generation Reanalysis," *Journal of Geophysical Research*, 109, (2004).

Sarkisyan, A. S. "Major Advances and Problems in Modeling Long-Term World Ocean Climate Changes." *Izvestiya, Atmospheric and Ocean Physics* 38 (2002): 664–681.

Schar, Christopher, et al. "The Role of Increasing Temperature Variability in European Summer Heatwaves." *Nature* 427 (2004): 332–336.

Schiermeier, Quirin. "Modellers Deplore 'Short-Termism' on Climate." *Nature* 428 (2004): 593.

Schmittner, Andrea. "Decline of the Marine Ecosystem Caused by a Reduction in the Atlantic Overturning Circulation." *Nature* 434 (2005): 628–633.

Service, Robert F. "As the West Goes Dry." *Science* 303 (2003): 1124–1127.

Shepherd, Andrew, et al. "Larsen Ice Shelf Has Progressively Thinned." *Science* 302 (2003): 856–858.

Sheram, Katherine, and Tatyana P. Soubbotina. "Economic Development and the Risk of Global Climate Change." Chap. 14 in *Beyond Economic Growth: Meeting the Challenges of Global Development*. World Bank, 2000. http://www.worldbank.org/depweb/beyond/global/chapter14.html (accessed January 2009).

Sloan, E. Dendy. "Fundamental Principles and Applications of Natural Gas Hydrates." *Nature* 426 (2003): 353–363.

Stainforth, D. A., et al. "Uncertainty in Predictions of the Climate Response to Rising Levels of Greenhouse Gases." *Nature* 433 (2005): 403–406.

Stokstad, Erik. "Global Survey Documents Puzzling Decline of Amphibians." *Science* 306 (2004): 391.

Sullivan, Rohan. "Australians Shed Light, Go Green." *Chicago Tribune,* February 21, 2007: 13.

Svensen, Henrik, et al. "Release of Methane from a Volcanic Basin as a Mechanism for Initial Eocene Global Warming." *Nature* 429 (2004): 542–545.

Swing, John Temple. "What Future for the Oceans?" *Foreign Affairs,* September–October 2003:139–152.

Tanser, F. C., B. Sharp, and D. le Sueur. "Potential Effect of Climate Change on Malaria Transmission in Africa." *Royal Society of Tropical Medicine & Hygiene* 97 (2003): 129–132.

Thomas, Chris D., et al. "Extinction Risk from Climate Change." *Nature* 427 (2004): 145–148.

Thomas, Helmuth, et al. "Enhanced Open Ocean Storage of CO_2 from Shelf Sea Pumping." *Science* 304 (2004): 1005–1008.

Thomas, R., et al. "Accelerated Sea-Level Rise from West Antarctica." *Science* 306 (2004): 255–258.

Toniazzo, T., J. M. Gregory, and P. Huybrechts. "Climatic Impact of a Greenland Deglaciation and Its Possible Irreversibility." *Journal of Climate* 17 (2004): 21–33.

Trenberth, Kevin, and Timothy J. Hoar. "The 1990–1995 El Niño–Southern Oscillation Event: Longest on Record." *Geophysical Research Letters* 23 (1996): 57–60.

United Nations Framework Convention on Climate Change (UNFCCC). Kyoto Protocol. http://www.unfccc.int/kyoto_protocol/items/2830.php (accessed January 2009).

Urban, Frank E., Julia E. Cole, and Jonathan T. Overpeck. "Influence of Mean Climate Change on Climate Variability from a 155-Year Tropical Pacific Coral Record." *Nature* 407 (2000): 989–993.

Verburg, Piet, Robert E. Heky, and Hedy Kling. "Ecological Consequences of a Century of Warming in Lake Tanganyika." *Science* 301 (2003): 505–507.

Visser, Marcel E. and Leonard J. M. Holleman. "Warmer Springs Disrupt the Synchrony of Oak and Winter Moth Phrenology." *Proceedings of the Royal Society B.* 268 (2001): 289–294.

Walther, Gian-Reto, et al. "Ecological Responses to Recent Climate Change." *Nature* 416 (2002): 389–395.

Whitfield, John "Alaska's Climate: Too Hot to Handle." *Nature* 425 (2003) 338–339.

Williams, Mark, and Ieva M. Augstums. "Gustav Damages Could Trigger $10 Billion in Insurance Claims." *Huffington Post,* September 2, 2008. http://www.huffingtonpost.com/2008/09/02/gustav-damages-could-trig_ n_123302.html (accessed September 23, 2008).

Williams, Stephen E., Elizabeth E. Bolitho, and Samantha Fox. "Climate Change in Australian Tropical Rainforests: An Impending Environmental Catastrophe." *Proceedings of the Royal Society B.* 270 (2003): 1887–1892.

Woodford, James. "Great Barrier Reef?" *Australian Geographic* 76 (2004): 37–55.

Zachos, James C., et al. "A Transient Rise in Tropical Sea-Surface Temperature during the Paleocene-Eocene Thermal Maximum." *Science* 302 (2003): 1551–1554.

Zeng, Ning. "Drought in the Sahel." *Science* 302 (2003): 999–1000.

Zuckerman, Seth. "My Low-Carbon Diet." *Sierra* 91. (September/October 2006). http://www.sierraclub.org/sierra/200609/carbon.asp (accessed September 2008).

WEBSITES

Acciona Company — Nevada Solar One. http://www.nevadasolarone.net (accessed September 2008).

Alaska Youth for Environmental Action (AYEA). http://www.ayea.org (accessed January 2009).

Annenberg Media. Learner.org. http://www.learner.org/interactives/ collapse/chacocanyon.html (accessed January 2009).

British Antarctic Survey. National Environment Research Council. 2004. http://www.antarctica.ac.uk/about_antarctica.

Calpine Corporation. http://www.geysers.com/default.htm (accessed January 2009).

Climateprediction.net. http://www.climateprediction.net

Commonwealth Edison/Excelon Corporation. http://www.exeloncorp.com/ ComedCare_Main (accessed February 22, 2006).

Energy Information Administration. http://www.eia.doe.gov (accessed January 2009).

National Air Traffic Controllers Association. http://www.natca.org/media center/bythenumbers.msp (accessed January 29, 2007).

National Climatic Data Center. http://www.ncdc.noaa.gov/oa/reports/ billionz.html#chron (accessed February 2007).

National Oceanic and Atmospheric Administration. Coral Reef Information System. http://www.coris.noaa.gov (accessed January 2009).

Nova. ScienceNow. Original broadcast July 26, 2005. http://www.pbs.org/ wgbh/nova/sciencenow/3210/03.html

Nuclear Energy Institute. http://www.nei.org./resourcesandstats/nuclear_ statistics/usnuclearpowerplants (accessed January 2009).

Reusablebags.com. http://www.reusablebags.com/facts.php?id=7

SPG Media Limited. Water-technology.net. http://www.water-technology. net/projects/perth (accessed January 2009).

Turnbull, Elizabeth. http://www.turnbulltinyhouse.blogspot.com.

Union of Concerned Scientists. http://www.ucsusa.org (accessed September 2008).

United Nations Environment Programme (UNEP). Environment Alert Bulletin. http://www.grid.unep.ch/product/publication/download/ew_heat_ wave.en.pdf (accessed January 2009).

U.S. Department of Energy. Energy Information Administration. http:// www.eia.doe.gov/oiaf/ieo/emissions.html (accessed September 25, 2008).

U.S. Environmental Protection Agency. http://www.epa.gov (accessed January 2009).

World Petroleum Council. http://www.world-petroleum.org/education/petref (accessed January 2009).

CREDITS

Use of Pitseolak Alainga quotations from the interview of September 27, 2007, courtesy of *The Story with Dick Gordon,* www.thestory.org.

Illustrations on pages 12, 18, 43, and 169 by Tony Frankhauser

Illustrations on pages 22, 34–35, and 76–77 by Karen Minot

pp. x–xi photograph copyright © 2008 by Jeremy Doorten/www.sxc.hu

p. 1 photograph courtesy of NASA/JPL-Caltech

p. 9 photograph copyright © by Audiffret/Dreamstime.com

p. 20 photograph copyright © 2008 by Alexey Stiop/www.stockxpert.com

pp. 29 and 30 photographs copyright © 2003 by www.e-Cobo.com, Nikolay Dimitrov

pp. 38–39 photograph copyright © by Fallsview/Dreamstime.com

p. 48 photograph copyright © 2003 by www.e-Cobo.com, Nikolay Dimitrov

p. 59 photograph copyright © 2008 by Makio Kusahara/www.sxc.hu

pp. 68–69 photograph copyright © by Audiffret/Dreamstime.com

p. 71 photograph courtesy of NASA/JPL-Caltech

pp. 84–85 photograph copyright © 2003 by www.e-Cobo.com, Nikolay Dimitrov

pp. 90–91 photograph copyright © 2008 by iStockphoto.com/RyersonClark

p. 95 photograph copyright © 2003 by www.e-Cobo.com, Nikolay Dimitrov

pp. 104–105 photograph copyright © 2007 by John Boyer/www.sxc.hu

p. 111 photograph copyright © by Michael J. Tyler

pp. 114–115 photograph copyright © by Audiffret/Dreamstime.com

p. 127 photograph copyright © 2008 by Sebastian Fissore/www.sxc.hu

pp. 132–133 U.S. Geological Survey/photograph by Dennis Demcheck

p. 134 photograph FEMA/Jocelyn Augustino

p. 138 photograph copyright © 2007 by Sara E. Moses/www.sxc.hu

p. 151 photograph copyright © 2003 by www.e-Cobo.com, Nikolay Dimitrov

p. 157 photograph copyright © 2008 by Santiago Masquelet/www.sxc.hu

p. 159 photograph courtesy of NASA/JPL-Caltech

p. 172 photograph copyright © 2008 by K. Tuck/www.sxc.hu

p. 177 photograph copyright © 2007 by Sara E. Moses/www.sxc.hu

p. 184 photograph copyright © 2008 by Alexey Stiop/www.stockxpert.com

INDEX

TIM FLANNERY is an internationally acclaimed scientist, explorer, and conservationist whose books for adults include *The Weather Makers: How Man Is Changing the Climate and What It Means for Life on Earth; The Eternal Frontier: An Ecological History of North America and Its Peoples;* and *The Future Eaters: An Ecological History of the Australasian Lands and People.* He is a contributor to the *New York Review of Books* and the *Times Literary Supplement* and is a familiar voice on ABC radio, National Public Radio, and the BBC. A former director of the South Australian Museum, he is an affiliate professor at the University of Adelaide and lives in Australia.

SALLY M. WALKER is the author of more than fifty nonfiction books, mostly science-related, including *Written in Bone: Buried Lives of Jamestown and Colonial Maryland; Secrets of a Civil War Submarine,* the 2006 Sibert Medal winner; and several books in the Early Bird Nature and Earth Science series. She lives in Illinois.